# HOW (NOT) TO FAIL AT CONSULTING

## JACK PRZEMIENIECKI

ISBN: 9798534287073

First published November 2021

Edited by Susan Gaigher
Caricatures by Marco Iwerten

www.hownottofailatconsulting.com

*To my family.*

# Contents

Introduction                           1

Change                                 5

Anatoly Roytman                       15

Communication                         25

Andrew Finlayson                      47

Adversity                             55

Jeremy Dalton                         69

Presentations                         77

Insights                              91

Andrew Hogan                         121

Leadership                           131

Failure                              169

Antoinette Kyuchukova                187

Feedback                             193

Mental health                        211

Stephen Knight                       231

Network                              237

Brand                                253

Richard Hepworth                     267

Progression                          273

Andy Woodfield                       285

Diversity                            289

Dola Fashola                         307

Exponential acceleration             315

Future of consulting                 335

Conclusion                           365

Further reading                      369

End notes                            389

# Acknowledgements

The wisdom graciously shared by both named and anonymous contributors has made this book possible. I am particularly thankful to the patient and understanding individuals that have gone out of the way to lend their time, encouragement and insights. Special thanks to Anatoly Roytman, Andrew Finlayson, Andrew Hogan, Andy Woodfield, Antoinette Kyuchukova, David Fowler, Dola Fashola, Henryka Bochniarz, James Easterbrook, Jer Lau, Jeremy Dalton, Jon Hughes, Magdalena Chrobot, Maria Axente, Melissa Max-Macarthy, Melville Carrie, Richard Hepworth, Richard Murton, Stephen Knight, and Tor Gisvold.

# Introduction

When I initially set out to write this book, my intention was to create a helpful, practical, contemporary guide to the world of consulting.

Having spent over two decades working with companies both big and small across four continents, I've seen the good, the bad, and the ugly. In the first decade of my career, I worked with innovative start-ups, entrepreneurial agencies, and on the client side. Then, when I entered the world of consulting, I had the good fortune of moving quickly up the grades, working with truly remarkable people and some of the world's most recognisable brands.

I picked up a few battle scars along the way, so I knew there were many stories and lessons learned I could share to benefit others. Yet, I was also conscious that the book couldn't be about my experiences alone. They were, after all, mine, limited in scope by my perception of the world. To expand that view, I interviewed some of the thought leaders, pioneers, and mavericks of the consulting world.

I deliberately interviewed consultants from various grades, industries, and backgrounds to gain a wide range of perspectives, who offered insights that would have never been discernible from their online profiles alone. They graciously shared their life journeys with me; how they first entered consulting, their experiences and fascinating adventures, and some of the things they learned throughout their careers.

During these interviews, several themes emerged. These themes started to form the overarching framework for this book and were then dichotomised into more granular, pronounced elements through further conversations and hours upon hours of research. From within each element emerged new stories to tell, experiences to share, and lessons learned to examine. The book began to take on a life of its own. It became more than a guide for those entering the consulting world, as the themes and ideas discussed were relevant to all consultants, no matter their grade level or industry.

My journey thus far has been an incredible one, marked by exhilarating highs and gut-wrenching lows, as is the nature of life. I made a conscious decision to share some of my own most personal experiences in this book, and not all of them positive ones. I'm also very thankful for the bravery and honesty of those who have shared their moments of adversity with me. I hope that these reflections will help others who may find themselves in similar situations. After all, there is a comfort to be found in knowing that we are not alone in facing adversity and value in learning from the missteps others may have made.

That being said, I've attempted to keep the book reasonably light, entertaining, and story-driven whenever possible. I've also added a fair bit of data and external references to contextualise further the topics discussed for our more analytical readers. Finally, I've endeavoured to avoid dusty theories in favour of focusing on authentic, real-world experiences, interesting people, memorable stories, and valuable lessons.

Thus, the book has become a practical guide to the world of consulting as told by the people who have experienced it and have the battle scars to prove it. It is my sincere hope that this book provides you, the reader, with insights, ideas, and points of reflection that will help you along your journey. If not, then I hope it at least becomes a handy paperweight.

"Change is not merely necessary to life — it is life."

Alvin Toffler

# Change

"So that, in a nutshell, is the problem," Joseph's colleague remarked as he motioned to the brochures laid out in front of them on the office desk. "We keep sending these out, but the feedback has been abysmal. No one seems to understand what it is we do."

"Let me have a think about this," Joseph replied as he picked up one of the brochures from the desk. "I'm sure there is a way."

"Thanks, Joe. Appreciate it," his colleague said as he turned and left the room. Joseph sat down behind the desk and looked over the brochure thoughtfully. It was an exciting challenge and one that he relished.

He had begun his career as an electrical engineer and lawyer by training. However, his real passion was the free market, which is why he started working with the Mackinac Centre for Public Policy in Michigan. The Mackinac Centre was a non-profit research and educational institute think tank with the purpose of advancing the principles of free markets.

He had been working at the Mackinac Centre for several months, and the same issue kept coming up. Anytime he tried to explain what they did, he was met by blank stares from his family and friends. Similarly, no matter how many brochures the Centre distributed, people continued to have a hard time grasping what a think tank was and what they did.

As he sat there looking out the window, he began to formulate the basis for his theory. Acknowledging that public policy is a spectrum, he thought, policymakers had to be sensitive as to where their ideas fell in this spectrum. Any idea too far outside of the acceptable range would be deemed too extreme to gain or keep public office given the climate of public opinion at that time. What would have been considered an extreme point of view a decade earlier may have become commonly accepted as public opinion shifted. Think tanks, such as the one Joseph worked for, made it their business to understand how public sentiment was changing, in what direction, and how quickly.

He contemplated that if public opinion shifted along a horizontal axis, from the very far-right views to those on the very far left, it would cover a range of policies rather than a narrow point. The policies in that range would be deemed as acceptable, while policies further outside of the range would be more challenging to explain and implement. Policies further outside the range would also encounter more vocal resistance from groups not aligned with the espoused views.

He called his colleague over to his office, "I think I've figured it out!"

He took a piece of paper and drew a horizontal line. Then he drew a box midway along the line. "So, this box represents the policies that the general public will find acceptable. Our job is to understand where this box is, where it is moving to, what policies are in this box, and how we can influence where this box shifts over time."

His colleague looked down at the paper. "That makes sense. Maybe we can include a diagram like this in our brochures to show how policy can shift and to explain the work we do. This is a great idea, but what do we call it?" Joseph thought about it for a moment and replied, "Let's call it the Window of Discourse."

# Overton Window

The "Window of Discourse" remained fairly obscure in Overton's lifetime. It was only after his tragic death in 2003 in an ultralight plane crash, at the age of 43, that his colleague Joseph Lehman formalised and named the idea after his late colleague. He presented the idea to fellow think-tank colleagues and the name stuck. The Overton Window quickly became conceptual bread and butter among activists, lobbyists, and politicians. In 2010, the controversial conspiracy theorist Glenn Beck published a novel called *The Overton Window*, and the term became mainstream.[1]

The shift of popular opinion is supported by extensive polling data throughout the years. For example, continual polling by Gallup over the course of more than two decades has shown that support for same-sex marriage has proliferated while the opposition to it has simultaneously collapsed. In 1996, 68% of Americans opposed same-sex marriage, while only 27% supported it. By 2018, 67% of Americans supported same sex marriage, while only 31% opposed it. These statistics are indicative of a relatively rapid shift in public sentiment, policies, and laws.[2]

Building upon the work of the Mackinac Centre, political commentator Joshua Treviño postulated that there were six degrees of acceptance, starting from the most unimaginable and moving steadily towards the middle of the Window: Unthinkable, Radical, Acceptable, Sensible, Popular, and finally, Policy. As the Window shifts to the left or the right, ideas that may have once been deemed Radical may become Acceptable or even Popular.[3]

## The Overton Window and the six degrees of acceptance

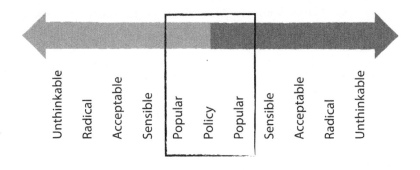

# Mind your Window

Much in the way that political advisors must consider where policy recommendations are positioned in relation to the Overton Window, consultants must consider the position of the Window within their client organisations and within their own firms. Rather than only focusing on public sentiment, we reinterpret the definition of the Window into a snapshot of an organisation's technology, ambition, politics, risk tolerance, culture, and policies at any given point in time.

As with think tanks monitoring the shifts in overall public perception, the role of consultants often tends to necessitate a similar understanding of where an organisation's Window resides and what it is moving towards. Gaining an understanding of the current state of an organisation, department, or team, serves to identify where any new idea or proposal resides in the spectrum from Policy or Acceptable to Radical or Unthinkable.

For example, in the 1990s, no one would have imagined a world where even relatively simple financial transactions could be completed through a mobile application on a touch-screen mobile device with built-in biometric user identity authentication. After all, the iPhone was only released in 2007 and the Apple App Store only launched in 2008.

However, as the technologies became universally available, customers' expectations shifted so dramatically that not offering sophisticated, user-friendly mobile banking options can profoundly negatively affect a financial institution's brand. The Window moved so quickly, in fact, that while legacy organisations were struggling to acknowledge the shift and adapt to it, agile app-based banking start-ups such as Revolut and Monzo moved in to fill the gap, achieving significant success.

There were undoubtedly voices advocating for a more rapid transition of focus to user-friendly mobile application-based banking options in legacy financial services organisations. However, depending on where the organisation's Window resided and where the proposed ideas were in relation to the Window, these new ideas may have been seen as Radical when they were first presented, resulting in considerable resistance to their adoption. When proposing a course of action, it is imperative to acknowledge where it sits in relation to the Window. If an idea is too far outside of the Window and is perceived as too audacious, a robust communication and change plan, alongside a coalition of like-minded colleagues and stakeholders will need to be convened to overcome the inevitable pushback.

# Butterfly effects

In chaos theory, the butterfly effect is "the sensitive dependence on initial conditions in which a small change in one state of a deterministic nonlinear system can result in large differences in a later state." The more straightforward definition is that even small events can have significant consequences. The classic example given is that of a butterfly gently flapping its wings and the miniscule variations in air pressure inducing a series of events that eventually contribute to the formation of a tornado elsewhere. Similarly, shifts in attitude and expectations are identifiable across industries and may be instigated by specific butterfly effect inducing catalysts.

Technology is the most obvious and prevalent culprit, as technology has had an incredible impact on all parts of our lives. As the pace of technological advancement accelerates, the associated butterfly effects may be significant and, at times, not widely understood or acknowledged. The impact of technological progress is made more difficult to predict as technologies continue to combine into new permutations while simultaneously shifting human behaviour and expectations.

In the 1990s, the notion of getting into a car with a stranger would have seemed ill-advised, if not dangerous. By 2020, a mere three decades later, the ride-sharing giant Uber claimed over seven billion trips per year globally.[4] The dramatic growth of Uber represents a profound shift in attitudes, enabled by technology, that occurred in a relatively short period. Organisations that were able to anticipate the shift of the Window were, therefore, able to gain a significant first-mover advantage. Of course, this shift has had several knock-on effects, some of which may have been easier to anticipate than others.

For example, the rise of Uber led to the downfall of many taxi and car-hire services around the globe, the proliferation of interdependent contract drivers, and the reduction in new car sales in cities where Uber began to operate. For every seemingly obvious consequence, there may be dozens that were not. Consider how the lack of health insurance or pension contributions in the emerging gig economy, of which Uber drivers are a part, presented new business opportunities as well as long-term policy headaches for governments around the world. An increase in Uber trips can also be connected to a decrease in walking and cycling, potentially contributing to adverse health impacts over time. Public transit may also suffer, not only because regular traveller numbers are reduced as more people opt for an Uber, but because politicians may use the very existence of Uber and other car-sharing services to rationalise decreased investment in public transport options overall.[5]

Similarly, the Window will continue to shift within an organisation based on the industry, policies, laws, technology advancements, customer expectations, and any number of other catalysts. In addition to that complexity, not taking the requisite time to analyse or anticipate the butterfly effects of initiatives may undermine their very intent. For example, a renowned hospitality client I had the pleasure of working with had spent millions on a business intelligence programme, wanting to provide their hotel managers with real-time data they would be able to use to improve operations. As an IT-led initiative, the focus was placed on identifying the best-in-class building blocks of the system, with little regard for change management and user experience ramifications. They implemented an incredibly robust system that required managers to move across multiple platforms to extract the information they needed manually. It was a tedious and time-consuming process. As a result, managers ignored the system, and the investment wasn't effective in what it was meant to achieve. The organisation failed to recognise the knock-on effect that the implementation of multiple systems would have and did not take the experience of the managers into account.

Elsewhere in the organisation, advances in technology and a subsequent shift in customer behaviour profoundly impacted how account managers interacted with their VIPs. Rather than using the legacy communication channels such as email or telephone, the VIPs preferred to communicate exclusively through the mobile communication application WhatsApp. They would book rooms, make inquiries, order room service, and carry out all other business with their account managers directly through the application. However, as the organisation was not aware of, nor did they anticipate this shift in behaviour, they did not have any policies or infrastructure to log, monitor, or standardise the new communications channel. This is an example of a larger scale butterfly effect, whereby two young men developed a mobile communications app in California, Facebook bought that app for $19 billion USD in 2014, and years later, a hotel chain based on a different continent was forced to rethink its systems, processes, and customer relationship strategy.

This is why it is essential to take a holistic view. We need to monitor advances in technology and emerging trends, considering how they may impact human behaviour and preferences. By anticipating these shifts and their potential butterfly effects within society, our organisations, and our clients' organisations, we will put ourselves in a better position to accommodate them and to identify new opportunities as they emerge.

# Audacity Ratio

Any policies that fall directly in the middle of the Overton Window will not be considered contentious. Equally, proposing new projects that fall in the centre of an organisation's Window will not be met with much resistance. While there may be much talk about "thinking outside the box", the reality is that most partners, directors, managers, or client stakeholders will be hesitant to promote truly ambitious projects that are well outside of the Window. After all, staying within the Window is safe, comfortable, and the perceived risk to their reputations is minimal.

Taking the more ambitious approach by pursuing opportunities outside of the Window will always be fraught with challenges. There may be pushback internally from those who had built their careers on not pushing the envelope. There may be pushback from the client, who may not feel ready to embark on the potentially perilous journey. Meanwhile, other stakeholders may naturally be suspicious of change, who may not be convinced of the value or understand the proposition itself. That being said, as we will discuss in later chapters, there are times when pursuing an audacious course of action is necessary for the organisation to survive. Hence, our main challenge is not only to identify these audacious ideas, but to also acknowledge the relative level of effort required to pursue them effectively. The further an idea or proposal outside the Window, the proportionally more time will be required to explain it, the larger the group of stakeholders that will need to be brought onside, and the more robust the planning and execution will need to be.

Truly audacious ideas require more effort to explain, more effort in the setup, and more effort in the execution. They need more effort to convince others that they are the correct course of action, and they may have more butterfly effect inciting variables to consider. Therefore, a proportional multiple of effort will be required to ensure the success of an audacious idea. The Audacity Ratio serves to remind us that the more courageous, risky, or challenging the idea, the more time will need to be spent presenting, explaining, lobbying, communicating, and explaining again.

## 1 [Audacity] : 2 [Effort]

No two scenarios or organisations will be the same. Understanding the position of the Overton Window for a given organisation will give us an insight into how far inside or outside of the Window any new proposals are. Based on that understanding, we will gain a better insight into how audacious our latest idea is in relation. The further the idea outside the Window, the more audacious it is, the more effort will be required to successfully convince stakeholders that it is the appropriate course of action. Even when stakeholders are convinced, the further the idea outside the Window, the more effort will be required to keep them informed and aligned throughout the execution.

By default, people fear the unknown and will be suspicious of new, audacious ideas. Too many times have great ideas been rejected by fearful stakeholders using the line, "Where has this been done before?" as a shield against ambition or progress. It's our responsibility to ensure that we put their minds at ease and clearly explain our approach and the benefits of the initiative. The Audacity Ratio serves as a reminder that we must devote an appropriate amount of effort to bring stakeholders onside and subsequently bring them along on the journey with us. The most successful consultants I've spoken to instinctively understood the ratio required, devoting a proportionate level of effort to ensure their ideas and projects were successful, no matter how audacious they were.

"The people who are crazy enough
to think they can change the world
are the ones who do."

Steve Jobs

# Anatoly Roytman

Anatoly's story is the real-world embodiment of several themes discussed in this book, but perhaps none more than having a vision and a structured approach for achieving it. He was mindful of the Overton Window and clearly communicated the way forward, effectively convincing those around him to share in his vision for the future.

I first met Anatoly when I was only starting my consulting career. After completing all the aptitude tests, case studies, and other interviews, I was to speak with the Accenture Interactive leader himself. It would be fair to say that I was intimidated, as Anatoly has the look and manner of speaking akin to an early '90s movie antagonist. I could imagine him explaining, in excruciating detail, his plans for world domination and the gruesome method by which the secret agent he'd captured would meet his untimely demise. In our conversation, however, my impression quickly changed. Anatoly was welcoming, kind, quick-witted, and did not shy away from a joke. He had a clear vision for Accenture Interactive and shared it in such a way that made me sure I wanted to be a part of it.

It was those qualities that propelled Anatoly to achieve a number of truly remarkable feats during his 11-year career at Accenture. Anatoly oversaw many of the most important early UK acquisitions, including design agency Fjord in 2013 and creative shop Karmarama in 2016.[6] Anatoly played an instrumental role in growing Accenture Interactive to become the largest digital agency in the world, reporting the highest worldwide revenue of any digital agency network at $8.5 billion USD for Accenture's 2018 fiscal year, reflecting an annual growth of 30%.[7] I wanted to find out how he became the renowned leader and innovator I knew, and what lessons he'd learned along the way.

Anatoly was born in Nizhny Tagil, an industrial Russian city located close to the virtual border between Europe and Asia. When he was young, he moved with his mother to Brest, Belarus, close to the border with Poland, where he later attended high school and university. He was very bright, but lacked direction.

"I just wanted to find something easy because I did not know what to do with my life," he admitted, smiling. In those days, anyone who did not attend university would be automatically drafted to serve in the army, which was all the motivation Anatoly needed. "I couldn't come up with anything, so at the end of high school, what became popular was anything related to computers. I didn't know much about computer science, but decided to pick something that would be related to computers. That was the only school in Belarus that offered this type of education, and my faculty was called Automated Systems. Back then, when you graduated in Russia, you're supposed to go to a pre-assigned place of work for three years. You're supposed to give back to the to the country. So, they assigned me to a shoe-making factory. I showed up there and they said, 'Well, they didn't want anyone and they don't have any computers to speak of.' I went back to the university and they said, 'Okay, well, in that case, you are free to go, but where do you go?'"

"Back then, in those days in the Soviet Union, you have to know somebody in order to get a place somewhere. My aunt had a connection in the ministry of, well, it was called the milk and meat-processing ministry. She found a place for me in that ministry. Unfortunately, the place of work was a meat-packing plant. So, if you haven't been to meat packing, imagine an office with a window looking at the wall and at the end of the wall, there is a pipe. At 3 p.m. every day, there's a lot of bones that would drop down in front of you into a pile of bones. This is where I did my best programming."

Anatoly worked on programming devices for automation, at times working with American processors that would have magically appeared at the ministry from sources unknown. Working without manuals, it was up to Anatoly to figure out how these processors worked and how to program them. All the while, the meat-packing activities went on around him. The pungent smell of those activities, as Anatoly recalled, "Was not just in the in the vicinity, but maybe as far as three, four miles away. You could smell this stuff, especially if the wind blew your way."

In 1987, the opportunity arose to leave the Soviet Union, and Anatoly jumped at the chance. "I lived in Italy for two months, and I worked as a teacher, teaching refugees computers. I was able to earn about $1,000, so this was my fortune." Having studied English for 15 years, Anatoly had his heart set on moving to the United States. He had connections in Boston and Minneapolis that would be able to sponsor him, and ultimately chose Boston as his destination.

"We didn't know much about anything outside of our borders. There was a book published in the '60s about America, and this is how I understood America to be. So, for example, it said that back then you could buy a house for $20,000, but I didn't realise that time had passed, but I knew that the people were making $50,000, even in the '80s. So, my God, you can buy two houses in one year! Can you imagine? So anyways, it was naïve and crazy, but I arrived in Boston."

Anatoly laughed, "By the way, I also did not know much about climate. I arrived in Boston in November 1987, and to my astonishment, there was about a meter of snow on the ground, was super cold, and I didn't have any winter clothes!"

Having arrived in the US with only $1,000 to his name, Anatoly knew he needed to get a job, and quick. He found a job in a hardware store but only lasted two weeks. "That was like a miracle, but two weeks later, I also got accepted to a software engineering shop. When I went to my boss and said, 'I'm sorry, but I have this offer. I have to leave.' He was amazed because I only worked for two weeks. I said, 'I am very sorry, but this is the offer I can't refuse.' And he said, 'What's the offer?' Well, first of all, I could develop software. But then, also, they offered me twice as much!"

Anatoly started his career as a software engineer, developing CASE (computer-aided software engineering) tools. From there he joined Digital Equipment Corporation (DEC), initially as a software engineer, but promptly made a move into technical consulting.

"Why did I move? Because I thought that programming by itself was not exciting me. I wanted to solve problems. I wanted to define things to do versus just simply executing somebody else's ideas. So, I went to technical consulting from there. I went to a very small management consulting firm. Why that, because again, even technical consulting was following somebody else's ideas, I was trying to get to the point where it was all about ideas. I left the strategy firm and started, with a few other people, what now would be called a digital agency. As the internet boom turned into a crash I had to find a new job and joined a direct marketing agency that was in the process of repositioning into a digital transformation shop. It was great fun because I met people who are really creative. It was very exciting to work with creative people. The only problem was that given my technical background, I was not front and centre of the agency."

"It was something that was secondary to what they do. It was one of few agencies that recognise that technology plays a role, but it was still secondary to creative and marketing. I mean, that was a good time. What I struggled with is how to fit into a creative shop. After the agency was sold I went to Sapient, because Sapient was on the other side of the scale at the time. It was more of a technology company, trying to be creative." Anatoly made the move over to Accenture in 2009, just as Sapient announced its merger with creative shop Nitro, becoming SapientNitro.

Reflecting on the challenges agencies face, Anatoly noted, "There are two things wrong with the agencies, one is that they cannot find a balance between technology and creative. So, it's either one or the other. The other part is more of an add-on; they're not equal. There is no equilibrium between capabilities. The other big problem is that the work that you do could be a very exciting and rewarding or could be really, really boring. It all depends on the brief. You only operate within the confines of the brief whereas at Accenture, at least the way I thought about it, it is a huge company that has all the big brands as their clients. If you have ideas, you can bring ideas to clients. You don't need to wait for the RFP or a brief. I love that idea. Also, it was the start-up within the established business. This is why I survived at Accenture for 11 years."

Thinking back to how it all started, Anatoly presented an ostensibly simple plan. "First of all, find the client. Once you find the client, you make sure that successful first project gives you a right to hire more people. Then you go find another client and then it grows from there, because at the same time, you have to maintain chargeability for the people, you have to be within the financial confines. Then you need to convince other people, the client partners, that this is something useful. The only way to convince them is to give them an example of how it worked with other clients. Then, when you're successful, everybody wants a piece of you."

Anatoly described a measured, iterative approach to building the practice. "If you look at the beginning, when there wasn't much, very few people and not even a name. I had this vision about creating something that is creative and technical and consultative. So, a three-legged stool. But if you think that you could imagine Accenture Interactive the way it is right now back 10 years ago, or 11 years ago, it would have never happened. So, for example, if you would present this as a destination, no one would accept it. What needed to be done is to take steps. The first step is more about technology. Can we find people who can build a website? We need to build a scaled capability. It's not too far from where the mothership was, right? So that was an understood mission. That was an understood market target. It is understood skill that we need to acquire or train some to develop."

"The next step is something like content, which can be positioned the way a BPO organisation deals with many other issues. It is a process. Content management is a process and if you explain it that way, then it becomes not as scary. It's not something that is totally different. Then design or service design, which is consulting in different words. Yes, it requires a little bit different methodology, but it is consulting. It is when you interview people, you go into a workshop, you present some outcomes, at the end of the day it's consulting. If you simplify things and present them in a way that is digestible to people who use different language, it becomes less scary. But then, of course, once you make this move, you need to present it as a success. Then you have credibility to make the next step. It was a long journey to go from convincing the firm that we need to have people who can build an app to the point where we need to have people who can advertise at the Super Bowl."

Anatoly was able to effectively gauge what the Window encompassed and instinctively understood the effort required to bring others to his way of viewing the world. He understood taking a big leap would require a lot of effort or be impossible given the current position of the Window.

That is why he identified milestones on the way to his desired destination. Each milestone would require its own analysis and, based on its audacity in relation to the organisation's Window, would require the proportional level of effort. By breaking up a big, incredibly audacious idea into smaller, iterative components and then explaining those in plain language, Anatoly was able to make them seem less scary; less audacious.

"I cannot even imagine that if anybody would draw a picture of the final destination, the whole journey, I mean, they would kill me, this idea would be killed. While you're doing it, demonstrate that this step is great, that it actually has some value, but when you combine it with the previous step, it generates even more value. There is a synergy in all of that."

Celebrating each success along the way allowed Anatoly to build credibility and trust among his stakeholders, giving him permission to move faster and introduce ideas that may have been more audacious than the ones that preceded it. With each success, he effectively shifted the Window within his organisation. All the while, he kept an eye on the larger objective, moving closer to that vision with every success.

"There are so many different stakeholders and they have so many different objectives, their own objectives. You have to find some connection with those objectives. There are people who care about one dimension of it, the people who care about the other dimension. You need to clearly explain what's in it for them to put it simply. And you know, some of these people, you have to be able to understand that some of the people get excited about doing something new. They are risk takers and for them, it is exciting to see the whole picture. For some other people, who are more careful, you need to break it down, make it simple, and connect it with their agenda and show them how we will make them successful. The real art is that figuring out more about the people and understanding what drives them and then finding a way to connect with them."

The ability to listen, to understand the motivations of his audience, and to subsequently tailor his message, served Anatoly well. He had a vision of what he wanted to accomplish and, step by step, success after success, he convinced others that his vision was one worth pursuing. As the coalition of like-minded individuals grew, he was able to take increasingly bigger, more ambitious steps. It was an approach that served him well throughout his career and his 11-year tenure with Accenture Interactive.

"You aren't learning anything when you're talking."

Lyndon B. Johnson

# Communication

"Communication is a skill that you can learn. It's like riding a bicycle or typing. If you're willing to work at it, you can rapidly improve the quality of every part of your life," noted business author Brian Tracy.

Consulting is all about relationships, meaning values such as honesty, transparency, and trust are as essential within our professional relationships as they are within personal ones. Perhaps the most crucial aspect of any relationship is effective communication. It should come as no surprise that a survey conducted by YourTango found that "communication problems" was cited as the most common factor that led to divorce, with 65% of respondents claiming it as the main reason for their decision to separate.[8] As within marriage, the importance of communication is paramount in any professional relationship. In fact, the Project Management Institute noted that high-performing organisations that finished 80% of projects were twice as likely to have communication plans in place compared to their low-performing counterparts.[9]

When done well, effective communication serves to bring stakeholders onside, ensures alignment across teams, and fosters a spirit of openness and collaboration. Poor communication, or a lack of communication, may foment feelings of suspicion, confusion, or doubt. It may lead to misunderstandings, arguments, and rejection of whatever new ideas are being proposed.

It is easy to dismiss the need for planned and structured communication as an apparent or implied aspect of a project. It is also deceptively easy to assume that communication takes place across all organisations or departments. However, as one of my teams learned the hard way, the assumption that something has happened by no means guarantees that it did.

Alongside several colleagues, we were working on a project with a local government council in a city outside of London, UK. The project had been discussed for weeks. The council stakeholders were to be made aware of what was about to happen by representatives within the council. Namely, one of the programme's main elements was the replacement of the existing council website with a new, improved offering. At the time, one of our tasks was to follow up with council stakeholders, after they were to be initially briefed by our council counterparts, as to the details of our approach, including the timelines involved in decommissioning their existing platform.

As my colleagues and I sat in the small meeting room within the city administrative building, we introduced ourselves politely to the council representatives. We were joined by one of the council communications leads and two members of her team. After we exchanged the customary pleasantries, we moved on to discussing the platform migration and associated timelines. As we began to go into the details, however, the council communication lead became visibly and increasingly more uncomfortable. She kept asking basic questions regarding our project that she should have known the answers to had she been properly briefed by representatives within the council.

Of course, we took time to answer each and every question, but the more we did, the more flustered and agitated she became. After several minutes of back and forth, we asked her if she had been told anything about the programme before our meeting, as was the plan. She told us she had not. To make matters worse, she had made the existing platform a pet project of hers and had worked on it diligently over the course of the previous year. While our intent was entirely benevolent, the communication breakdown resulted in emotions running high. When we explained that one of the critical objectives of the programme was to replace the existing platform, the very platform she had been working on, the communications lead broke down and began to cry.

Once we took a break in the meeting to allow the communications lead to collect herself, we returned to the meeting room to discuss the other details and timelines of the programme. But the damage had already been done. In conjunction with our assumption that the message had been delivered, the lack of communication within her organisation resulted in a remarkably uncomfortable situation. While some of the blame would undoubtedly have to be attributed to the communication failings within the council, the ultimate responsibility fell on us, as we failed to ensure that we validated all our assumptions.

# Listen

Talking too much is, unsurprisingly, a common trait amongst consultants. With so much emphasis on being, or at least sounding like, the experts in the room, talking becomes an instinctive act. The compulsion to say or write more than needed is particularly noticeable amongst some new consultants, who typically send excruciatingly long, unstructured, jargon-filled emails where a few sentences would have sufficed. Likewise, some consultants tend to focus on what they want to convey due to inexperience or insecurity rather than creating space for a two-sided dialogue.

According to Dale Carnegie, the famous American writer, lecturer, and author of *How to Win Friends and Influence People*, "If you aspire to be a good conversationalist, be an attentive listener. To be interesting, be interested."

Taking the lead in a call or meeting and purposefully asserting the role of a moderator may be helpful but should not be confused with launching into a monologue or undermining voices that would have otherwise been inclined to contribute. Also, as we learned the hard way in that meeting with the council representatives, it is never advisable to assume anything. Each participant will come into a call or meeting with their level of knowledge of the subject matter, their own motivations, and their own view of what the outcomes should be.

Taking the time at the beginning of a call or meeting to validate the stakeholder's understanding and objectives will help prevent uncomfortable situations and give stakeholders the satisfaction of knowing they are being listened to. The theme of empathy will be touched upon several times throughout this book. During meetings and calls, empathy plays a vital role, as we need to tailor our approach and message to the audience. We need first to strive to understand where the other participants are coming from and what they want to achieve rather than forcing our own agenda.

This is where listening plays such an important role. Listening is one of those things that we all know we should do but sometimes simply forget to do. We get so wrapped up in showing off our knowledge or asserting our intellectual superiority that we forget one of the most basic communication principles. The Greek philosopher Epictetus lived approximately 2,000 years ago and captured the need for listening in a remarkably insightful quote, stating, "We have two ears and one mouth so that we can listen twice as much as we speak."

Whenever we find ourselves in a conversation, call, or meeting, it's worth remembering that two-to-one ratio. If, at any point, you find yourself monopolising the conversation, ask the opinion of others. Soliciting the views of others will help them feel included and involved while allowing you to listen and learn. Take a moment, as the moderator, to involve and solicit the voices of those who would not otherwise engage.

Any meeting or call is your opportunity to ensure that everyone feels that they are part of the team and have an active voice in the discourse. Every client meeting or call is an opportunity to ask questions, listen and learn, and apply the ratio that Epictetus advocated.

"The reality is the solution to the majority of our client's challenges is already within their organisation." Andy Woodfield of PwC observed. "So, the only way to find the right answers is to listen. People should always be given a thorough listening to and we must make sure we really hear them and that we're not just listening to wait for a gap in the conversation to remind them how clever we are. We must focus on listening to understand. I'm always intrigued, 'How did you get to today? How did you get there?' Then, in that knowledge and understanding, you often find a lot of the mechanisms that you can make use of, levers for change, to help take the next step. So, for me, it's only by listening, and critically, hearing your client and your team, that you find a way of moving forwards, together."

Truly listening to our colleagues or clients and asking questions, even if they may seem like "dumb" questions, will present us with insight and understanding that would have otherwise been missed. By listening, we create a space for information to be shared and for others to feel appreciated, valued, and respected. It is perhaps the most powerful tool that we have in truly understanding any individual or situation we encounter.

# Unsilenced

There are sure to be a few extroverts, a few introverts, and a few individuals who are somewhere in between in any randomly selected group of people. Consequently, whether leading a workshop or a call, there will always be a few individuals who will monopolise the conversation and be very vocal on any subject raised. There will also be a few individuals who may not be very vocal, who will not be very loud, and who will not interject at any opportunity. As moderators, it becomes our responsibility to ensure that we involve everyone in the conversation, meaning we need to be particularly mindful to include those who may not otherwise speak up. However, it is essential to keep in mind that we may be making those who are more introverted feel uncomfortable when singled out, so our approach to soliciting their opinions needs to be measured.

Karl Moore, professor at McGill University, wrote, "Introverts have a wealth of natural strengths — they assess situations before acting, they listen to the ideas of others, and they are skilled at taking independent action. By understanding the needs of introverted employees, managers can harmonise those strengths and successfully encourage their introverts to be their 'best selves.' Which in turn leads to a more balanced team. If there's a meeting, discussion, or anything you want their opinion on, it might be a good idea to wait a while before asking them for their thoughts. Again, they need time to process, digest, and formulate a smart response. And when you follow up, make sure it's one-on-one, not in a group setting."[10]

I've encountered exactly this type of challenge when leading a workshop for a global consumer goods client. In the sessions, we created three teams comprised of individuals from across the business. As we began going through the ideation exercises, the imbalance within the teams became apparent. Two of the teams were working well, with all the participants being active contributors, while one of them was not.

The team in question had one very outspoken, brash, loud individual who would effectively quash any other input if it did not align with his thinking. As a result, some of the other team members simply stopped contributing. Had we not quickly taken action to shuffle the teams and to engage individually to solicit opinions, we may have lost out on many great ideas from individuals who were effectively silenced by their rowdier counterpart.

As consultants, we must be the listeners; we must be the moderators. We must empower those who would not otherwise contribute, creating a safe environment for them to have their voices heard.

# Bridging the gap

"My first week on the project is always very simple. It is talking to people," Tor Gisvold, formerly of Capgemini and PwC, confessed as we discussed his approach. "If you're going to be a technical manager, you'll have to say that your door is open and you're willing to talk to people. You have to spend time doing that. What I'd done many times is come in as a consultant trying to sort out a problem between management and the engineering teams."

As a technical architecture lead, Tor would find one of his roles became to be the translator between technical teams and non-technical stakeholders on his projects. "They still have an enormous gap where people think, 'Oh, I can just keep on changing things and meddling with it forever.' Management want to change some text on a page; engineers want to play with new technology. Someone needs to sit in the middle and pull both of those sides together to talk and actually have the product folks get the product out the door."

Tor identified that, as a leader, he would need to tailor his message depending on the group he was speaking with. On the one hand, engineers would need to be given direction with enough time and freedom allocated to allow them to play with the technology and explore different alternatives.

On the other hand, Tor was mindful not to overwhelm non-technical stakeholders with too many options, presenting them with a limited number of easy-to-understand alternatives.

"What you need to do is to try find a way where both groups are happy. The engineers do something fun, just slightly differently, and you start pointing them in the right direction, and management are told what their options are. You always tend to end up with, 'You have a plan, A, B, C, these are the pros and cons of each of them. It's up to you what you do.' If you're going to ever deliver something in this day and age, you need to do something about what you're doing."

"Make a change; fail fast. You have failed; go forward. That's not easy, because then politics come into the whole thing and then it gets weird and wonderful and starts taking a lot of time. Often, I keep on saying, 'Make a decision, any decision, but don't stand still, that's the worst thing you can do in the digital world.' But getting them to make that decision is really hard. I've struggled with that so many times, both in start-up companies and in big companies. So, of course, it's still the same communication gap; it all comes back to it."

Tor recalled a time when he visited a client site to rescue a project. "I went into a project where it turned out they hadn't really had any meaningful discussions with the client for six months. They've been running demos every two weeks and they thought that running a demo and telling the client what they've developed, with no input from the client, meant that it was accepted by the client."

When he spoke with the client, the client said, "You haven't done any of the things we asked you for in the beginning."

The engineers retorted, "No, we didn't, we've done something much better."

"But that isn't what we asked for!" the client snapped back.

Reflecting on the situation, Tor freely admitted, "This is a typical situation you get into."

As consultants, there are times when we will be called upon to act as translators between teams. They may be internal teams, client teams, or a combination of both. We need to be mindful of the way we tailor our communication to each distinct group. The way we communicate with technical teams, for example, will not resonate with non-technical stakeholders. Tor identified this when he would only present a limited number of options to management, making it as easy as possible to decide.

Our opportunity resides in identifying where organisational silos exist and then orchestrating occasions to break those silos down. We have a chance to facilitate communication, bring people into the same room, and collaborate to identify the best way forward. We can never assume that communication is taking place or, as Tor illustrated, that all parties are on the same page.

# Words matter

As a teenager growing up in Toronto, Canada, one of my first "real" jobs was working at a sports footwear and apparel shop called Champs Sports in the local Fairview Mall. As it was the mid-1990s, the world looked very different to what it does today, and malls across North America were booming. Amazon was founded in the garage of Bezos's rented home in Bellevue, Washington, and had only started selling books online in 1995. It would take years before Amazon and other online retailers began effectively decimating the mall industry. Hence, in the mid-1990s, people from all walks of life would descend on their local shopping malls to wander, meet with friends, shop, visit the food court, or go to the movies. I recall my experience selling sports shoes and apparel as overwhelmingly positive.

While it was not the most glamorous job, I worked with a great team, and most of our days were spent joking around with our customers and with each other. Sometimes the jokes may have bordered on the inappropriate, but we were young, we didn't know any better, and the customers kept coming back.

One day, a young couple came into the shop. It was a busy afternoon, and the shop was packed. I quickly helped them find what they were looking for and led them to the cash register to ring up the order. It was then that the young woman made a comment, one that I can't remember after all these years, but one where she made a casual observation about something irrelevant. While I don't recall the exact comment she made, I certainly remember my response when I said, "Welcome to Canada."

It wasn't a comment meant to belittle or insult. It was, what at least I thought was, a humorous barb in response to the comment the young woman had made. There wasn't much of a reaction at the time, but I did feel a brief sense of unease. Had I overstepped? We completed the transaction, and they made their way out of the shop. It was only 20 or 30 minutes later that the young woman came back to the shop.

"Is there anything else I can help you with?" I asked.

"Yes, I'd like to talk to your manager," the young woman replied.

My heart sank.

I felt like there may have been unease in our previous exchange, but I had quickly brushed it off as I made my way to help other customers. When I asked the young woman what the issue was, she proceeded to inform me that, as an immigrant, she did not feel like my comment had been appropriate. She said she felt insulted, mainly as she felt like I had just belittled her recent arrival to the country.

I was shocked. As an immigrant myself, I knew first-hand how much words could hurt and would never want to hurt others in that way, but inadvertently, I had. One careless remark had caused this young woman pain. I profusely apologised to her, and after hearing my story, she accepted my apology and went on her way. The shame I felt for the incident, however, remained.

Looking back at the situation now, I can't help but be impressed by her. Rather than simply brushing it off, she stood up for herself and made it clear that she did not consider what I had said to be appropriate. Of course, I never meant to insult her, but what we say will be interpreted by others based on their context, not our own.

For me, that one interaction that happened in a busy sports apparel shop decades ago has stuck in my mind and will be with me forever. It serves as a reminder that we need to be mindful of the words we use, as one wrong comment in the wrong circumstances may have severe ramifications. That is why we need to be mindful of what we say, how we say it, and when we say it.

In the business world, there is no shortage of stories recounting instances when leaders said the wrong thing. There's the example of Dennis "Chip" Wilson, the founder of the yoga apparel company Lululemon, who made an appearance on Bloomberg Television in 2013 in order to address a recall of the company's signature yoga pants. Customers had been complaining that the yoga pants were too sheer, prompting Chip to say, "Some women's bodies just don't actually work for it. It's really about the rubbing through the thighs, how much pressure is there. I mean over a period of time, and how much they use it." What followed was a firestorm of controversy, with his seemingly half-hearted apology doing little to assuage outraged customers. In the 50-second apology video, Chip did not apologise to the customers he may have offended, but only to his own employees. He eventually stepped down as chairman of the company's board.[11]

In 2014, John Legere, CEO of T-Mobile, derided his rivals at AT&T and Verizon by saying "These high and mighty duopolists that are raping you for every penny you have... they f*cking hate you."[12] He was later forced to apologise for his remarks.

In 2013, just before boarding a flight to South Africa, Justine Sacco, senior director of corporate communications at IAC, tweeted, "Going to Africa. Hope I don't get AIDS. Just kidding. I'm white!" Justine only had 170 followers on Twitter, but her tweet was soon trending worldwide alongside the hashtag #HasJustineLandedYet. Of course, Justine didn't know any of this during her long flight. She landed to a slew of angry texts, tweets and emails. Shortly thereafter, she was also fired from her role at IAC.

Then, of course, there's the example of a former presidential candidate, whose open-mic audio recording was released as he was running for president in 2016. On the audio recording from 2004, he was heard saying, "I just start kissing them. It's like a magnet. Just kiss. I don't even wait. And when you're a star, they let you do it. You can do anything. Grab 'em by the p*ssy. You can do anything." Unlike the other examples, however, the repercussions for this incident weren't nearly severe enough. The man went on to become the President of the United States, meaning "Grab 'em by the p*ssy" may one day, tragically, appear in the "Presidential Quotes" category of the quiz game show *Jeopardy!*.

More recently, in 2021, the world of consulting was shocked when the KPMG UK chair resigned after comments made in a virtual town hall session attended by approximately 500 people. Bill Michael, who had headed the company since 2017, said, "I have spoken to a lot of partners, and people at all sorts of levels, where it almost feels like this [pandemic] is being done to them. Well, you can't play the role of victim unless you're sick. And I hope you're not sick, and you're not ill, and if you're not, take control of your life, don't sit there and moan about it."

In another part of the video, Bill also questioned whether unconscious bias training, which attempts to challenge people to consider any stereotypes they hold without realising it, was effective. "There is no such thing as unconscious bias," he said. "I don't buy it, because after every single unconscious bias training that's ever been done, nothing has ever improved. So, unless you care, you actually won't change." Whatever his intentions were in saying these things at the time, a scandal erupted when his comments were made public. The damage to his reputation and to the reputation of the firm had already been done. Bill, who had made over £1.7 million GBP in the previous year, issued an apology, described his position as "untenable" in the wake of the scandal, and promptly resigned.[13]

"Michael's departure was no surprise, after he failed to meet the standard required of leaders," commented Gemma McCall, the CEO of Culture Shift. "Leaders really do need to take heed and exceed expectations when it comes to creating safe and supported environments for all employees. Organisations should absolutely be putting equality, diversity, and inclusion at the heart of their practices, and this should be coming from board level down."[14]

If there is anything these stories teach us, it is that we need to be mindful of the words we use, as one poorly chosen statement in front of our team or with client stakeholders may have severe ramifications. As Warren Buffett, famed investor and the "Oracle" of Omaha, once stated, "It takes 20 years to build a reputation and five minutes to ruin it."[15]

# Structure

In our everyday conversations with our family and friends, we tend to ramble, jump wildly between ideas, and inject references or jokes that no one else would understand or appreciate. Obscure references from *The Simpsons* may be hilarious to those closest to us but will be met with confused stares when shared elsewhere.

It's almost as if we develop our own language with those closest to us, where we forego any structure favouring an improvisational, lyrical jazz of seemingly random thoughts and emotions. That sort of understanding is a beautiful testament to the bond that is built over many years.

With our clients or our co-workers, however, the way we communicate and share ideas changes. We do not have the luxury of assuming that they will instinctively understand everything we say or not say. We cannot expect our clients to read between the lines or for our colleagues to understand obscure references they'd have no way of knowing. Developing rapport takes time, which we may not have with all our clients or colleagues. Hence, we need to be mindful that our communication is clear, concise, and without ambiguity.

Ensuring that we are structured in our communications will have several positive ramifications. First, it allows us to consider what we are trying to convey. Second, it will make it easier for those listening to or reading our communications to understand our ideas. Third, adopting a clear structure will present an opportunity for improved collaboration.

Applying the appropriate structure allows us to be more deliberate, to consider all the different aspects we may have missed if we only rambled off the cuff. Without becoming mired in agonizing levels of detail, there are several popular approaches worth mentioning. For example, when answering competency-based questions, a popular approach is to employ the STAR structure. STAR stands for Situation, Task, Action, Result.[16] When asked to give an example of a time when we faced a difficult problem at work and how we solved the problem, our response could be:

> **Situation:** "I was working as a retail manager at a department store during prom season. A customer purchased a dress online and had it delivered to the store. One of my associates accidentally put the dress out on the floor, where another customer immediately purchased it."

**Task:** "I knew I needed to make this right for the customer to meet my own service level standards and to uphold the reputation of the company."

**Action:** "Before calling the customer to let her know about the mistake, I located the same dress at another store location nearby. I ordered it to be pressed and delivered to her home the morning of prom, along with a gift card to thank her for her understanding."

**Result:** "The customer was so thankful that she wrote us a five-star review on several review sites."

While the STAR structure is primarily used for behavioural and situational interview questions, we can readily adapt it to any other communication. When sending an email to a group, for example, consider whether the situation or the actions are clearly articulated. Our objective is not to identify a structure and then shoehorn it into every situation. Rather, it is to adapt to our circumstances to ensure we structure our thinking and present our complete thoughts and desired outcomes clearly to others.

Stanford Graduate School of Business lecturer Matt Abrahams introduced a slightly different variant for organising information when writing an email or when presenting ideas. In his book, *Speaking Up Without Freaking Out*, he proposes a three-pronged approach that answers three basic questions:

**What:** Identify the context of the situation.

**So what:** Develop further ideas from the context that will resonate with your audience.

**Now what:** Present the next steps for moving forward.

This is a simple method to add structure to any communication. For example, rather than sending a long, rambling, convoluted email about the office party, consider following the structure by writing, "The office party is tonight. It will be a great opportunity to meet folks from across the teams. Please be punctual and don't forget about the raffle."[17]

Again, the purpose of structure is not to find one approach and to stick to it at all costs. It is to facilitate our own thinking and craft a message that is easy to understand, no matter who is on the receiving end of that message.

If, for example, we find ourselves pitching an idea, a slightly different structure may be more appropriate:

**Problem/Opportunity:** Expose an issue, or explain how an existing product, service, or practice can be improved.

**Solution:** Your company's future or existing plan to address the problem. Stronger if supplemented with facts and figures.

**Benefit:** What the customer will directly experience as a result.

On the other hand, if we are preparing a presentation or report, a pyramid approach may be more appropriate. In the late 1960s, Barbara Minto, working at McKinsey, created the Minto Pyramid Principle. In the pyramid, the key message is supported by any number of arguments, with each argument being supported by sub-arguments. This logical structure can be further improved by removing, as much as possible, overlap between the arguments and sub-arguments. The MECE principle entails grouping arguments and sub-arguments in such a way that they are mutually exclusive (ME) and collectively exhaustive (CE). By challenging ourselves to follow the MECE principle in conjunction with a pyramid information structure, we will effectively improve the logical flow of our presentations or reports.[18]

## Minto Pyramid

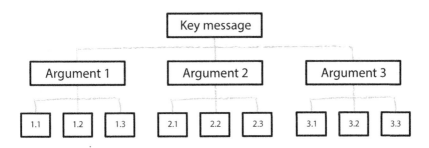

Establishing a clearly laid-out structure should apply to all our communications, including emails, status reports, team updates, or meetings. Structured communications also present an opportunity to collaborate with other stakeholders or clients. When we solicit input when defining and agreeing on the structure, we create a chance to turn an us-versus-them relationship into one based on collaboration and co-creation. For example, the simple act of starting a meeting by asking all of the participants if they agree with the agenda or if there are any amendments or additions creates a sense that their input is valuable and appreciated. Furthermore, given the high cost of meetings, we need to ensure that the time is spent as efficiently as possible.[19] There are several ways this can be achieved, including making the objective clear, validating the agenda with stakeholders, subsequently sticking to the agenda and finishing the meeting on time as stakeholders may have other commitments to attend.

By being structured in our communications, listening and tailoring our approach, we will be in a much better position to ensure our stakeholders are aligned and engaged. I recall working with a telecommunications firm in South Africa, developing a high-level customer experience strategy. To do so, our team would need to work with all of the department heads. Unfortunately, each of the department heads considered themselves the king or queen of their own siloed empire, not incentivised or particularly eager to collaborate with anyone, much less external consultants.

In one of the introductory meetings, the head of the mobile department, in no uncertain terms, let us know he didn't like consultants, didn't know why we were there and didn't want us there. By no means the introduction we were hoping for.

It was only through listening to his concerns, acknowledging him, and pragmatically answering his questions that we were able to get our foot in the door. By structuring our communications, keeping him and other stakeholders engaged, we proved the value of our approach. Additionally, we used workshop sessions as a means by which to break down the organisational silos and encourage the department heads to collaborate. We eventually convinced him and other reluctant stakeholders to become more engaged, open, and trusting in us and our approach through our frequent and structured communications.

Effective communication is the bedrock upon which relationships are built, ideas shared, and engagements successfully navigated along their way to completion. Not communicating effectively, using the wrong or ambiguous language, or assuming communication is happening without a plan in place, will only result in misunderstandings, assumptions being made, and the occasional, unfortunate tears.

Our responsibility is to listen with the intent of understanding, to be the moderators that create a safe space for others to contribute their ideas, and to build bridges between organisational silos where none may have existed before. In conjunction with a structured approach, we will build better relationships with our stakeholders, facilitate more effective exchanges of information, and increase our engagements' probability of success.

"Stick to your true north—build greatness for the long term."

Ruth Porat

# Andrew Finlayson

"I never, ever wanted to explore consulting as a career opportunity. So, I am a consulting denial person," Andrew Finlayson said with a wry smile. We were sitting in the Accenture headquarters in London, located on Fenchurch Street in the city's Square Mile. The floors occupied by Accenture Interactive had changed quite a lot since I had last visited, with a new open concept interior design meant to convey a more contemporary, start-up feel.

I first met Andrew during my time at Accenture and was immediately impressed by his charisma, easy-going nature, and ability to put those around him at ease. He gave the impression of being a truly authentic, genuine individual, taking a real interest in those he was speaking with. He had a glowing reputation among other consultants and clients, quickly rising up the ranks at Accenture. I was keen to speak with Andrew about his life, the adversity he'd faced along the way, and how he'd become so well-regarded amongst colleagues and clients alike.

Andrew was born in Southport, a large seaside town south of Blackpool in the UK. When he was five, his family moved to Nottingham before moving to Blackpool when he was in high school. His father had been a butcher most of his life, but once in Blackpool, he began running a hotel and opened a shop. Andrew helped where he could, reminiscing, "I'd do everything. Cook breakfast, cook dinners, maybe stepping behind the bar. Yeah, it was a shop, so jewellery and brass. Worked at buying inventory stock, helping with where stock levels are, stock takes, all the things you do when you run a business. I didn't call it entrepreneurship; I just needed to make a living. My parents didn't know about careers and things, that wasn't their background."

"My mom started working at 15, and my dad started at 12. My mum worked in retail all her life and can tell you lots about Royal Daulton pottery but very little about consulting! My dad has been a delivery driver, taxi driver, rag-and-bone man and warehouse operator before settling in on being a butcher at 16. His early life was very hard and he knew poverty. He wasn't a big talker and just got stuck into his work. He was select mute for a number of years following a traumatic incident and made him a brilliant listener. I got my listening skills from dad."

Andrew attended Blackpool college, thinking, "I'm gonna be a chef because I know how to cook." He continued, "There was a module that was eight weeks to write recipes on the computer. I didn't read the eight weeks, so I did the assignment at home and brought it in. I finished it in the first week and the lecturer, who was also lecturing full-time in computing in the broader courses, was just questioning my decision of being a chef." Andrew took the advice and began to take on more computer-based courses. In the meantime, he needed to keep working. "I was looking for jobs to do what I did, but I have people skills and technical skills. I saw a job during training, so I went for that."

He taught courses in WordPerfect, DataEase, Lotus 1-2-3, Aldus PageMaker, and Windows 3.1 in addition to a variety of other computer related subjects. In time, as his skills and knowledge improved, he began to write and deliver courses himself. It was then that he thought, "Why am I doing this for someone else? I think I'm okay, I'll start a training centre." Andrew established his own training centre and ran it for two years. He soon learned the value of self-promotion, making himself available for local radio shows so that he would be able to promote the business.

"It was good, I liked it a lot, but after a couple of years of that, there was a company we were training who was starting a multimedia company. After doing all the training for their staff, they said, 'Okay, you need to run our team, so how about you come in.' So, I became a founding member for a larger ambition that they had."

Andrew went from organising corporate training sessions to running a multimedia company that produced CDs and websites. The CD-production side of the business was considerable, mass manufacturing more than three million CDs at a time. Andrew had an opportunity to learn and be directly involved in all sides of the business, including resource planning, resource scheduling, logistics provisioning, creative direction, product manufacturing, investor relations through to being the product owner for new offices. The company was growing quickly, looking to secure funding for faster expansion and to float on the stock market. Then tragedy struck.

"We were going to float in October or November. It's very fuzzy now to recall as I lost time in the chaos of that particular September. It was devastating for so many people. We'd done all the fundraising rounds. I can't tell you how many investment banks I'd worked with, but we did a lot of fundraising rounds. Then there was this thing on the telly. We all knew." Andrew recalled the moment the attacks of 9/11 happened in New York.

"We were doing international work. I was working with people in New York at the time. We knew as soon as that happened that there'll be a delay or an impact. So, there was no flotation." The impact on the company was substantial. "It's hard to let individual people go. We've got a great thing here, now we're actually gonna start shutting it down. We're gonna try and find a buyer. We actually had to find some buyers. A few people move over there, few people over here, but that's the rub. I mean, we were working with some fantastic people; the board was people I now see are CEOs of good, wholesome firms."

The next few years were a whirlwind for Andrew, who freely admitted as much. "So, from multimedia, to retail, to then software retail, to merchandising specialist retail, to then retail again, to then moving into a bit of software again, and then going into life sciences due to the life event."

"So, my second daughter's birth created an inflection point of what is meaningful, what is important, versus what can you get paid for. The Japanese Ikigai is quite an easy way of structuring that. We can all do what we want, to remember what the world will pay for, and what difference we're making. There's a nice full aspect to your 'raison d'être'"

"So, actually, I began working in life sciences 15 years ago after the birth of my youngest daughter. I was happily married to Tracey, had a daughter already and she was active, loved to dance, and everything was 'normal'. My youngest daughter, Georgia, was born with severe disabilities, and that was very difficult. I started to suffer from extreme anxiety and had a mental breakdown. A practical step to help me handle that was to quit my job and my roles in retail and focus on something that helped me. I was health illiterate, and I felt I needed to learn about healthcare and learn fast. Our family life was never to be 'normal' again, and I had the pressure of knowing this but not knowing what to do all hitting me all at once."

"I've worked in retail, media, public services, consumer tech, catering, and conferences. I'm a qualified mortgage broker, I'm an ISO auditor, I'm a developer, I'm a trainer, I'm a waiter, I'm also a chef, but it wasn't enough. I've worked around in different patches and I needed to answer a lot of questions about the health system I didn't know. I joined AstraZeneca as the company itself was going through a lot of changes. I was quite enjoying the industry but didn't want to work in some of the areas that they had, only because I didn't feel personally passionate about some of the areas. There was a guy from Accenture that called me, along with a number of other companies, but the guy from Accenture I quite liked. He told me the company was changing and they wanted people with diverse backgrounds, so I thought, 'Sure'."

"I took the role as a manager because I didn't know what the roles and grades were, so it made no difference to me. As long as I was paid enough to pay the mortgage," Andrew joked. Joining from industry was a challenge for Andrew. He went through nine interviews, with every single interviewer telling him the same thing: "You are absolutely the right person for this firm, but I think I'm the wrong area for you. You should go and work over there." He had come into the process thinking that he would be joining the firm, not realising that a firm of this scale would have its fiefdoms. He didn't know until much later that some interviewers passed on his application as he didn't have a degree-level education. It was a socioeconomic block he wasn't aware of, despite his wealth of experience.

"The firm does have pockets; it has areas; it has departments; it has practices. So no, it took four months to do something which other companies could probably do in a day, but the ultimate result is I did join the area that I think I'm happy with. In hindsight, I think if I had joined some of the other areas that I now know, or that I was ruled out of, then I don't think I would have been happy. I think it takes a little bit longer to join, but actually, most people are trying to get you into the right place because it is such a large organisation."

"If you wanted to, you could work 24/7. The company is on 24/7; it's in over 100 countries. If you don't suffer from natural curiosity, companies like this aren't very good for you because there's so much on. If you feel that you need to know everything, companies like this aren't very good for you. The first year was not me trying to learn everything; it was me trying to find people that knew more than I did." Andrew instinctively understood the need to network, to find those who knew more than he did, as they would be able to guide his career and be there when he had questions pertaining to specific subject matter.

"I'm very patient. I'll try and listen, and I meet as many people as I can. I still put down at least four hours a week to meet people I've not met before. That excludes community events. I make time to do that even though it's personally inconvenient, so I can meet people. I think active networking is a good phrase for it. Sometimes it's just being personable and showing people what your motives are versus their motives and appreciating that. I think it goes back to my foundation principle of appreciating diversity. I don't have a problem if somebody doesn't agree with me. I don't have a problem if you're from a different culture. I don't actually get annoyed or bitter if you talk differently than I do. It is not a thing. Networking is easy because it's not a chore; it's normal. Yeah, and I think most of the people I've got working on some fantastic projects have been from that sort of proactive networking and just getting used to people."

Andrew explained that his daughter, Georgia, was diagnosed with DDX3X, a very rare, spontaneous genetic mutation, and understood everything he was told by the geneticist due to his life experience thus far. According to the DDX3X Foundation, the mutation was only discovered in 2014 and has only been identified in about 300 individuals. However, doctors believe it is the cause of one to 3% of all intellectual disabilities in females.[20]

"It was diagnosed a couple of years ago through a trial that David Cameron helped set up with Genomics England, which is a trial called 'The 100,000 Genomes Project.' People that didn't have a reason for their condition or one for those they cared for. Also, one that harmed the ability to get the most appropriate treatments and social care considerations. They were put into this trial, and they would help to try and find out what went wrong using whole-genome sequencing and analysing DNA. It was pretty cutting-edge, and I'm now privileged to be working with Genomics England, and I have attended their forums, and I can't be more thankful."

Taking a moment to reflect, Andrew noted that, "I suppose we're on, and I don't want to make this too full of philosophy, we are all on our individual quests and journeys." His approach dealing with others, undoubtedly influenced by his own experiences, continued to evolve and mature. The traits of tolerance, acceptance, and openness to others, which he honed growing up around hotels and shops in Blackpool, became even more distinguishable as his career progressed.

"I suppose there's an added layer of depth that I now appreciate that I didn't appreciate before. I always appreciated people, but not quite to the same level. I now have clients and I want to understand what their motivations are, not just what they want delivered. What are their motivations, what are their passions, how do they feel successful? I have relationships with clients where I know a bit more about their personal lives, only because occasionally you share a few things and you want to be good citizens and good people. Sometimes I have found clients who were on this similar quest to me for very similar reasons, and you find a common bond with that."

"Are they better clients? Well, we both got our companies to work with; they've got their companies, I've got my company, but if we can find common ground between it then business can be done. People are people; diversity is inevitable."

"If you are not interested in inclusion, respect, and diversity, you will cap out in your career at a certain point. In the end, a P&L isn't the only thing; in the end, cash is not an ultimate driver. In the end, mutual respect and shared benefit wins. I always had that in my mindset."

No matter the challenges he faced in his personal or professional life, Andrew was always able to adapt, count on his support structure, identify solutions, and map out a way forward. A combination of hard work, innate honesty, positive attitude, and openness with those around him propelled Andrew's career to the upper echelons at Accenture. He joined as a manager, quickly rose to the role of senior manager, and became a managing director in 2014. He advanced again in December of 2018 to senior transformation executive, leading the Health & Life Sciences Client Group for Accenture Interactive UK&I.

"A step backward, after making a wrong turn,
is a step in the right direction."

Kurt Vonnegut Jr.

# Adversity

Santi Cazorla started playing football in Spain, joining the club Villarreal six months before turning 18. At five foot six, he was never going to compete for headers against the likes of Ronaldo or Bale, but he was fast, agile and had great vision in identifying opportunities for passes.

He famously rejected playing for Real Madrid when rumours of his departure began circulating in 2008, saying, "There are many other things in football besides Real Madrid. It's clear that it is possible to say 'no' to them, there is no doubt that they are a great team, but I also feel very satisfied and valued at my club." He added, "I hope I can continue growing at Villarreal because I am young, and I'm only starting off with the national team."

After several successful years at Villarreal, he joined Malaga in 2011 and helped the club qualify for the Champions League for the first time in its history, before going on the join the mighty Arsenal Football Club in 2012.[21]

Based in north London, Arsenal was and continues to be one of the top clubs in Europe and consistently superior to their diminutive north London rivals, the Tottenham Hotspur. Over the course of the next four years, Santi became a fan favourite. He helped the club qualify for the Champions League in 2013, winning the 2014 and 2015 FA Cup and became one of the most accurate passers in the league.

Unfortunately, Santi struggled with injury throughout his career. He could even recall the moment it all began, back in 2013 when playing in a friendly between Spain and Chile. He broke a small bone in his ankle, and while it was painful, it did not prevent him from playing. However, the injury continued to cause him pain during every game he played. He fought through the pain until 2016, when he sustained a severe injury to his right Achilles tendon while playing in the Champions League fixture. "Half-time killed me, because it got cold, I'd be crippled at the start of the second half, and the pain got worse and worse," he recalled. "That night, I cried; it had become too much. I had to stop. Then the problems started."

Surgery after surgery, his wound continued to become infected, prompting the need for more surgeries. At one point, skin from his forearm was needed to rebuild his heel. The tattoo of his daughter's name, which he had on his forearm, is now partly located where his heel used to be. He underwent ten operations, had 10 centimetres of his tendon rebuilt, missed deadlines, developed gangrene, and faced the possibility of losing his leg and never being able to walk again.[22] His family, the fans, the players, and the Arsenal manager at that time, Arsène Wenger, supported Cazorla throughout his operations and subsequent recovery. Of Wenger, Santi recalled, "He renewed my contract before the first operation, which was an incredible gesture. He called me in: 'Santi, I'm going to give you the optional year. It's here, sign it, have your operation with peace of mind.' That helped me focus on my rehabilitation without fear. I'm eternally grateful for that."

After months of rehabilitation, he played his first game in 636 days when he appeared for his home club of Villarreal in a friendly against Hercules, later signing officially with the club. Not many people gave him much of a chance to succeed, but Santi was determined to return to form and play consistently for the club.

In the 2019–2020 season, he had 30 goal contributions across all competitions and earned a recall to the Spanish national team for the first time in 1299 days.[23] After he moved to Qatar for the 2020-2021 season, he registered 18 goals and 13 assists in 30 games and was named Qatar FA Best Player of the Year at the age of 36.

# Action

While being a football fan may help relate to Santi's story, it is by no means a requirement to appreciate the determination he showed in the face of adversity. Adversity is an inevitable part of life, but how we deal with it plays a pivotal role in our personal and professional lives. There are three main learnings we can take from his story that are applicable to consulting. First, his immediate support structure helped him get through the most challenging moments. Second, he did not dwell on the negatives but focused on the path forward. Third, he had a methodical, structured approach to getting back on track.

Supporting others, helping them, or being there for them when they need it most, is a potent catalyst to spur a positive work culture. It helps build team cohesion, reduces friction, and effectively instils those positive actions as part of the organisation's makeup. The movie *Pay It Forward*, released in 2000, was based on the premise that for every good deed or favour, if the recipient were to pay it forward to three other people, the exponential nature of the process would create a better world. It is up to us to what degree we go out of our way to perform good deeds, or if we pay it forward at all, but the positive impacts of taking action will be undeniable.

These actions do not have to be overly dramatic or elaborate to be effective. For example, I recall a late Thursday evening at PwC when a collective decision was made that all those in the immediate team would head out to the local bar for a well-deserved, post-work drink. As we started packing up and heading out, there was one colleague who did not move. Seeing the colleague not getting up to join the rest of the team, Steven MacLellan made his way over to inquire as to why he wasn't joining us.

It turned out he was frantically trying to complete a relatively simple, but onerously time-consuming task that was due the next day. He was the only one left to complete the job, meaning he would have had to stay at the office for a few hours, missing out on drinks with the team. Without a second thought, Steven took off his jacket, sat down, opened his laptop, and proceeded to help with the task. Several others promptly did the same, myself included. With the collective effort, we were able to make quick work of the undertaking, and we were at the bar in no time.

Steven had a decision to make in this scenario, and he chose to support his colleague. His actions inspired others to do the same. It was a real-world example of positive actions and support propagating throughout the team. There is no question that if any one of the team members were presented with a similar scenario in the future, they would not hesitate to help others based on that experience. It was the real-world embodiment of the Pay it Forward premise. Even small acts of kindness or support, particularly when performed by leaders, have the power to inspire others to do the same when the opportunity arises, improving the overall team culture and cohesion.

While it is essential to be there for others, it is equally vital to ensure that we have a support structure of our own. For Santi Cazorla, the support of his family, his team, his friends, his coach, and the fans played a vital role in his ability to persevere through and overcome the adversity he faced. Likewise, we must ensure that we have a support structure in place to overcome our own hardships.

The composition of our support structure will vary from person to person. Still, the fundamental principle is that we should not bear any burden alone, nor should we consider asking for help to be a sign of weakness remains the same. As the often-cited slogan reminds us, "Sometimes asking for help is the bravest move you can make. You don't have to go it alone."

Actively building out a network within our organisation is key to ensuring that we will have people to turn to with questions and when we need an extra pair of hands. David Fowler, formerly of PwC and KPMG, took two steps to build out his network.

He recalled, "One was taking advantage of all of the different events that were offered. There are lots of networking events, and there are lots of team events. The second thing is probably a bit more structured. I've done it a couple of times, thinking through 'Whom do I need to know?' In my world, I'm going to need to know people who work in technology; people who work in utilities. You can always think through the different dimensions of 'Where's my network going to be' because of roughly how the organisation is structured. Basically, seeking out those people; having coffees. I must have spent 200 quid on coffees here. Joking aside, go out and mind map what people you're going to need and find those people."

David adopted both an organic and structured approach to building out his support network. Should he ever find himself in a position where he has a technology question, he will have someone to reach out to for support. Having these people in his network will also increase the probability that they will want to make time to help him, in contrast to him frantically contacting them at the last minute, out of the blue. In addition to his professional support structure, David also had a personal support structure that he could look to when needed. Building out a robust support structure will help us overcome challenges that we will face along the way. Like David, Santi had built a robust support structure that was able to help him through his most challenging moments.

Second, Santi did not dwell on the problem but instead focused on the way forward. After he had gone through surgery after surgery, there may have been times when self-pity, anguish, and frustration could have overcome him. Likewise, we will face challenges both big and small in our daily lives that threaten to overwhelm us. The instinct to curl up into a ball in the face of a mountain of adversity is not uncommon.

Yet, Santi did not give up and did not spend time focused on the adversity he faced, but instead identified his objectives and began working towards them. Sometimes, while standing at the base of a mountain, the challenge ahead may seem insurmountable, but the only way to get to the top is to take that first step, then another, and then another.

Jacqueline Susann, the famous American writer and actress, captured this sentiment perfectly by writing, "When you're climbing Mount Everest, nothing is easy. You just take one step at a time, never look back, and always keep your eyes glued to the top."[24]

Some of the decisions we make, while at times poor in hindsight, are an opportunity for reflection and learning. Everyone makes mistakes, everyone faces adversity, everyone stumbles along the way, but the key is not to become so overly focused on what could have been that attention is taken away from what needs to be done. Dwelling on past mistakes or errors for too long prevents us from focusing on the path ahead.

In the 1997 movie *The Edge*, a plane carrying the two men crashes down in the Alaskan wilderness. While the ensuing struggle for survival against the wilderness and the elements makes for an entertaining film, there was one exchange that was particularly relevant. As Charles Morse (Anthony Hopkins) was speaking with Robert Green (Alec Baldwin), shortly after their crash, Morse observed: "You know, I once read an interesting book which said that, uh, most people lost in the wild, they, they die of shame."

"What?" Green replied.

Charles Morse continued, "Yeah, see, they die of shame. 'What did I do wrong? How could I have gotten myself into this?' And so they sit there and they...die. Because they didn't do the one thing that would save their lives."

"And what is that, Charles?" Green inquired.

"Thinking," Morse concluded.

The exchange highlighted our tendency of spending too much time thinking about what we could have said or done differently rather than focus on what needs to be done to move forward. There will always be time for detailed introspection, analysis, and corrective plans to be implemented later. However, when we are in the middle of a crisis, we need to focus on how to overcome the challenges ahead of us, not things that already happened that we no longer have any control over.

First, Santi had a robust support structure. Second, he did not dwell on the problem. Third, he had a methodical approach to his recovery. Likewise, we must identify the appropriate structure to help us overcome whatever challenge we are facing. A straightforward approach is to determine where we want to get to and when we need to be there, then work back in time to identify the milestones along the way to that objective.

Jessica Wiese, Roger Buehler, and Dale Griffin noted the challenges associated with planning in a report on the subject, stating, "In many contexts, people strive to predict accurately when a task will be finished. They may be called upon by others to provide a realistic estimate, or may privately seek an accurate prediction to guide their own decisions. Moreover, people make important decisions and binding commitments on the basis of these predictions, and thus errors can be costly."

They continued, "For example, individuals may rely on task completion predictions to decide which projects, and how many projects, to tackle in the coming month. A tendency to underestimate completion times can result in over-commitment, stress, and aggravation. People frequently underestimate the time needed to complete tasks and we examined a strategy—known as backward planning—that may counteract this optimistic bias. Backward planning involves starting a plan at the end goal and then working through required steps in reverse-chronological order, and is commonly advocated by practitioners as a tool for developing realistic plans and projections."[25]

For Anatoly Roytman, for example, scaling Accenture Interactive required many milestones on the way to his desired objective. It was only when he understood what those milestones were that he could set upon taking the appropriate actions to achieve them.

For Santi, it was being able to play football again. To do that, there were a number of steps he'd need to take. For example, if the stated objective was to play his first game, working backwards, he would have to train with the team, train individually, build up his fitness, undertake physiotherapy, recover from surgery, and go through surgery. Each milestone along the way would require him to complete a number of activities, at set times, before being able to move to the next phase. There would be no shortcuts.

Returning to the analogy of climbing Everest for a moment, there has never been a mountaineer whose plan consisted of a single item: "Reach the summit. Celebrate!" Any successful expedition requires meticulous planning and preparation preceding the climb. Each factor is considered in detail, be it the equipment, the route, the weather, the team, the support, or the conditioning required to take on the arduous challenge. Tragically, even with all the preparation and training, more than 300 people have perished on the mountain, highlighting the fact that no matter how good the planning and preparation, things may still go horribly wrong.

A structured approach will reduce the risk of failure, as it will help us identify critical measures and milestones in the journey to overcome any challenge. Simply hoping that things will work out or curling up into a ball under the desk has never been an effective strategy to overcome adversity. Instead, having the proper support, not dwelling on the problem itself, and implementing a structured approach to move forward will serve to help us overcome any challenge in our way.

# Don't sweat

When it comes to not dwelling on the negatives or on the problem itself, Melissa Max-Macarthy of Accenture offered a key piece of advice she learned when supporting a financial services client project focused on updating their call-centre infrastructure: "Don't sweat the small stuff."

She'd been entrusted with being one of the project leads on the high-profile engagement. "I remember my first ever project at a global bank. I was running a team and all of a sudden you couldn't call this bank and you couldn't find what your balance was. Everything was going well as we were migrating from a London voice data centre to one outside of London. I was there until 5 a.m. when I left to go back and get some sleep. I get a call from my managing director saying everything was down. This was back in 2014 when people still called into the bank."

Melissa now found herself in a precarious position whereby the bank's clients were unable to contact the bank by phone. With every minute that passed, the bank's customers would be trying to reach the bank with questions, with issues, or with amendments to their accounts, but would ultimately not be able to get through to anyone with the system malfunctioning.

"We get fined £100k every time we bring down one of the systems, and at this point we had press reports, news on Twitter, Facebook, and others, so we were really struggling," Melissa recalled.

Outages of this sort do not go unnoticed, and within an instant, everyone within the bank and within the consulting firm was aware of the issue. The matter was escalated to the CIO and to all the technical teams.

"There was no blame culture at all. Like it doesn't matter, it failed, and it was more about how you respond to it. So now the reason I said, 'Don't sweat the small stuff' is unless a service, a global service, has been taken out, it's never that bad." For Melissa, the experience with the bank put all other challenges she would face into perspective.

"Things are never as bad the next day; for me, that's a general life lesson, but definitely applicable in projects. One day you'll be tracking red (underperforming versus plan) and you're like, 'Oh my God, oh my God, oh my God, what am I doing?', and the next day the state of play has changed, and it's all okay."

No matter how overwhelming a crisis may seem at the time, Melissa's experience reminds us that it's essential to put the situation in perspective. Take a deep breath or go for a walk to overcome the initial wave of panic, fear, and frustration. Then, as Santi Cazorla's example taught us, seek out your support structure for perspective, focus on the path ahead, and plan what actions need to be taken to get back on track.

# Own it

"The buck stops here" is a phrase that was popularised by U.S. President Harry S. Truman, who kept a sign with that phrase on his desk in the Oval Office of the White House. The phrase refers to the notion that the President must make difficult decisions and accept the ultimate responsibility for those decisions. Likewise, we should own up to the mistakes we make and take the appropriate corrective actions.

Unfortunately, when we make a mistake, our instincts will throw us to either side of a wide spectrum. According to Ashley Cobert, a public relations professional, "On one end, you may act too quickly—saying too much and overcomplicating a situation in your attempts to recover quickly. On the other, you may be tempted to hastily cover up what happened and look for ways to defend yourself. While seeking help and self-preservation are both natural, neither extreme is the most effective when it comes to owning up to a mistake at work."[26]

She continued, "Just like Goldilocks and her porridge, somewhere in the middle is just right when owning up to a mistake. Here's your game plan: Upon realising your error, don't react right away. Instead, take a deep breath and analyse possible solutions. If the mistake is something that you can address, act immediately. For example, if you pushed send on a press release that was supposed to be on hold until tomorrow, call the distribution company right away and see if you can catch it before it goes live."

"If your mistake isn't retractable (or your attempt at retracting would cause more harm than good), devise a couple solutions to the problem before even stepping away from your computer. Decide who the most appropriate person to talk to would be, and approach that person (and only that person) with a clear, concise description of what happened. Tell her you'd appreciate her help and understand you're utilising her valuable time. Apologise—once—and then present your solutions. The less time you spend hemming and hawing and the more quickly you fix the mistake, the more your boss will see you as someone who does well under pressure and cares about the success of the company."

"We're all human, and we all make mistakes," noted Tammy Perkins, chief people officer at PMI Worldwide. "Keep in mind that the moment you say or do something, it becomes a fact with your employees, so it's important that you own it and take responsibility for it. A sincere apology can make a difference in your relationship with your team and reinforce trust."[27]

Everyone makes mistakes, but not everyone is able to overcome those mistakes with grace. The Forbes Coaches Council offered the following advice:

### Admit the mistake and identify solutions
When quickly admitting a mistake, also share your honest assessment of the impact of what happened and several options for resolving or lessening that impact.

### Protect the business, not your ego
Ask for help from your boss if needed. If not, keep them updated.

### Focus on the "next shot"
Rather than focusing their attention on the last shot they missed, great athletes will shift their attention to the next shot they need to make.

### Demonstrate you've learned from the mistake
Analyse what went wrong, make the correction, and put measures in place to prevent a repeat.

### Focus on the opportunity to improve
Taking responsibility is important, but don't overdo the "mea culpa". Rather, discuss the situation, what you've learned, and how you will improve.

### Start with "I'm sorry"
Simple, but powerful, it communicates that you recognise the error and any unintended circumstances.

### Think like the boss
Put yourself in the shoes of your boss and consider what they would expect you to do or say.

### Choose an audience-focused approach

Consider who your audience is and tailor your message to them.

### Use a "reframing" technique to help everyone calm down

Put the situation in perspective and present a clear remedy
and prevention plan.

### Preserve your integrity over your image

Own the mistake early, transparently, and be serious
about making things right.[28]

Adversity is an inevitable part of life. Sometimes, it will be of our own
making, as we will all make mistakes. Other times it may be any number
of external factors that will create challenging situations that will need to
be overcome. As we learned from the remarkable recovery of Santi Cazorla,
having the proper support, focusing on the path ahead, and structuring the
approach to recovery helped him through one of the most challenging times
in his life. Taking inspiration from Melissa Max-Macarthy, we must not lose
our heads, remain calm in the face of adversity, and put whatever challenge
we face into perspective. It is only then, after we've taken a deep breath,
accepted what has occurred, and analysed the situation, that we will be able
to identify the appropriate path forward.

"Whether you believe you can do a thing or not, you are right."

Henry Ford

# Jeremy Dalton

Anytime someone explicitly states they do not want to mention a company name, chances are something did not go well. That is precisely how Jeremy Dalton began recounting his first experience out of university. Having met Jeremy at PwC, I was always impressed by how well he crafted his brand, how well he seemed to get along with those around him, and the ease by which he commanded the room's attention when presenting in front of hundreds of people.

Now a widely recognised figure in the virtual reality (VR) and augmented reality (AR) field, and a prominent public speaker and published author, I was curious about the path Jeremy had taken and the challenges he faced along the way. I wanted to find out how the once shy and self-conscious young man had transformed into someone who would command the attention of a room of hundreds of senior partners.

"I'd say my lack of confidence became apparent in high school, when I started to develop my soon-to-be adult personality," Jeremy recalled. "I noticed that I was becoming more withdrawn, not in a super negative emotional sense, but withdrawn in the sense that 'introverted' would probably be the right descriptor. I didn't really want to participate in class. I was happy to work hard, but I had no interest in putting my hand up. I would work fine in groups, but I wouldn't love it. Socialising with people was not one of my priorities."

Jeremy identified his lack of confidence as one of the areas he wanted to improve. He always attained good grades in school but felt like his lack of soft skills held him back. He wasn't very confident, but, as life would have it, he would be presented many opportunities to assert himself.

"Just after university, I had a job offer from a software development company, which I definitely do not want to name," Jeremy recollected with a smile. He had taken mathematics in university, even though he readily admitted not to have ever been passionate about it. When he graduated, he was offered a role with this unnamed firm. "It's in another city, and I moved there, stayed in a hotel nearby, and put a deposit down on an apartment." The company advertised that development skills were not required, and that comprehensive training would be provided. Excited to get going, Jeremy arrived at the office on the first day to no induction, no welcome from anybody, and no program of any kind.

"Well, where do I sit?" he inquired.

Uninterested, someone replied, "Oh, I think your seat is over there."

Jeremy made his way to the seat, sat down, and turned on the computer next to him.

"Okay, well, what do I do?" he asked.

"Oh, I guess, do the training," came the reply.

Jeremy looked around. There were no materials available. Eventually, someone told him to have a look at a PDF file on his computer's desktop.

"Are you f*cking kidding me?" Jeremy thought to himself. The company had clearly oversold their 'comprehensive' training programme.

In the same way we evaluate and seek to improve the experiences of our client's customers or employees, Jeremy's story reminds us that every journey or interaction within an organisation represents an area for potential improvement. In his case, the onboarding journey was so abysmal that he decided he'd had enough by the third day.

"I packed my bags that day, took a train back to Southampton and knocked on the door of my two friends who were doing their master's degrees. I just showed up at their doorstep with luggage in hand. And well, thankfully, they took me in."

"I applied to PwC, John Lewis, and to IBM, for completely different roles. For IBM, I got to the last stage of the application process and then crashed and burned. I had to deliver a presentation to sell a particular product to a senior manager at IBM. I didn't have a lot of confidence back then, and I needed a script to follow. I practised as best as I could, and went into the lion's den with my detailed script, and was completely flummoxed when he didn't accept it. He kept pushing me towards different conversational paths and not allowing me to talk about what I had prepared. I didn't know how to respond because I didn't have any ability or experience to adapt at that point. I pretty much just shoehorned my script into that conversation, which definitely didn't go down well. That resulted in my application being rejected, so IBM was out of the window."

In a previous chapter, we discussed the need to listen and adjust our presentations to our audience in terms of style and substance. As Jeremy's experience highlighted, we also need to adapt, in real-time, to the feedback we receive from our audience, even being willing to forego our prepared materials if required, to better tailor our messaging.

Jeremy continued, "I also made it to the last stage with John Lewis. As with IBM, I had to travel from Southampton to London for the assessment. Unfortunately, the bus near my house was running tremendously late, which led to me getting to the train station just in time to see the train disappear into the distance. I hopped on the next train to London, and I knew it was going to be tight. I sprinted across London's underground network, bashing into people, and leaping through closing train carriage doors. I finally ended up at John Lewis; and dashed inside, sweating profusely through my suit and tie. I let the receptionist know that I had arrived for the assessment centre but she looked confused and it took her a while to figure it all out. Then she said, 'Yes, sorry, they've already started.' I responded desperately, 'Can't you call them or do something?' No luck there. I didn't push it because again, I didn't really have the confidence at the time. I left the building and boarded the next train back to Southampton. It was a miserable journey."

Given the commonly available advancements in technology, whereby mapping applications will calculate optimal routes, considering traffic, weather, road closures, and many other factors, there is little excuse for anyone being late anymore. As the bestselling author Eric Jerome Dickey stated so succinctly, "Early is on time, on time is late, and late is unacceptable!"

Jeremy laughed, "Then PwC's final assessment came, and I have to admit, it wasn't my finest hour either! During the group exercise session, each person is given two unique solutions to a business problem that is being discussed."

"You're supposed to prioritise those unique pieces of information because you're the only person that can see them, communicating them to your team members to a successful conclusion. Now, being the perfectionist that I was at the time, I was desperate to process all the information in front of me. In doing so, I fell into a deliberately placed trap: there is too much information that you can analyse in the mere 10 minutes that you have to prepare. I spent too long on the generic company case study information and had just gotten through the first unique piece of information and they said, 'Right, time is over, let's start discussing what you found.'"

"The first thing that the candidate opposite me says is, 'I think it's a good idea to go through our unique pieces of information,' and I cringed internally. As the conversation travels around the table, each candidate reels off beautifully summarised versions of their two solutions. Then it comes to me and the proceedings are brought to a screeching halt as I announce sheepishly, 'Look, guys, I'm sorry, I didn't actually have time to do my second one, but then I came up with an idea. Why don't we continue going around the table, and meanwhile, I'll try and summarise my second solution and bring it into the conversation?' My suggestion was accepted with mild indifference. Fortunately, within the next minute or two, I had already ascertained that my second solution was not viable because we already had better options on the table. Consequently, I was able to recover from that situation, which probably saved me, despite my poor time prioritisation."

As a lot of the challenges are timeboxed, it is imperative to manage the available time effectively. We've previously discussed working backwards from the set objective. In this case, that objective may be to complete the report in a set amount of time, 40 minutes, for example. Working backwards from the 40-minute mark, assuming we want a five-minute buffer at the end and at least five minutes to check our work, we are left with 30 minutes.

If we give ourselves 10 minutes to write out details under each header and 10 minutes to decide on the structure and the headers themselves, we are left with 10 minutes to review the data provided. All these actions and timings are arbitrary and can be amended to the time, the tasks, and the objective. However, the method of working backwards from an objective helps reduce the optimistic bias and prevents us from spending too much time on one task at the cost of others. While Jeremy was aware of this as he began work on his second assignment at the assessment centre, one of the other participants evidently was not.

"I was very conscious that I had to get this right. I kept my game plan front of mind: I am going to literally skim through this and start writing down headers and sub-headers. Only when I've done that am I going to go into the content. So, it doesn't matter when they take the paper off me; the report will be as complete as it can be given the time constraints. That mental preparation served me well, but not everyone followed suit. It was an agonising situation for the chap across me because he obviously had his moment, his equivalent of what I had in the group exercise, and he just looked completely distraught. All he said was, 'I didn't write anything on the paper because I was still reading the material.' He knew, and we knew, it was all over for him."

A week later, Jeremy flew to visit his parents in Cyprus. Just as he landed at Larnaca and was waiting at baggage claim, he received a phone call from the UK. He answered tentatively, to hear, "Hi, Jeremy, I'm calling to give you some news." PwC had offered him the job.

"It was a delightful start to my holiday in Cyprus," Jeremy reminisced. "I joined PwC and attended a comprehensive induction; I was super excited and in awe of everything. I was told, 'Your first six months are going to be in audit, then you're going to be joining business recovery, and for the next two years, you're going to be working on your ACA [Associate Chartered Accountant] qualification.'"

Throughout the recruitment process, his first months at PwC, and the ACA qualification process, Jeremy continued to grow in confidence. "It wasn't was an overnight thing," he admitted. "Although it did feel that way once the dust had settled following my qualification as a Chartered Accountant."

For Jeremy, the ACA provided a means by which to boost his confidence and prove to himself, and others, what he was capable of. The rest, as he recalled, was built up gradually through day-to-day experiences and efforts. Through his work as a consultant, he was able to step outside of his comfort zone time and time again. With each new experience, he gained more confidence in himself, his abilities, and his presentation skills. In time, he recognised that audit and business recovery were not for him.

In what has become a common theme amongst successful consultants I've spoken with, Jeremy took charge of his career trajectory. He identified a new, rapidly expanding team within PwC that was at the forefront of emerging technologies and digital. He effectively navigated the politics of the organisation, supporting the team for several months and building up his network before officially aligning himself to the new team.

It was there that, given his interest in VR and AR, he began to shape his brand. He continued to challenge himself, taking on more public speaking engagements. With every presentation and every speech, his skills improved further. He had come a long way from being the timid, insecure young man he was in high school. He identified the areas where he wanted to improve and methodically set upon improving those areas. He established his personal brand and went on to become one of the foremost experts in VR/AR at PwC. He also authored a book on the subject in 2021 entitled *Reality Check: How Immersive Technologies Can Transform Your Business*.

"Designing a presentation without an audience in mind
is like writing a love letter and addressing it 'to whom it may concern.'"

Ken Haemer

# Presentations

I was standing on stage in front of over 200 other consultants and lecturers. The gravity of the situation had just hit me. The fight or flight instinct kicked in, overriding any haze remaining from the previous evening's festivities, sharpening my every sense of the surroundings. The all too familiar surge of adrenaline followed shortly thereafter. Cold sweat. Clammy hands. The microphone that I was holding in my hand began to shake a little. Then, just a little more.

At that point, I was all too aware that everyone in the cavernous hall was looking at me, waiting for me to speak. Was my fly down? No time to check. The microphone was shaking uncontrollably from side to side at this point. I reached up with my other hand to steady the first, holding the microphone with both hands as if I were about to break into a moving ballad. I took a deep breath and began to speak.

I had arrived in Chicago three days earlier for the integration and education programme organised by Accenture. Several days of lectures, workshops, and networking events were scheduled on a campus approximately an hour west of the city in a place called St. Charles. One of the organised activities was a large-scale business simulation, wherein 40 teams of five would compete against one another. Virtual supply chains had to be orchestrated, manufacturing runs coordinated, and product-feature sets decided upon. With every round of the competition, dozens of decisions needed to be made that would have an impact on the potential success or failure of the enterprise.

My team, comprised of consultants from across the world, had picked me to be the CEO of our virtual enterprise. We agreed on a strategy and proceeded to see it through. While a few miscalculations cost us the early lead, we bounced back, and we were on a promising trajectory as the final day approached. During the last session, the host began to unveil the scores, starting with the lowest. The teams in the top 10 were revealed one by one, with each successive unveiling garnering more and more applause. Finally, the host reached the top three. First, he unveiled the third place, and it was not our team, meaning we had either finished first or second. The tension was palpable as we awaited the unveiling. Then, in an instant, the final results appeared on the giant screens. We had won!

Unfortunately, this meant we had to go on stage and, as the CEO of our virtual enterprise, I had to say a few words. After I overcame the initial burst of adrenaline and succeeded in steadying the microphone in my hands, I did finally manage to string together a few semi-coherent words. As I recall, I thanked my team and the organisers before, to the host's dismay, launching into an unplanned Q&A session. He graciously allowed me to embarrass myself a little longer before gently ushering our team off the stage.

In addition to being very proud of what my team accomplished, it was a meaningful experience that exemplified a well-run project. In a short period of time, working with an international team I'd never met before, we formed a plan, delegated responsibilities, communicated well, trusted each other and stuck to our strategy, even in the face of adversity, making incremental corrections along the way as required. The experience was a remarkable one and one I will remember. Beyond the lessons learned, it was also a stark reminder of the visceral, physical reaction that being on stage in front of an audience elicited. I had presented hundreds of times before that day and have presented hundreds of times since. Still, the all too familiar feeling of adrenaline kicking in before taking to the stage has stuck with me every single time, perhaps never more visibly or forcefully than on that day.

Being able to present effectively is one of the cornerstones of a successful career in consulting, yet it is also one of the most dreaded undertakings. Nick Morgan wrote in *Forbes*, "About 10 percent of the population loves public speaking. That group experiences no fear and get a huge buzz being in front of a large crowd. Another 10 percent are genuinely terrified. Those are the people who are physically debilitated by even the thought of public speaking. True glossophobics will go to great lengths to avoid speaking in a group situation, and will experience nausea, panic attacks and extreme anxiety. The rest of us—roughly the 80 percent in the middle—get butterflies, get anxious, don't sleep much the night before—but we know that we're going to live through it. It's just not much fun."[29]

There is some solace to be taken in the fact that even fantastic presenters, those that make it look easy, will statistically be as prone to nerves as the majority of us. When observing someone giving a presentation, take note of what the presenter is doing with their hands. Chances are they will fidget or exhibit another tell that, even though they may appear composed and collected, they are actually nervous themselves.

Jeremy Dalton recounted a similar experience, "I watched some partners deliver talks at a repeating series of Digital Masterclass events that I was hosting. Because I had seen their presentations many times before, I turned my attention to their body language. When they paused between gesturing wildly, I could see their hands subtly, but visibly, shaking on stage. I knew that feeling of fear and anxiety in having to deliver a presentation in front of a crowd. But, remember, these were people who had been in the firm for 20 or 30 years: delivering high-pressure talks to senior business leaders was par for the course with them. This presentation was not high stakes. It was a communications and branding exercise for an internal audience. Yet, despite that, they too were fearful of public speaking. I often recall that and conclude that you can never get rid of the feeling of anxiety, fear, or trepidation of public speaking; you just learn how to manage it better."

Supposing we acknowledge being able to effectively present in front of others as a valuable, necessary evil. In that case, we must consequently consider what can be done to reduce the stress involved and how to improve the effectiveness of our presentations.

# Practice

"It's a lot of practice." Jeremy Dalton admitted as we were discussing how he overcame his fears of public speaking. I had seen Jeremy present in front of hundreds of people, making it look effortless, blending bits of personality, charisma, and innate likability to command the attention of the audience. Yet, as he explained, it wasn't always easy for him.

He continued, "Public speaking has always been difficult for me. For anyone that is interested in it, public speaking is not an inherent skill; it is a learned skill that you can develop through practice. Start with low-risk presentations and build from there. Initially, these might be to a few people in your team, and then you can test your skills on more senior individuals."

"From there, you can grow your audience size, presenting to a larger group of people you're less familiar with. Recognise the experience you're gaining as the variables of your presentations change: the number of people, their seniority, their level of knowledge on the subject of your presentation, as well as your confidence on that subject. I ramped it up bit by bit in terms of all those factors, and it got to the stage where I was presenting to hundreds of unfamiliar faces."

When I inquired as to his method, Jeremy replied that he took an incremental approach to his craft, stating, "I did read up a bit on the theory, and I experimented with different techniques in every talk that I gave. For example, sometimes, I would try not to have any speaker notes. Sometimes, I would try walking towards the crowd when I felt nervous because that was a way of convincing your lizard brain that you are not the prey in this situation. Projecting, gesturing, delivering with a dynamic tone: the more you practise incorporating these elements (and others) into your presentations, the more they become an inherent part of your public speaking delivery."

"Breathing exercises are vital to reducing anxiety. You can even do some breathing exercises while on stage before it is your turn to speak. For example, if you're on a panel and the moderator calls on your fellow panellists one by one, each of whom confidently delivers fantastic responses, prep the gist of your response and consider your breathing. If you can get control of your breathing, then you can get control of your public speaking. It's a way of convincing your mind that you're in control, even though it's a completely unrelated subject. So that's one tip. The second tip, takes place at the very beginning of your delivery, where the first few minutes are pretty gruesome. You can get over that hump really quickly if, again, you convince your mind that you're in control. Either you or the audience determines the atmosphere of a presentation. Take the initiative and make it clear from the beginning that you are leading the session."

"For example, ask how everyone is doing or thank them for being there and giving you their attention. Take your time and scan the entire crowd purposefully. You are in control; you are in the position of delivering. As a result, you will naturally become more confident and less anxious when it comes to delivering the rest of your presentation."

Maria Axente of PwC added, "Besides prepping, you first need to understand who your audience is. Ask the organiser, 'Who am I speaking to?' I create some talking points with three key messages. This is one of the best things I've learned. Make sure that in every single presentation communication, you have three things that you want to communicate. People will only remember three things. So, if you do this and make sure that those three are infused and part of your narrative, and at the end, you repeat them, you are more likely to have a memorable experience. Preparation is key; don't just show up and blabber on."

In a previous chapter, we discussed the importance of applying structure to our communications. It helps to challenge our thinking while simultaneously ensuring our communications are easier to understand by our clients and colleagues. In presentations, the same principles apply, as Maria highlighted, referring to the Minto Pyramid Principle.

Born in 384 BC, Aristotle is credited with the triptych principle for effective presentations.[30] The principle may be almost 2,400 years old, but it holds as true now as it did then:

**Tell them what you will tell them**
This is your opener in which you lay out why
you are speaking to the audience.

**Tell them**
This section is open-ended. This is when you pour out
all your content and explain the details.

**Tell them what you just told them**
Reiterate your salient points, summarising your
main messages and call to action.[31]

By putting in the necessary time to prepare, tailoring our presentation to
our audience, structuring our thoughts into a few salient points, and then
practising our delivery as much as we are able, our presentation skills will
only continue to improve.

# Suggestions

Marjorie North, of the Harvard University Extension School, wrote
extensively about public speaking and executive communications skills.[32]
She stated that, first and foremost, communication is never perfect
and that nobody expects us to be perfect. Melville Carrie, formerly of
Genpact, agreed, "I don't think that practising will make you perfect,
but it will make you better. It'll make you be honed. But actually, you don't
need to be perfect. I think that's the key thing; perfection is unachievable for
99% of the time of your life. So, don't try and attain it; just be the best you
can be in that moment."

Putting in the requisite time to prepare will help us deliver a better
presentation. While we may not be able to shake our nerves completely,
we can learn to minimise them. Marjorie summarised her top-10 public
speaking tips as follows:

**Nervousness is normal. Practice and prepare!**
All people feel some physiological reactions like pounding hearts and
trembling hands. Do not associate these feelings with the sense that
you will perform poorly or make a fool of yourself.
Some nerves are good. The adrenaline rush that makes you sweat
also makes you more alert and ready to give your best performance.

The best way to overcome anxiety is to prepare, prepare, and prepare some more. Take the time to go over your notes several times. Once you have become comfortable with the material, practise, a lot. Record yourself or get a friend to critique your performance.

**Know your audience. Your speech is about them, not you.**
Before you begin to craft your message, consider who the message is intended for. Learn as much about your listeners as you can. This will help you determine your choice of words, level of information, organisation pattern, and motivational statement.

**Organise your material in the most effective manner**
Create the framework for your speech. Write down the topic, general-purpose, specific purpose, central idea, and main points. Make sure to grab the audience's attention in the first 30 seconds.

**Watch for feedback and adapt to it**
Keep the focus on the audience. Gauge their reactions, adjust your message, and stay flexible. Delivering a canned speech will guarantee that you lose the attention of or confuse even the most devoted listeners.

**Let your personality come through**
Be yourself; don't become a talking head—in any type of communication. You will establish better credibility if your personality shines through, and your audience will trust what you have to say if they can see you as a real person.

**Use humour, tell stories, and use effective language**
Inject a funny anecdote in your presentation, and you will certainly grab your audience's attention. Audiences generally like a personal touch in a speech. A story can provide that.

**Don't read unless you have to. Work from an outline.**
Reading from a script or slide fractures the interpersonal
connection. By maintaining eye contact with the audience,
you keep the focus on yourself and your message. A brief
outline can serve to jog your memory and keep you on task.

**Use your voice and hands effectively. Omit nervous gestures.**
Nonverbal communication carries most of the message.
Good delivery does not call attention to itself, but instead conveys
the speaker's ideas clearly and without distraction.

**Grab attention at the beginning, and close with a dynamic end**
Do you enjoy hearing a speech start with "Today I'm going
to talk to you about X"? Most people don't. Instead, use
a startling statistic, an interesting anecdote, or a concise
quotation. Conclude your speech with a summary and a
strong statement that your audience is sure to remember.

**Use audio-visual aids wisely**
Too many can break the direct connection to the audience,
so use them sparingly. They should enhance or clarify your
content or capture and maintain your audience's attention.

There is a big difference between a document meant to be read and a
document meant to be used alongside a presentation. While the former will
inevitably use a mix of words and images to illustrate the significant points,
the latter presentation document should have as few words as possible,
if any words at all. Presentation visual aids should, ideally, only feature a
few keywords in a large, legible font. Alternatively, they may only feature an
image or graph to support the point you are trying to convey. Remember,
any time your audience spends reading presentation slides is time they are
not paying attention to what you are saying.

# How you say it

"One of the key things I've learned, is that it's not about what you say, it's about how you say it. I've missed points during my presentations because I prioritise delivery over completeness and therefore don't refer to written notes. This is a worthy sacrifice, in my opinion, because if your objective is to convince others, it really is largely about how you deliver your presentation. There obviously has to be some substance, but once you've ticked that box, it really is just about how you say it," Jeremy Dalton explained as he reflected on the importance of attitude, body language, and energy when presenting.

With over a decade of experience in communications, Sarah Walker agreed, noting, "Research suggests that we more readily believe a poor argument explained to us in a convincing manner than one based on sound logic but presented by someone who sounds unconvinced or uninterested. It was Professor Albert Mehrabian who established a classic rule on the effectiveness of spoken communication, which helps us understand how and why we do or do not trust people who are speaking to us—and thus the degree to which they can influence us."[33]

While the studies Mehrabian undertook were admittedly limited in sample size, rendering the findings inexact, he played an essential role in highlighting the importance of non-verbal communications. Mehrabian found that where there seemed to be an inconsistency between the speaker's words, tone of voice, and body language, we would tend to read their meaning in the following way:

> **7%** of meaning is in the words that are spoken.
> **38%** of meaning is paralinguistic (the way that the words are said).
> **55%** of meaning is in facial expression.

His experiment showed that tone of voice and facial expressions could enormously influence an audience and the degree to which they trust a speaker. Arguably, much of what people take away from a presentation may be from the non-verbal: body language, appearance, and delivery style.

Jeremy continued, recalling a time when he observed the power of non-verbal communication, "I was 23 when I married a Turkish lady, whom I met while I was on the Erasmus program at university. We got married in Turkey, and her family invited a friend to commemorate the event with a speech that I couldn't understand most of because it was delivered in broken English."

"But it didn't matter because it was delivered with passion. Everybody felt what he was trying to convey as he managed to do so on an emotional level. That is a moment that I always remember when I'm doing public speaking. Because most of the time, it doesn't matter what you say. If you can deliver with enough energy, you can transmit key messages convincingly to another party."

"The energy you give off during a presentation, is the energy you will receive from the crowd most of the time. If you give off a sense of fear, embarrassment, anxiety, then the audience is going to sense that, and they're going to feel bad for you. If you give off a sense of confidence, it won't matter if you make mistakes during your presentation, because everyone's comfortable that you're comfortable with it. I tested this point out during one of our digital master class sessions by attempting a complicated and risky session. We gave all 15 tables (approximately 120 people) a Raspberry Pi with a set of wires, a transistor, and a temperature sensor. We attempted, in the space of one hour, to get each table to hook it all up, such that it would not only detect the temperature in the room, but send that to a cloud-based database and display each table's results on the main screen for everyone to see."

"I knew something was going to go wrong, but being able to manage that with confidence was part of the exercise. I announced up front, 'This hasn't been done before, and it may not work, but we're gonna give it a go anyway.'"

Jeremy took his experiment a step further, announcing that there would be an anonymous survey at the end of the session to gauge how engaging the exercise had been. Each participant was asked if they had found the exercise interesting and if they would ever do it again. The results would be immediately displayed for everyone to see.

"Soon enough, a few people voted, 'This is excellent. I definitely want to do this again.' Eventually, 'Definitely, do it again,' was second place and 'Do it again with a few changes,' was in first place. In last place, with a very small minority of votes was 'No, never do it again.' I was very happy with those results and because of the energy that I conveyed in the room, everyone, myself included, was comfortable with the session 'failing.'"

# Don't rely on anything

Presentations are stressful enough in their own right, and much more so when things go wrong. Thus, it's imperative to prepare for any eventuality. If your laptop fails, make sure someone else has the presentation ready to go. If you don't have a suitable display connector, make sure the client was sent the document beforehand so they can open it from their own device. Should everything not work at all, make sure to have a printed version that you can review. While these may seem like obvious steps to take, everyone from partners to associates has been guilty of wasting valuable time at one point or another, frantically scrambling to get their presentation to display correctly.

"Never put yourself in a position where you are 100% reliant on anything or anyone but yourself," Jeremy noted. "Throughout my all presentations, yes, I'm expecting the slides to work. But, if they don't, I always have an idea of what I want to talk about that I can deliver without those slides."

"I'll tell you one story," Jeremy continued. "I was delivering a paid talk for an organisation in Sweden. I was one of a handful of key speakers that they flew over for this event so there was a lot at stake. There were 200 people in the crowd, including some governmental officials; it was clearly an important event. My slides, timings, and key points were well-prepared and well-rehearsed. I even had my laptop on my lap in the front row, so that I could get going as quickly as possible after my name was called. The time comes so I jump up on stage, place my laptop on the podium... and it crashes."

"After taking a second to curse my unfortunate luck, I accepted that I wouldn't have slides for at least a few minutes. I used the free time as an opportunity to introduce myself and my story in long-form fashion, connecting it to the innovation theme of the event. I joked about the slides not working and how that might be a relief to some. The audience laughed, comfortable that I was taking this disaster in my stride. Within a few minutes, I had my slides back up and could continue the presentation as I had planned — but it wouldn't have mattered either way as I was prepared to deliver that presentation with no supporting material. I got lucky on that occasion that my slides were resurrected but I've had systems fail for the entirety of my presentation before, leaving me feeling naked on stage and speaking for 30 minutes based on memory. In these situations, you've got to have a plan B. Never be 100% reliant on anything external."

Presentations and public speaking are an integral part of the life of a consultant. Yet, a survey by Chapman University found the fear of public speaking was the biggest phobia among respondents, with 25.3% stating they feared speaking in front of a crowd.[34] Overcoming our fears will require persistence and practising at every opportunity, improving our skills with every attempt. By understanding our audience, tailoring our messaging, and structuring our thoughts, we will be more effective at engaging and succinctly conveying our message.

"Your most unhappy customers are your greatest source of learning."

Bill Gates

# Insights

"There is no way that is correct, is it?" I was taken aback. Amid a busy contact centre, with dozens of people answering calls and moving about, it seemed like everything slowed down for a split second. The near-constant drone of background noise seemed to dissipate, even if only for a moment. The realisation of what was just explained to me began to sink in. The contact centre lead had just outlined, in no uncertain terms, how we could save the company millions.

I had been working with one of the leading global broadband and media organisations in the UK for a few weeks at that point, helping them gain a better understanding of their 'single customer view' approach. The project was focused on understanding how they were interacting with their customers across different channels, identifying where they could improve, and prioritising opportunities into projects to be taken forward. In short, a very typical consulting assignment.

Using an experience-based approach rather than solely relying on departmental metrics meant that we could uncover a much more holistic view of the organisation, its people and customers, and thus the opportunities for improvement.

According to Anatoly Roytman, "Clients are struggling with similar issues. Now they recognise that it is all about the experience. It is a relationship between a brand and consumer, and they are organised by function: sales, marketing, service IT. Each one of those departments has different KPIs [key performance indicators]. None of these departments, in isolation, can actually solve this problem."

Each department, in isolation, lacks the necessary insights to improve the end-to-end experience of clients or employees. An ancient parable, the earliest versions of which can be found in Buddhist, Hindu, and Jain texts, highlights the limits of perception and the importance of sharing information to gain a more complete, holistic context. It describes a group of blind men hearing that a strange animal, called an elephant, had been brought into town. Curious about what this animal looked like, the blind men decided to make their way into town to examine the animal in the only method available to them; by touching and feeling the animal's form. The first blind man reached out and touched the elephant's trunk. He exclaimed, "This being is like a thick snake!" For another, whose hand reached the elephant's ear, it seemed like a kind of fan. As for another, whose hand was upon its leg, he said that it was like a tree trunk. The blind man who placed his hand upon its side said, "This is a wall." Another, who felt its tail, described it as a rope. The last felt its tusk, stating the elephant was something hard, smooth, and like a spear.[35]

Each man described the animal from their own limited perspective. Similarly, organisational departments are typically only focused on their view of the world, each tracking and prioritising activities in their own areas at the cost of the holistic view.

Sitting in the contact centre, listening to the contact centre lead outline the problem, the need for a holistic, experienced-based approach became very evident. As the contact centre lead described it, any time one of their customers had an issue with their router, they were prompted to go through a multi-step online diagnostic. The process itself took approximately five minutes. The customer would answer several questions to identify potential root causes of the issue they were experiencing. If they were unable to find a solution, they were prompted to call the contact centre.

If we were to stop there and only analyse that part of the customer journey in isolation, everything would appear to be working according to plan. The customer had an online process by which a percentage of customers would find answers to their questions or solutions to their problems. Those customers would not call the contact centre, therefore saving the organisation considerable sums they would have otherwise had to pay for contact centre support. Had we only considered the process or the KPIs for the online diagnostic, everything would appear to be working in line with expectations.

However, the customer journey did not stop there. At the end of the diagnostic, if the issue remained unresolved, the customer would be prompted to call the contact centre. The contact centre support person receiving the call would not have been made aware that the customer had just finished the online diagnostic through any flag on the customer's account. Without that information, the contact centre support person would spend the next five minutes going through the same diagnostic process with the client that they had just completed themselves.

While it may be an unpleasant and time-consuming activity for the customer, the consequences were much more costly for the organisation. When those five minutes of redundant contact centre support were multiplied by the hundreds of thousands of similar calls coming into the contact centre, the annual cost was estimated to be in the millions.

If we had only examined the processes during the online diagnostic, everything would have seemed satisfactory. Had we only considered the data for the contact centres, nothing would have appeared out of the ordinary. In fact, as most organisations will allocate KPIs based on department, both the online team and the contact centre team would report that everything was working as it should. They would be satisfied that they were meeting their department-specific targets, entirely unaware of the significant opportunities for improvement.

Only when we considered the entire end-to-end customer journey could we identify opportunities that would not have been evident otherwise. By taking a holistic view of an organisation, we discovered friction points and opportunities for improvement that may not have been apparent to departments only focused on their narrow view of the world. Furthermore, rather than only speaking with senior stakeholders at the head office, we uncovered valuable insights by talking with those on the frontlines every day. After all, they would know their business better than anyone, acutely aware of the day-to-day operating realities compared to the theoretical view of those far removed from them.

## Planning versus behaviour

Walking the streets of Warsaw, Poland, I've often encountered living examples of the significant difference between design and human-centred design. After Nazi troops destroyed more than 85% of buildings in Warsaw during World War II, the city had to rebuild. As the country was under the Russian sphere of influence at the time, the official style of Social Realism was imposed in 1949.[36] Grand buildings such as the Palace of Culture and Science were constructed, with the architects being given free rein to design parks, walkways, and boulevards in a similar style of straight lines and a focus on symmetry. While some of the designs were breathtaking in their grandiosity, they did not take human behaviour into account.

Streets and parks were designed to look good in propaganda materials, not to cater for the needs of the people living in the city. The results were predictable. While the city has much green space, there are areas where the otherwise pristine green lawns are intersected with well-worn dirt paths where countless people had traversed. Most commonly, these dirt paths could be found as shortcuts running between two perpendicular walkways. The architects had thought their grandiose designs were perfect, but they did not account for where people actually wanted to walk.

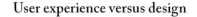

## User experience versus design

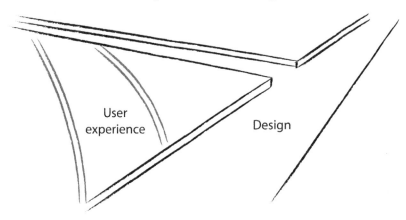

Warsaw is by no means the only city designed to look good rather than cater to its citizens' needs. Brasilia, the Brazilian capital city, was built from scratch between 1956 and 1961. The grand design by Lucio Costa featuring majestic avenues and impressive buildings has since been labelled a 'cautionary tale' for urban planners.

"The problems Brasilia faces today include inequality, congestion, and sprawl—which are far from unique in this city and common throughout the world. They're direct ripple effects of the utopian thinking that went into its design," Diana Budds wrote for Curbed.[37] The city designers did not consider the butterfly effects of their design decisions, resulting in a multitude of adverse, unanticipated consequences.

The city quickly sprawled beyond the initially built Pilot Plan area. Of the over 2.5 million people living in the Brasilia metropolitan area, only 300,000 live in the Pilot Plan area, with the rest living in suburban areas and many forced to commute through the city centre every day.

Jorge Guilherme Francisconi, a retired architect and urban planner, has lived in various areas of Brasilia since the 1970s. He summed up the experience of living in Brasilia by saying, "I have a beautiful quality of life, but I live in the Plano Piloto."

"Elsewhere there is poverty and slums...[Costa] was a pure urbanist; he didn't know about land economics and urban economics. Brazilian architects are interested in the formal point of view versus the functional point of view. Costa never thought about pedestrians. The design of the streets was just terrible. They're not for leisure or walking or meeting." He added that due to high rates of violence in Brazil, shoppers feel safer going to malls instead of storefronts on inhospitable streets.

Many have criticised the design of Brasilia as being designed from space rather than from street level, literally being designed from the top-down rather than from the bottom up.

Designing anything, be it cities, products, interfaces, processes, or user journeys, without considering human experience will result in humans rejecting the proposition outright and finding their own paths. Rather than expecting humans to conform to a system, we must strive to understand human behaviour and design solutions that put the human experience at the centre of all we do.

# Observation

To truly understand an organisation, relying only on numbers provided by the client or on outdated process flows provided by the head office will only ever tell part of the story. By taking a more holistic approach, acknowledging that each parcel of data is only a piece in a larger puzzle, we can better understand an organisation and opportunities across each area.

This is where consultants can really make a meaningful impact; by taking a step back, understanding the whole picture, and subsequently uncovering valuable insights. Sometimes, the most straightforward answer to uncovering insights is remarkably low tech but staggeringly powerful: observe, ask, and align. The seemingly simple act of observing how people behave or what employees do during a typical day, combined with asking the right questions and forcing stakeholders into situations where they must align, often yields invaluable insights. When combined with reliable data, we can map out journeys that form the foundation for experienced-based transformation.

The act of observing and asking questions may not seem like a ground-breaking idea, but it is taken for granted too often. Organisations tend to place too much stock in outdated documents outlining the theory of how processes should work without considering how customers or employees interact with existing systems. This is where we can uncover to what degree the theory of a process or workflow correlates to what actually happens in the real world.

I was able to observe the disconnect between theory and practice first-hand when working with a leading fast moving consumer goods (FMCG) company. They had gone through a massive initiative to merge their supply and planning centres around the world into nine global hubs. Each of these hubs employed hundreds of people responsible for overseeing the entire supply chain, from raw product to store shelves. It was a remarkably complex endeavour.

Every day, hundreds of planners would coordinate between manufacturers, logistics firms, local governments, and individual stores. They would be responsible for dealing with the seemingly endless barrage of logistics issues, from strikes at local manufacturers to trucks being delayed at borders to the quality of goods not meeting predefined specifications. They also had to consider and forecast the number of goods making their way across the entire supply chain. Too few items would result in lost revenue, and too many would mean items were taking up valuable storage space that could be allocated for better selling items.

During the consolidation of the planning centres into the nine global hubs, specific processes were set out for the planners. Given the ambition of the undertaking, developing strict guidelines and procedures was seen to be necessary to ensure the young workforce would carry out the essential tasks uniformly across teams and geographies. Every day was meticulously orchestrated out for the planners, consisting primarily of meetings followed up by individual working time to address the issues raised in the sessions. The theory of what was supposed to happen began diverging from reality when the planners set to their tasks.

The processes and tools provided to the planners by the organisation all made sense in theory. However, in reality, finding the prescribed tools lacking, planners began to develop their own tools, algorithms, and approaches to tackling the issues they faced daily. Rather than interact with company-provided platforms, planners developed their own Excel spreadsheets, which they would often not share with others.

Again, had we only relied on process flows or KPIs provided by individual departments, everything would have seemed in order. The reality, however, when taking human behaviour into account, was much different. Asking the right questions and observing behaviour played a vital role in identifying opportunities for improvement.

On paper, the business and the planners were functioning within acceptable parameters. In reality, there were many areas of improvement that would benefit the organisation and the quality of life of the planners. Each redundant step eliminated or more intuitive dashboard created would improve operations while also giving more time back to the planners to focus on more mission-critical, value-adding activities.

IDEO, one of the most innovative and award-winning design firms in the world, emphasises empathy when designing anything. They believe that the key to figuring out what humans really want depends on doing two things: observing behaviour and putting oneself in the shoes of the end-user. According to IDEO, to understand how people behave, we must observe them. For example, if we're designing a vacuum cleaner, we need to watch people vacuum. When we put ourselves into the user's shoes, we understand what the user experience is really like and feel what users feel.

By observing how people interact with or within organisations, we will gain valuable insight that will better position us to identify areas of improvement. As we then implement improvements, we need to be mindful to continue to observe, as with the introduction of any new element that behaviour will continue to change. As we continue to observe, improve, and then observe some more, we create a continuous improvement loop based on real-world human interactions and experience rather than theoretical and outdated process flows provided by the head office.

# Data

While observation plays a foundational role in understanding real-world behaviour and identifying opportunities for improvement, data serves as a valuable objective layer. Through data, we can identify patterns, validate insights, guide our thinking, or track incremental improvements over time.

Returning for a moment to the example of paved walkways and dirt paths where humans actually wanted to walk, we can't help but wonder how differently the designs would have developed if the designers had been more focused on human behaviour. Through observation and inquiry, they may have identified the most common routes that people would take through a particular part of town to be in a better position to design walkways that accommodated the most common paths. It would be interesting to see how different their designs would have been if they also had access to sophisticated modelling applications that used thousands of data points to augment their thinking further.

As technology has evolved, so have the tools by which consultants, designers, architects, and others can better quantify human behaviour to identify patterns, predict needs, and improve existing designs. Urban planners and architects can now use sophisticated tools to simulate how crowds would move through a virtual building or landscape. Through these simulations, they can make the necessary amendments to, for example, reduce congestion in a part of a building foyer before construction even begins. Similarly, city planners can use digital twins of their cities to understand population growth to anticipate infrastructure needs. They can use virtual city topographies to gauge the impact of a new building on direct sunshine availability or a proposed building's effect on the wind velocity around it. These types of tools provide an opportunity for observation, but at a larger scale, supported by many more data points than would be otherwise available had the technology not existed. Hence, the principle of observing behaviour to gain valuable insights, even if the behaviour is only simulated, remains unchanged.

Technology allows us access to vast data sets that will either support or challenge any hypothesis. For example, when optimising a website for conversation, we may consider several options to improve performance, including improved text, different arrangements of the content on the page, or different colours of the call-to-action buttons.

We will test the site with real users within our target demographics and gain valuable insights into how they interact with the page. We may also use a multi-variate testing tool on our live site that will randomly change some aspects of the page for some users, while it may change other parameters for others, tracking the effectiveness of those changes. One visitor may see a green button on the left with a short slogan, while the next visitor may see a red button on the right with a wordy description. By tracking the effectiveness of each combination, these tools present us with the optimal configuration to achieve a specific objective, such as increasing conversation on a page, meaning the percentage of users that complete a desired action. Even a slight improvement in conversion will have a significant impact when multiplied by tens of thousands of visitors.

Using data to augment our ability to observe, analyse, and improve, bolstered by increasingly sophisticated algorithms, can be found in every industry. In retail, for example, organisations are turning to machine learning algorithms that mimic human eyes and the visual cortex, interpreting images and video to gauge the effectiveness of store displays across the paths shoppers take. Using these tools, retailers can improve physical store displays to draw the shopper's gaze by appealing to the subconscious part of the human brain responsible for prioritising what we notice first. They accomplish this by breaking down the basic rules for how our brain subconsciously interprets images even before it has had a chance to understand what it is seeing. They can develop heat maps based on what our brain will notice first and what elements blend into the background.

Online tracking behaviour is made significantly more accessible by the thousands of data points each customer journey generates. Every action can be tracked, quantified, and fed into sophisticated algorithms that choose what messaging, product or image to show to the user from the time a browser is opened and the first search query entered.

These algorithms have become so sophisticated that they essentially form a digital identity for each user, carefully monitoring behaviours and changes in behaviour, making adjustments along the way to optimise for experience and conversion. Again, observing behaviour, augmented by these algorithms, creates opportunities to anticipate needs or improve user experience.

A famous example of how companies use data to improve the experience by anticipating customer needs and increasing average revenue per user (ARPU) comes from retailers endeavouring to ensure that expecting mothers become loyal customers. Charles Duhigg wrote an interesting piece in The New York Times where he observed how Andrew Pole, a statistician at Target, used disparate data points to anticipate customer needs.

Charles explained, "Pole ran test after test, analyzing the data, and before long, some useful patterns emerged. Lotions, for example. Lots of people buy lotion, but one of Pole's colleagues noticed that women on the baby registry were buying larger quantities of unscented lotion around the beginning of their second trimester. Another analyst noted that sometime in the first 20 weeks, pregnant women loaded up on supplements like calcium, magnesium, and zinc. Many shoppers purchase soap and cotton balls, but when someone suddenly starts buying lots of scent-free soap and extra-big bags of cotton balls, in addition to hand sanitisers and washcloths, it signals they could be getting close to their delivery date."

Using scent-free soap and cotton ball purchasing patterns as an indicator of potential pregnancy would allow Target to tailor communications to their customers. If approached correctly, they would be able to anticipate customer needs and tailor their experience to increase revenue and loyalty. Of course, there is a fine line between being helpful and being creepy. The article goes on to recount the time an angry man went into a Target outside of Minneapolis, demanding to talk to the manager.

"My daughter got this in the mail!" the angry man exclaimed. "She's still in high school, and you're sending her coupons for baby clothes and cribs? Are you trying to encourage her to get pregnant?"

The manager didn't have any idea what the man was talking about. He looked at the mailer. Sure enough, it was addressed to the man's daughter and contained advertisements for maternity clothing, nursery furniture, and pictures of smiling infants. The manager apologised profusely and called the man a few days later to apologise again.

On the phone, though, the father was somewhat abashed. "I had a talk with my daughter," he said. "It turns out there have been some activities in my house I haven't been completely aware of. She's due in August. I owe you an apology."[38]

While there is an inherent risk to using customer data, as the example illustrated, companies are finding that the benefits of leveraging these insights far outweigh the occasional missteps. The streaming giant Netflix, for example, was able to attribute a large part of their success to an impressive customer-retention rate, which was 93%, compared to Hulu's 64% and Amazon Prime's 75%. One of the ways in which Netflix was able to keep their customers happy is by effectively using the data they collect from their millions of subscribers and implementing data-analytics models to discover customer behaviour and patterns. Through those algorithms, they were better able to offer precise recommendations based on customer behaviour. According to Netflix, more than 75% of viewer activity is based on personalised recommendations.[39] Amazon earns approximately 35% of their annual sales thanks to product suggestions that they can make to customers based on their behaviour and the ability to analyse shopping patterns effectively. Facebook, the democracy undermining social networking giant, continues to profit from increased engagement achieved by showing users posts that they know will make them angry or frustrated enough to comment or share.

McDonald's uses data to customise digital drive-through menus that change on an assortment of factors, including time of day, weather, and historical sales data. Meanwhile, Starwood Hotels were able to increase their per-room revenue by dynamically adjusting pricing based on various factors, including local and global economic situations, weather, availability, and even local event listings.[40]

As these examples illustrate, data has become an increasingly valuable, if not crucial, asset for organisations. Regardless of industry or area of focus, data is quickly becoming the foundation on which organisations win or lose. Therefore, as consultants, we must be aware of the increasingly important role of data in our engagements and within our own organisations. As technology and best practices continue to evolve, a broad spectrum has opened up in terms of organisations' readiness and ability to take advantage of complex data.

On one end of the spectrum are organisations that have articulated complex data strategies. Terms such as data lakes, data warehouses, data fabric, and hubs enter the lexicon, opening a proverbial can of worms that would require its own series of books to properly unravel, particularly as trends and technologies continue to evolve at a rapid and accelerating rate.

However, most consultants will not have to contend with these advanced topics because most organisations are not nearly advanced enough in their data strategy to warrant these discussions. Some organisations are very advanced on the bell curve, while the majority are somewhere in the middle. Concurrently, organisations on the other end of the curve are only beginning to consider the data they collect and how they use it. I've witnessed organisations that were, by all measures, operating successfully and yet could not confidently define their customer segmentation or what information they were gathering from existing customers or for what purpose.

That broad range represents a treasure trove of opportunity, both for the organisations themselves and the consultants that can guide clients along their data strategy roadmap. Helping organisations understand what data is relevant and how to collect it, how to store data responsibly, the associated legal ramifications, and how to use it effectively will continue to become increasingly fundamental for consultants in all industries.

For example, working with the client at an early stage of their data strategy roadmap, my team quickly conducted a customer segmentation exercise. We uncovered that they didn't have only one customer type but five distinct segments. Customers in each segment had their own motivations, buying patterns, and means of interacting with the organisation. It was a small but meaningful step toward using the data they had to better understand and service their customers. Again, it was only through observation and asking the right questions that we were able to identify the opportunity, which subsequently led to several distinct workstreams of activity.

According to a report by Allied Market Research, the global big data and business analytics market size was valued at $193.14 billion USD in 2019 and is projected to reach $420.98 billion USD by 2027, growing at a compound annual growth rate (CAGR) of 10.9% from 2020 to 2027.

**Big data and business analytics market**

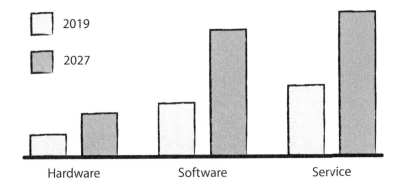

Big data analytics is an increasingly significant strategic investment, as it helps organizations manage, process, and streamline large datasets in real-time and improve their organizations' decision-making capability. In addition, the primary objective of big data and business analytics is to help organizations gain a better understanding of their customers and help narrow down their targeted audience, thus improving companies' marketing campaigns.[41]

At a high level, organisations will increasingly need to understand what data they need, how they will procure it, how they'll store it, and how they will effectively use it. Data will serve to augment our ability to observe behaviour, identify new opportunities for improvement, validate our assumptions, formulate our supporting business case, and provide an objective measure of success. As we embrace a data-driven, iterative, continuous improvement approach across all touchpoints, we will more effectively identify new innovative ways of anticipating needs and improving experiences.

# Human-centred

"In 1894, W.K. Kellogg made a discovery that would forever change what we eat in the morning. Seeking a more digestible breakfast alternative to baked bread for his brother's hospital patients, the bespectacled former broom salesman accidentally left a pot of boiled wheat out overnight. The wheat became softened, and when he rolled it out and baked it, each grain became a crispy flake," Dave Thomsen wrote for *Wired Magazine*.[42]

Kellogg tried the technique on corn, and over the course of several years, he perfected the tasty flakes by experimenting with different formulas. He tested his invention with patients at the Battle Creek Sanitarium wellness spa he owned with his brother. He had invented, or designed, corn flakes.[43]

"But Kellogg didn't stop there," Dave continued. "He believed that the entire population—not just hospital patients with special diet restrictions—would enjoy the new food, and he carefully positioned and marketed it. He created a recognisable brand and set about continually improving packaging that kept the product fresh. The product went on to sell 175,000 cases in its first year, laying the foundation for the $22.5 billion company that still bears Kellogg's name."

"Kellogg's genius came not just in his flair for food product invention, but also in his customer-centric approach, iterative prototyping process, and careful consideration of the entire product experience—from the cereal itself to its packaging, marketing, and distribution. Kellogg was more than a brilliant food scientist and marketer. He was also a brilliant designer."

Kellogg took a holistic approach, considering every single touchpoint as an opportunity to surprise, delight, and deliver benefits to his customers. Human-centred design considers the end-to-end experience that a customer or user may have with an organisation or system. Every touchpoint represents an opportunity for consideration; an opportunity for improvement.

"All design should be human-centred, it's as simple as that," wrote David Townson, an independent design and innovation strategist, "and I mean human-centred, not 'user-centred' or 'user-friendly', because users are human beings after all. But, more importantly, because being human-centred is not just about your user. Human-centred design takes into account every single human being that your design decisions impact on."[44]

The theme of empathy is intertwined with all aspects of our personal and professional lives, which is why it is mentioned several times throughout this book. In this context, empathy serves as an important reminder that we need to put ourselves in the shoes of those we are designing for rather than expect others to act as we would.

For example, several years ago, I worked with a large UK telecommunications client to improve their online presence. We were helping them redesign some of their online sites and wanted to understand how real users interacted with those sites. We identified an agency that specialised in this sort of testing. They arranged for a dozen participants from across all age groups and technological proficiencies to spend 30 minutes exploring the sites under the supervision of one of their analysts.

During the 30-minute session, the analyst would ask the participant to perform specific actions, such as navigating to a particular section or identifying a piece of information. Each session was recorded, including a screen capture of where the user moved their mouse pointer and where they clicked. At the end of every 30-minute session, the analyst would ask a series of questions to understand better how the participant felt about the experience and the site's design.

The results were interesting because they validated several of our assumptions while blowing others out of the water. We discovered that older users, for example, were not aware that they were able to scroll down the page to uncover further information, meaning they would be more likely to call the contact centre. Given that older users represented a significant percentage of the total user base and that contact centres are expensive, the designs were quickly amended to accommodate them better.

Had we limited the analysis of the sites to our own experience and technical proficiency, we would not have been able to address the needs of other human beings using the sites. Our opportunity, as consultants, is to embrace empathy by putting the human experience at the centre of any process, platform, or journey. As Anatoly Roytman explained, "Experience is the battleground. To win in today's market, brands must offer experiences that create value across every interaction throughout the customer journey."

# Journey mapping

In order to take a holistic view that puts a focus on experience, we must employ an approach that considers the entire end-to-end user journey. Through it, we examine how humans behave across every single touchpoint, across all channels. Journey mapping allows us to empathise with customers or colleagues, helping us improve our understanding of their experiences. Regardless of our industry or alignment, it is a powerful exercise by which we can gain valuable insights, collaborate with others, and uncover new opportunities for improvement.

The first step in gaining a better understanding of our users is developing a persona. According to the Interaction Design Foundation, "Personas are fictional characters, which you create based upon your research in order to represent the different user types that might use your service, product, site, or brand in a similar way. Creating personas helps the designer to understand users' needs, experiences, behaviours, and goals."[45]

We create personas as distilled essences of real users based on our observations and understanding of our users. In the persona-creation process, we challenge ourselves to think about the persona's motivations, needs, and attitudes to gain insights into how real users would interact with our organisation. Sometimes it may be helpful to think about the primary segments of users our organisation serves and identify a persona or multiple personas representing those segments.

The level of detail and number of dimensions we capture for our personas will depend on our needs and will typically include a name, short description or biography, motivations, and technical proficiency. There are numerous resources and frameworks to be found online that will serve as guides. No matter the framework, the exercise of creating personas follows the human-centred design principle of empathising with our clients, users, or colleagues, effectively putting ourselves in their shoes.

**Illustrative persona template**

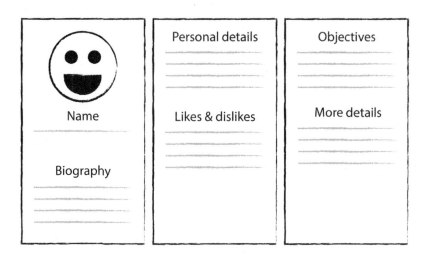

Alan Cooper, software designer, programmer, and the "Father of Visual Basic," said, "Personas are the single most powerful design tool that we use. They are the foundation for all subsequent goal-directed design. Personas allow us to see the scope and nature of the design problem... [They] are the bright light under which we do surgery."[47] Once we've identified a persona, we then need to consider how that person would interact with our organisation. In the entire life cycle, there may be several common journeys that the persona would undertake, ranging from, for example, initial contact or registration, when they have questions about their service, or when they want to cancel their account.

Of course, the life cycle and journeys themselves will differ from industry to industry and from one client to another. In its most basic form, journey mapping starts by compiling a series of user actions into a timeline. Next, the timeline is elaborated upon with items such as user activities, objectives, or emotional state. [47]

## Illustrative user journey map

| Persona + Scenario + Objective | | |
| --- | --- | --- |
| Step 1 | Step 2 | Step 3 |
| Emotions | | |
| Activities | Activities | Activities |
| Opportunities | Opportunities | Opportunities |

For our purposes of illustrating what a typical journey may look like, let's consider a hypothetical of a person renewing their mobile phone contract. What are the steps along the journey they'd undertake? Perhaps their journey would begin when they are notified that their contract is about to expire via email. They may be directed to review their options on a webpage. They may have questions about their options and will explore the website to find a contact number. They may then pick up the phone and call the contact centre to ask questions before returning to the webpage to complete the renewal. Once the renewal is complete, they receive a confirmation email.

In one form or another, the aforementioned journey of a customer interacting with an organisation to achieve a specific outcome occurs thousands of times, every hour, across industries and around the world.

Once we understand the journey itself, the motivations, and the user's emotional state undertaking that journey, we are better positioned to ask further questions such as: How easy was it for the user to achieve what they wanted? Were there steps that left the user frustrated? Could we have better tailored the tone of our communication to the user's emotional state? What are the opportunities to improve each step in the journey and the overall experience? Are there opportunities to anticipate user needs and offer moments that will delight them?

As we map out the journey, we will better understand the opportunities across each step in that journey. For example, in the initially sent email, can we personalise the message or offers based on what we know of the user? When the user visits the webpage, can we improve the layout of the information? If the user has questions, can we pre-empt the most common ones and present the information on the page? Rather than prompting the user to call the contact centre, can we offer a chat interface to make it easier to achieve their objectives?

These are only a few of the many questions we can ask as we review the journey. Once we identify opportunities for improvement, we can consider the value and complexity of the initiatives to gauge which we should prioritise. Assuming that we have timely, relevant data to track key performance indicators across each step, we can use that information to expand our investigation further. Data will also enable us to create rough, back-of-a-napkin style, high-level business cases to understand the value the organisation can potentially unlock by acting. Suppose our main objective is to deflect calls from the contact centre, for example. In that case, we can prioritise opportunities for improvement in that area, using the available information to articulate a rationale for why a particular initiative is favourable over others being considered. This is, of course, only one hypothetical journey of one persona within a much larger scope of the client life cycle, which illustrates the challenge that organisations face as they consider hundreds of internal and external journeys.

Organisations need to identify these journeys across multiple departments that typically do not interact as often as they should. These organisational silos complicate any holistic approach. The marketing department may be responsible for sending the emails, and the webpage may be administered by IT, while the contact centre may be its own independent department. Each department will have its own priorities and performance metrics, which may not align with the other departments' performance metrics. Worse yet, as organisations report performance on a departmental basis, they may not be aware of any areas for improvement nor incentivised to identify them beyond their own department.

Thus, taking a human-centred approach to articulating the customer's journey in this instance would enable us to break down the departmental silos within the organisation and focus on what is most important: the experience of the customer or employee. The exercise of striving to understand the experience through persona development and journey mapping becomes a compelling opportunity for departments to ideate, co-create, and align to identify opportunities for improvement across the organisation, not limited by departmental silos.

In the real world, working with a consumer goods client, we identified the different internal users interacting with the systems and proceeded to workshop solutions to address their specific needs. We effectively cut across departmental silos by including representatives from across the organisation and the different grades. We rapidly developed personas, mapped journeys, identified concepts, developed prototypes, tested with real users, and iterated on the designs. Within a short period of time, we had identified tangible solutions that would have a meaningful impact. The client feedback was remarkably positive, as they had not worked in such a manner before and were impressed by how quickly we were able to demonstrate tangible value.

Because the client was an integral part of the ideation, they felt both engaged and empowered. Thanks to that engagement, the buy-in for the program of work increased, with other leaders across the business taking note and wanting to carry out similar exercises within their teams.

Therefore, the power of human-centred design resides in guiding the improvement of organisations, systems, platforms, or processes that take the human experience into account and serving as a powerful collaborative, co-creation approach to rapidly identifying opportunities alongside our clients or colleagues. The technique can effectively jumpstart or refresh existing accounts or be used as a strategic investment to uncover opportunities within new accounts.

Furthermore, once a journey map is articulated and aligned between stakeholders, it effectively becomes a bridge between different departments that facilitates further collaboration. For example, rather than tracking performance indicators by department, organisations can begin to track performance within a customer journey. In this way, departments will be encouraged to collaborate to address the needs of the organisation's customers or internal users rather than only focus on their narrow department-specific view of the world.

The user journey maps become a perpetually evolving, collective reference point by which organisations can bring disjointed departments together and map the way forward. Incremental improvements across the different steps can be tracked and their butterfly effects considered thanks to the holistic nature of the exercise. Once agreed upon, key performance indicators can be captured within each step of the journey and measured over time, allowing organisations to use the journeys as benchmarks, monitoring their progress towards improving the experience of their customers or internal users.

Therefore, journey mapping is not a one-off exercise whereby a few documents are created and then promptly stored away, never to be seen again. Journey mapping can be a powerful catalyst for organisations to break down internal departmental silos. The approach allows organisations to engage with a broader cross-section of their employees, empowering them to contribute insights across every single step. Finally, journey maps are perpetually evolving reference points organisations can use to reposition their focus from narrow departmental objectives to a holistic view of the world that encourages collaboration and the free-flowing exchange of ideas.

# Suggestions

According to the Nielson Norman Group, "Journey mapping is a process to help you understand a holistic view of the customer experience by uncovering moments of both frustration and delight throughout a series of interactions. Done successfully, it reveals opportunities to satisfy customer pain points, alleviate fragmentation, and, ultimately, differentiate your brand by exposing new opportunities to provide additional value to your customers."[48]

David Townson, contributing for the Design Council, compiled a list of seven principles to get the most out of a human-centred approach:

**Get past your own great idea**
Examine the way real people interact with systems and don't let your own assumptions limit the exploration of other ideas.

**Don't be restricted by your own knowledge**
Be mindful of the fact that you may not know everything. Ask smart, naïve questions.

**Spend time with real people in real environments**
Validate or challenge your hypothesis by observing how people behave.

**Identify other users**

Consider the different types of users, not only your core group.

**Follow your users lead and needs**

Understand the specific needs of your users and design for them.

**Think about the whole journey**

Acknowledge that the end-to-end experience is important.

**Prototype and test your ideas**

Identify areas of improvement quickly by testing
with real users and iterate as required.[50]

Putting ourselves in the shoes of the humans interacting with our organisations forces us to challenge our assumptions and will undoubtedly uncover new opportunities for incremental improvement.

# Omotenashi

Omotenashi captures the way in which Japanese hosts pay attention to detail and anticipate their guests' needs. According to a *Japan Today* article on the subject, "Omotenashi involves the subjugation of self in service to a guest, without being 'servile'. Anticipating needs is at the heart of the concept, and it is certainly fair to say that in Japan, acting on others' needs without being asked to do so is at the height of savvy."[51]

When we consider our clients' experiences, their customers, our colleagues, or our managers, we need to consider how we can best anticipate their needs in the spirit of Omotenashi. For example, when improving user journeys, we need to challenge ourselves to go beyond delivering "good enough" and consider how we can create moments of delight. A truly well-orchestrated journey will anticipate needs and present users with something they were not yet aware they needed.

Throughout my career, I've had the pleasure of travelling across the UK by train. Every time I travelled, the experience was very similar. First, I'd make my way down to the station and rush to the ticket terminal, usually running a little late. I'd frantically fly through the menu options to purchase a ticket, with the departure time fast approaching. Once the ticket was purchased, the next step in my journey was to run over to the massive, billboard-size listing of departing trains. There, surrounded by dozens of people doing the same, I would strain my eyes as I scanned the listing for my train in order to identify from which platform it would be departing. Once I identified the platform number I needed, I would navigate through the throngs of people only to catch the train with minutes to spare. If you've ever travelled by train in the UK, there is a reasonable probability you've experienced something similar.

Several years ago, however, I was travelling by train outside of the UK. I approached the ticket terminal, purchased my ticket, and as the ticket was being printed, I looked around the hall to identify where the departures would be listed. Then, to my surprise, as the ticket finished printing, the ticket terminal display changed to show the departure time of the next train heading to my destination, alongside the platform from which it would be departing. It was a tiny tweak to the overall experience, but one that saved me time and effort by anticipating my need at that moment.

When a new bridge is being proposed, its utility can be calculated, at a high level, by multiplying the number of people making a trip that could be shortened thanks to the bridge by the travel time saved if the bridge existed. In the same way, the business case for tweaking the ticket purchasing user journey can be calculated by multiplying the number of people using it and the time saved searching for the departure time and platform information elsewhere. Even small numbers, in this case the time saved looking for the departure listing, when multiplied by big numbers, in this case the number of people using the machines annually, become significant in size.

Of course, beyond the time savings for travellers, there are ancillary benefits to consider. For example, the positive impact on the brand, fewer people making use of information stations, or the avoided rebooking costs for people who may have missed their train because they did not find the information they needed in time.

When evaluating user journeys, there are three key moments we need to consider:

### Pain points
Touchpoints where there are challenges or frictions faced by the persona or where a business feels it fails to meet expectations.

### Moments of truth
Touchpoints that are the most important or critical because they have the most impact on the long-term loyalty of the persona.

### Moments of delight
Touchpoints where a business identifies and executes on opportunities to exceed the expectations of the persona in question.[51]

Anticipating the needs of others requires a great deal of empathy. To truly understand other human beings, we need to put ourselves in their shoes to consider their feelings, frame of mind, and motivations. Only then should we begin to contemplate the appropriate interventions. In our personal and professional lives, it may be as simple as an act of kindness, when performed at the necessary time, that will put a smile on someone's face or make them feel appreciated. Within journey maps, the interventions we identify may save our clients millions while simultaneously improving their customers and employees' lives. When we strive to understand others, we will be better able to orchestrate moments of delight that will be the difference between an ordinary experience and an extraordinary one.

"There's no shortage of remarkable ideas, what's missing is the will to execute them."

Seth Godin

# Andrew Hogan

"I did a four-year undergraduate degree in politics and economics and came to the end of my four years and found I wanted to do more," Andrew Hogan recalled as we were sitting in the futuristic PwC offices in central London. As a partner with the firm, he undoubtedly had many things on his plate. Still, despite his busy schedule, he had not hesitated when I initially contacted him to participate in an interview. I interpreted his willingness to find the time necessary as a testament to his generosity with others, as was his reputation, or to his innate friendliness as a Canadian, or both. I was curious about the career path that had led him to become a well-respected partner at one of the leading consulting organisations in the world and what lessons he had learned along the way.

"I did a master's degree in political science, so I decided to do that in French in Quebec City," Andrew continued. "While I was putting myself through university, I was also working during the summer breaks and the winter breaks as an analyst at CIBC [Canadian Imperial Bank of Commerce] in Toronto."

"It was great, because I was getting great experience; I was getting paid enough to live at university and pay tuition. It meant that when I was finished with my politics MA, I had an opportunity to go back and work on Bay Street for a few years before leaving Canada."

"I worked for three years in the customer team at CIBC in Toronto, doing what now looks like the dark ages of data analytics, customer insight, and data-informed marketing. I had a very important mentor, career mentor, at CIBC who had been my mentor as a student and who was instrumental in bringing me into the bank. He had done his MBA and there was one of those conversations you have over a pint which is, 'You know, you're doing really well and you're progressing well here, but you need to think about the next steps; you need to think about what you want to do.'"

Andrew spoke very fondly of his mentor, an individual who would force him to consider the difficult questions that required introspection, decisions to be made, and subsequent planning. As we were speaking, I considered that perhaps one of the reasons he was so willing to spend time with me to share his knowledge was that someone had once done the same for him. Like all the other individuals I had interviewed, there was an underlying spirit of generosity and willingness to pay it forward. It was symptomatic of successful consultants to acknowledge that they would not be where they are if it had not been for others helping them along their way. It was an appreciation of those efforts that drove them to emulate that supportive behaviour, being kind and generous with others in turn.

Andrew continued, "I remember at that time there was this group of guys on the floor, they were from this company called McKinsey, I've never heard of before. They were doing all kinds of management consulting, which was completely unknown to me. The more I learned about it, the more I thought, 'Actually, that sounds quite interesting.'"

"To be able to be a professional problem-solver working with different clients, potentially in different industries, in a high-paced, high-pressure environment with lots of learning. The more I researched it, the more I realised that a good stepping stone into consulting would be to do the MBA. I looked at most of the American schools, but at that time I figured two years was a long investment, so I decided to go for the one-year program at INSEAD in France, and so spent 1998 doing my MBA in France."

"I think doing an MBA without having done some work experience is a bit risky. When I look back on my MBA experience, I was pretty much right on the norm in terms of the number of years of work experience. I kind of fit the profile. There were people there that were younger than me, there were people there that were older than me, but in terms of work experience, having had that two and a half to three years gave me something in the MBA context to reflect upon. Something that I could, as I was learning the theory of business, to be able to root it in personal experience and that was important. Not only that, but also the personal experience of my classmates. Being in a classroom where people were coming from lots of different backgrounds. Some of them were from financial services, some of them were from the military, government, advertising, manufacturing. A lot of the learning in an MBA program is from the interaction you have with your fellow classmates. So being in small groups, large group discussions where people were talking about their experiences and I could share mine; that was really valuable."

The MBA continues to be an important differentiator within the consulting world, but that is not to say that all consultants are required to complete an MBA. Kevin Sneader, McKinsey's global managing partner, told the *Financial Times* he wanted the proportion of staff with MBAs to decrease from 37% to "less than a third." One reason he gave was that firms were looking to hire people from a more diverse range of backgrounds, such as those from creative industries.

Nick South, a partner at BCG, said, "Whilst we are continuing to recruit MBAs and they remain a strong source of talent for our business, the relative share of MBAs in the overall mix of people we are recruiting is changing."[53]

That being said, a former colleague of mine once illustrated the desirability of an MBA in terms of fish, saying, "With every new qualification and bit of experience, you effectively jump from a bigger pool of fish to a smaller one, then to a smaller one, and then again to a smaller one. That is why an MBA matters; because you are automatically jumping to a smaller pool of candidates. Pursuing an MBA also allows you to build a broader professional network, with the friendships formed through the programme remaining for years, if not decades, after graduation."

Andrew continued, "I'm still very good friends with a lot of my old classmates, but I also have good connections and acquaintances in maybe every part of the world now because of that program. I was also saying that the content of their experience is part of my learning, and the content of my experiences in business was a contributing factor through their learning." Andrew was fortunate to be offered a role straight out of INSEAD.

"That's the thing," he said, "that at all these top business schools, you don't have to go looking for jobs; the jobs come looking for you. Every firm, every bank, every major corporation globally recruits at INSEAD. General Electric or British Petroleum or all the consulting firms. They all go on campus events called 'milk rounds'. It's a very efficient way to job search. I was engaged to be married at the time and my fiancé, a Brit, lived in Toronto. So, we decided, 'Yeah, we'll see if we can get jobs in London. We'll live in London for a while and see what happens.' Well, that was 20 years ago now, so I've been in London for 20 years, and this is now home."

Andrew joined Mitchell Madison Group (MMG) and received some excellent advice from one of the partners as he was kicking off his career in consulting. In his very first week on the job, one of the partners told him, "You know, my advice to you is to keep your eyes and ears open; there are a lot of people here who have been doing this for a long time. They are going to want to teach you and help you, but you're also going to have to learn from them. There's no shame in if you see a great deck, a great document by your partner, to learn from it and be inspired by the ideas that are in it. Realise that consulting is an apprenticeship model; you learn it by doing it. You can't really learn by watching a screen or being in a classroom; you need to get your hands dirty."

As Andrew grew into his role, he was inspired by the intellectual curiosity he saw in the partners. He admired their unrelenting inquiry of "Why is it like that, why are things the way they are, how could they be different, how could they be made better?"

At its core, consulting is about that type of curiosity, continuously identifying areas of improvement in any scenario. Of course, Andrew also identified a type of bravery in asking these questions, as sometimes the answer to "Why is it like that?" may be a stubborn and belligerent, "That's the way we've always done things!"

He continued, "I think having that ability to question and be intellectually curious is something I found inspiring. Intellectually curious, also, on a wide variety of things. The partners that I admired, they were very good at what they did, but they also had lives outside of work; they were interesting. They were in hobbies, or passions, or interests that made them interesting people as well. If you got stuck next to some of these people on a long flight, it wasn't unpleasant. You could actually have a conversation and learn a lot from outside of work too."

"The partners that I think of were incredibly organised and structured in the way that they thought about things. They weren't intellectually lazy; they were willing to go through difficult thinking, data-informed thinking, in order to drive to a conclusion to earn an answer for their clients. That sometimes means delivering bad news to the client, telling them what they need to hear as opposed to what they want to hear."

"There's an integrity and an honesty approach too, which is sometimes what's best for the client is not necessarily best for the partner of the firm. It might generate more money for the firm to do one thing, but the right thing to do by the client is perhaps something that is less revenue-generating for the firm." The theme of honesty that Andrew touched upon was one that had been repeated time and time again by other leaders I had spoken with. Honesty within teams, within relationships, with yourself, and with your clients had been discussed repeatedly as a foundational element for personal and professional success. Building trusted, long-term relationships with clients required an honesty and transparency when discussing opportunities for collaboration.

"When I was back at Mitchell Madison, there was an engagement we'd come to the natural conclusion of the project. I think there was an opportunity to drag it out and potentially 'feather the nest' a little bit."

"We had an information asymmetry, where we knew more about the situation than the client did. The partner just said, 'No, it's not the right thing to do. You know we're not gonna take advantage of this client, we've done a great piece of work, we're gonna draw a line under it.' I remember thinking, 'Well, that's taking a bit of a short-term pain, but it's actually the right thing to do and it's also a business-wise a smart thing to do.' Because a lot of times these things can come back to bite you. When the client finds out that you feathered your nest, then you've burnt a bridge and you've cut out potential revenue in the future."

The most successful consultants that I'd spoken with or observed throughout my career instinctively understood the importance of maintaining trusted relationships with colleagues and clients alike. They were able to do so by being authentic, by listening, and by seeking to support others, as Andrew recounted when he was introduced to a potential client at a leading bank. "We had an initial meeting and there wasn't really much to go on, but it was just a kind of a personal introduction. What I did deliberately is not to show up and say, 'Right, what do you wanna buy?' because nobody wants to be spoken to like that. It was more of an opportunity to say, 'So, tell me about you, what are you looking at now, what are your problems now, what do you want to be doing?' Probably not as direct as that, but through a natural conversation I got to know him as an individual and likewise revealed stuff about myself. We happened to get along because there was a little bit of a chemistry there. It was the beginning of the relationship and we were able to, just through that conversation, find a small little problem. It wasn't a big RFP [Request for Proposal] or anything, it was a small little problem that he was struggling with. I said, 'Well, if you don't mind, I'll just take it away and see what I can come up with in terms of an option or some sort of some solution.' That kind of got the ball rolling." Andrew took the problem away, discussed it with his team, and came back with a proposal for how to address it. Satisfied with what was presented, the client awarded Andrew the contract, and then the client called Andrew back to look at other areas where they could collaborate.

"It became obvious that I wanted him to be successful because I wanted him to be successful, and he recognised that. He could see that I had his best professional interests at heart. Likewise, he wanted me to be successful in the firm. So, there was a certain amount we could do to help each other be successful. Part of that was, as I say, delivering value when asked and called upon, but I also recognised part of it was delivering the not-so-nice messages."

"It's like when you take golf lessons. If you go to the golf course, to the driving range, and you pay somebody to teach you to be a better golfer. If all he says is 'Keep going, you're doing great, that's brilliant, just keep doing that do exactly what you're doing.' Well, that's not very helpful. It's more helpful when the guy says, 'Look, you do some things really well, keep doing those, but if you did some things differently, let's try it and see what happens.' All of a sudden, that's how you learn; that's how you make progress. I would go to him, and I'd say, 'I don't think you're doing this well' or 'I think he could do something slightly differently.' I didn't do that in the first meeting because he would say, 'Who the hell are you?!' But, after I had built up the trust and some credibility, he started to think, 'Okay'. I became a sounding board before he did things. I thought, 'Okay, now we've moved beyond consultant-client. Now I am a trusted advisor because he's asking me some very personal questions about what he should do with his career.' I can honestly say I started doing the same back to him. We've become very good friends as a result. I've been 'round to his place for dinner, our wives have met, our kids have met; but that all started with a kind of a very vanilla, face-to-face, 'Hi, this is who I am and what I do.'"

The potent mix of honesty, generosity, and curiosity has served Andrew well throughout his career. After MMG, he went on to work with Capco before joining PwC as a director in 2007. He was promoted to partner in 2011, continuing to build successful, trusted relationships both within PwC and across client organisations. Even as he reached the upper echelons of consulting, he remained humble and continued to pay it forward by making time to support others, much in the same way his mentor had done for him years ago.

"A leader is best when people barely know he exists,
when his work is done, his aim fulfilled, they will say:
we did it ourselves."

Lao Tzu

# Leadership

"Great leaders aren't managers," Stephen Knight of Accenture and formerly of CGI and PwC stated plainly, yet profoundly. "They're not controllers of you. They are there to inspire you, and, in my view, they're there to set the direction, to set the demonstration, and to give you freedom within bounds."

The question of what makes an effective leader is as old as time. It has been the subject of countless books analysing the behaviour of leaders throughout history to quantify what great leadership is. Yet, for all that has been written, when most people are asked what makes a great leader, the answers are typically the same. We instinctively know good leadership when we are in the presence of it, much in the same way as we know bad leadership when we have the misfortune of encountering it. I've been privileged to have worked with several truly inspiring leaders, some of whom have contributed to this very book. They have inspired people, supported people, and guided people on their journeys. They displayed great deals of empathy with their teams, colleagues, and clients, building trusted relationships that have stood the test of time.

Conversely, I have also worked for and alongside genuinely terrible people that, in broad strokes, could have been grouped into three categories. First are those that have arisen in the ranks above where their natural ability warrants. For them, it is not as much about malice as it is overall ineptitude. They are simply ill-equipped to lead and, at times, will mask their insecurity by shifting blame or outright aggression. Second are the a\*\*holes, whose severe character flaws create a hostile, unpredictable and ultimately destructive environment. Finally, and perhaps the worst of the three, are those that hide behind an aura of propriety, all the while harbouring sociopathic tendencies towards narcissism, arrogance, and selfishness. They perform incredible feats of cognitive gymnastics to justify their behaviour while hurting others without remorse. In each case, we must be wary as these people are unpredictable and untrustworthy. We must protect ourselves by creating distance and forming solid coalitions. The onus is on organisational leaders to identify and adequately address these individuals before their influence rots the organisation's culture from the inside out.

In American films of the Western genre between the 1920s and the 1940s, white hats were often worn by heroes and black hats by villains to symbolise the contrast in good versus evil. Unfortunately, we are not afforded such an easy means to distinguish the good from the bad in the real world. Yet, there are certain traits that we should look for that will make it easier to discern between the heroes and the villains. We should aspire to cultivate the positive attributes within ourselves and seek them out in our leaders, colleagues, and client stakeholders.

In a McQuaig survey, human resources professionals from around the globe were asked what they thought the essential positive traits of an effective leader were. The results were hardly surprising, with "empowers others", "builds trust", and "strategic thinker" in the top-three responses. "Embraces change", "energy/enthusiasm", "decisiveness", "empathy", "market knowledge", "independent thinker", and "ambitious" rounding up the top 10.[54]

## Traits of an effective leader

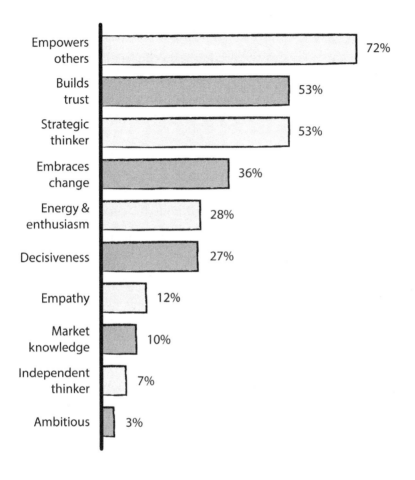

One distinction worth making is that effective leadership does not equal position within a hierarchy. I've had the pleasure of working alongside individuals across all grades in my teams that displayed leadership characteristics well beyond their years. Therefore, there is no specific time or grade level in which to begin working on developing or displaying these traits; instead, it is something that is honed over time regardless of organisational structure or our position in it. Through introspection and an ongoing desire for personal growth, we can identify which of these traits we exemplify and which we need to develop further.

Unsurprisingly, these traits were mentioned, time and time again, by effective leaders across industries, including those that have kindly contributed to this book. Through their stories, they have brought examples of these traits to life. They have also discussed the need to keep challenging ourselves to be better, to step outside of our comfort zone, and to seek out mentors or other support structures that will help guide us on our way.

# Empowers others

"The best example I can think of was with one of my biggest projects," Stephen Knight recalled. "McKinsey had gone in, completed a piece of strategy work, and said, 'You need to reinvent your electricity supply business into a new digital business.' It goes back to a McKinsey theory from about six, seven years ago called the digital attacker by which you bring a new piece, a new company, or a new entity into your organisation and it attacks the old business, becoming a totally digitally first company."

The client let him know that, while they did not have the budget for Stephen and his team, there would be opportunities for the implementation of the McKinsey strategy once it had been defined. He reached out to one of the partners with a proposal: "I need to go to Berlin for three months and help McKinsey be successful in defining the strategy. I think if we do that, we'll be able to work with them to do the roll-out and it'll be a substantial project if we roll it in."

"Well, what do we need to invest?" the partner replied. Stephen outlined the need for himself and another consultant to fly to Berlin to support the definition of the strategy. While the costs associated were not insignificant, the partner knew that it could position the company well in taking on the implementation of the strategy itself. The partner also trusted Stephen's judgement, promptly signing off on him and the other consultant to fly to Berlin.

Stephen continued, "We spent three months commuting to Berlin, and I wrote the whole technology strategy. As you know, I'm not a deep technologist, but I talk to people all over the world. Then it came to a bid process and we were trying to bid. We were working from the most grandiose McKinsey office; 27th floor with panoramic views in the tallest building in the city."

"We got a call on the Friday and we were asked to do a three day proof of concept on a Monday, Tuesday, Wednesday, and now its three in the morning on the last day. We've got to finish the answers to our questions on Wednesday and I've got this really difficult question I don't know the answer to. I knew lots of people in Accenture that would have the answer, but it's three in the morning; who can I call? I remember that the partner was in Chicago doing a training program."

Given the time difference between Berlin and Chicago, there was a chance that the partner would be available. Stephen picked up the phone and called. The partner picked up right away, "Hey, how are you doing?" Stephen detailed the problem they were facing and the fact they needed to have the answers completed that very morning. The partner listened to the challenge Stephen described and replied without hesitation, "We'll fix that. Give me an hour. I'll call you back."

As Stephen recounted the story, something that happened years ago, his tone changed when he thought back to that night. Unexpectedly, he did not recount the situation he found himself in with a sense of dread due to the gravity of the situation, or the predicament he found himself in, or the pressure that he and his team were under at the time. Instead, he smiled, as one would when recounting a moment of solace in otherwise troubled times. His tone reflected the gratitude he felt for the support he received when he needed it most.

"An hour later, she called me back," Stephen continued, "and said, 'I've got 20 people in the room who I think can answer the problem for you.' She basically got across to all the managing directors. She'd worked a room of 500 people to find the 20 people that could answer the problem from all over the world. She just said, 'Okay. I can fix this for you.' She used her amazing ability to leverage her network because she knows she's so brilliant in networking." Working with the people the partner corralled, Stephen and his team were able to identify the best way forward to complete all the questions they needed by the deadline. Thanks to the partner's trust, in conjunction with support, when it was required, Stephen and his team were able to succeed.

"I remember going in when we were doing sales pitch and the CEO of the company saying to me, 'So how can I be sure that Accenture is behind you?' I was able to turn and say, 'Well, now I've got the support of a whole European leadership team; our global leadership team,' I said, 'Now we will make this happen.'" Stephen was given a mandate; he was given the freedom to operate and was provided with timely, meaningful support from the partner when he needed it most. He was able to prove to the client that he had an entire organisation behind him. He felt empowered and confident, ready to conquer any challenge, in large part thanks to the partner's effective leadership.

"You know, that's like when you're given the wings to fly, and someone keeps on giving you those wings. That's great leadership. Great leadership isn't controlling and tightly gripping and saying, 'What are you doing?' It is giving you the inspiration to go forward and that's, I think, what I took from the partner and I tried to do that with my teams. I tried to give them enough guidance, inspiration, and freedom to fly. If you do that, they will grow. When they go a bit wrong, they can ask for help and you help them and you steer them, then they grow a bit more. You get great consultants that come out of that."

He concluded, "I can think of lots of really strong people that grow because you give them the space to grow. The best consultants are the ones that come back and say, 'Really, is that really what you want to do? What I see is this, this, this, and that, and you've not thought about that.' It's about being able to challenge based on insight and based on experience. While you might not be very deep in a specific business, you will be very broad, and that breath gives insight. Having that willingness to challenge and the ability to do that in a nice way, and sometimes in a very blunt way, is something else."

In 2018, Allan Lee, Sara Willis, and Amy Wei Tian conducted a meta-analysis of all available field experiments on leaders empowering others, examining the results of 105 studies, which included data from more than 30,000 employees from 30 countries.[55] Their analysis yielded a number of findings, two of the most important being, "First, empowering leaders are much more effective at influencing employee creativity and citizenship behaviour (i.e., behaviour that is not formally recognized or rewarded like helping co-workers or attending work functions that aren't mandatory) than routine task performance. Second, by empowering their employees, these leaders are also more likely to be trusted by their subordinates, compared to leaders who do not empower their employees."

"We found these effects happened through two distinct psychological processes. First, employees who thought their leaders were more empowering were indeed more likely to feel empowered at work—they felt a greater sense of autonomy or control in their work, they felt that their job had meaning, and it aligned with their values, that they were competent in their abilities, and that they could make a difference. These feelings of empowerment helped to explain the effects of such leaders on both employee creativity and citizenship behaviour. Empowered employees are more likely to be powerful, confident individuals, who are committed to meaningful goals and demonstrate initiative and creativity to achieve them. They typically have the freedom to generate novel ideas and the confidence that these ideas will be valued."

They continued, "Second, employees were more likely to trust leaders who they perceived as more empowering. They had greater faith in their leaders and were more likely to put in effort without feeling that they would be exploited. This is not as intuitive as one might think. When a leader tries to empower employees, he or she asks them to take on additional challenges and responsibilities at work. Employees could interpret such delegating as the leader's attempt to avoid doing the work him or herself. But we found that when empowering leadership is also about mentoring and supporting employee development, this can create a trusting relationship. Like psychological empowerment, we found that this feeling of trust helped to explain the effects of empowering leadership on both creativity and citizenship. This is because trust reduces uncertainty in the environment by instilling a sense of safety, which enables employees to take on more risks without feeling vulnerable."

No matter where in an organisation hierarchy we find ourselves, it is never too early to begin identifying opportunities to empower those around us. By empowering others, we will create more effective, creative, and engaged teams and build more robust, trusted relationships along the way.

## Builds trust

"So now you earn trust," Stephen Knight commented as we were discussing the importance of trust in business relationships. "It's a very trite thing to say, but you get trust because you say you'll do something; either you do it, or you do it better. Trust is something that comes from time and relationships. It's very hard in the virtual world, in the digital world to do that. What I'm finding is trust is actually also built in lots of small conversations. I don't think I do it intentionally. I just try to be very honest and very genuine with people. Therefore, the things I don't like is when people aren't honest and genuine."

"If they're doing something behind your back or if they're undermining you, whether deliberately or accidentally, I tend to call that out and bluntly. I walk away from situations where I feel that is the way it is, because I know how badly it affects my mental health. When I feel I'm in that situation, I get very nervous; stressed out."

Stephen recalled a challenging situation from his past. His tone changed again when reflecting on the events, as they were evidently difficult for him then and challenging to discuss even years later. He was brought in to work on a significant deal with what he described as "the second-worst client I've ever worked for." The client was incredibly demanding, constantly changing their mind and then making up stories about the decisions they had made. It wasn't an ideal situation, but Stephen did what he could to deliver on an engagement that had the potential to lead to a more significant piece of work.

Ultimately, the client did not choose the consultancy Stephen was working for at the time. It was then that the partner who was responsible for the account began to blame Stephen for the loss.

Stephen was unceremoniously replaced on the account and heard that the partner was spreading misinformation about him. Stephen escaped to work on a different project, where he achieved significant success. "We did great things because the project was the best project of my career. It won awards in the consulting awards; everyone got promoted. We made a lot of money out of it; it was very profitable. It gave me back my confidence and the confidence to say, 'Right, okay, and I need to move on.'"

The prospect of returning to work alongside the partner that betrayed him was too much to bear. He concluded, "It was all about the breach of trust. There's a concept in HR called the psychological contract. The partner broke that by throwing me under the bus. That's why trust is so important to me."

Jack Zenger and Joseph Folkman conducted a study on trust published in the *Harvard Business Review* in 2019.[56] By analysing over 80,000 360-degree reviews, the authors found that there are three elements that predict whether a leader will be trusted by his reports, peers, and other colleagues:

### Positive relationships

Trust is in part based on the extent to which a leader is able to create positive relationships with other people and groups.

### Good judgement/expertise

The extent to which a leader is well informed, knowledgeable, and experienced.

### Consistency

The extent to which leaders walk their talk
and do what they say they will do.

They concluded, "When a leader was above average on each of these elements, they were more likely to be trusted, and positive relationships appeared to be the most important element in that, without it, a leader's trust rating fell most significantly. Trust is an important currency in organizations and any leader would be wise to invest time in building it by focusing on these three elements."

Published in 2000, *The Trusted Advisor* explored the complex elements of what it means to become a trusted advisor in business.[57] The authors developed an equation with the aim of illustrating the multifaceted nature of trust, aptly naming it the Trust Quotient. According to the authors, the equation is comprised of:

### Credibility

Has to do with the words we speak and whether others acknowledge our expertise on a particular subject.

**Reliability**
Has to do with whether our actions align to the things
that we say we will do.

**Intimacy**
Refers to the safety or security that we feel when
entrusting someone with sensitive information.

**Self-orientation**
Whether the person's focus is primarily on him or herself,
or on others.

Be it in our personal or professional lives; trust plays a foundational role in building successful, long-lasting relationships. Trust is built over time; something that needs to be consistent; something that, when tarnished, will be increasingly more challenging to restore. Therefore, we must be vigilant and do the best we can to build and maintain trusted relationships within our personal and professional lives.

# Empathy

Successful leaders provide encouragement and support where needed while also trusting their team and giving them the freedom to act. Effective leaders also develop an instinct for when to step up to truly make a difference. As it was in Stephen's case, it may be that they step up when support is required. In other cases, it may be a small kindness that makes their team members feel valued and empowered.

Maria Axente of PwC recalled, "I don't think I've had ever had a person in my life, like my former boss, to do this for me. I'm just going to give you an example of what he did that will show his character."

She continued, "We were both flying to Washington, where we had a presentation for our global project, and I was supposed to present the next day. I was supposed to prepare a presentation. The reason I didn't do it earlier is that there were multiple problems with our tech provider in the UK. I had to work on the plane as we were flying during the day to do this. And guess what he's doing? He switches places with me."

"He sends me to business class, he goes to economy, so that I can have enough champagne and good food, and a lot of room for me to finish the presentation. I'm still amazed to the day how anyone can do this. That will say a lot about his personality and how much he cared about the person that I was. So yeah, that's what makes a leader; a great leader."

Prudy Gourguechon, a psychiatrist and psychoanalyst, wrote, "Empathy is the ability to understand another person's experience, perspective and feelings. Also called 'vicarious introspection', it's commonly described as the ability to put yourself in another person's shoes. But make sure you are assessing how they would feel in their shoes, not how you would feel in their shoes. This is the tricky part."[58]

Purdy continued, "There is a significant business cost when leaders lack empathy. Just ask United Airlines which earned the dishonour of having committed 'one of the worst corporate gaffes' ever, according to Bloomberg's Christopher Palmeri and Jeff Green, when a physician was dragged off a plane to empty his paid seat for an employee."

"It took United's CEO, Oscar Munoz, three tries before his public response showed any empathy. Munoz's first and woefully inadequate statement, 'I apologized for having to re-accommodate these customers,' seriously missed the mark in attempting to relate to his customer's experience."

"In his second statement, Munoz compounded the error by blaming the victim—describing the passenger as defiant, belligerent, and disruptive. Only with his third try, when Munoz said, 'I promise you we will do better,' did he demonstrate an empathic understanding of his current and future customers."

It is unsurprising that, according to the 2021 State of Workplace Empathy study, seven in 10 CEOs said it was hard for them to consistently demonstrate empathy in their working life. Meanwhile, only one in four employees believed empathy in their organisations was sufficient, while 72% of employees surveyed believed empathy drove motivation.[59]

In a previous chapter, we discussed the importance that empathy plays in crafting personas, striving to understand the mindset and behaviour of individuals across user journeys. We purposefully try to put ourselves in the shoes of others to understand their experience better, broadening our perception of the world to uncover opportunities for improvement across all touchpoints. Much in the same way, effective leaders will strive to put themselves in the shoes of their colleagues, team members, and client stakeholders. Through that exercise, they will be better able to understand the motivations and challenges faced by others, allowing them to take meaningful action.

For Maria, the simple act of changing seats so that she would be more comfortable when finishing a presentation mid-flight had a profound impact. That simple act of kindness helped her feel empowered and valued while fostering positive feelings of appreciation and trust towards the partner she was working with. Much in the same way, when Stephen was in a bind, his partner went out of her way to make sure that he received the support he needed. In both scenarios, the partners instinctively knew to act because they were able to put themselves in the shoes of others and understood how much their actions would be appreciated.

Conversely, showing a lack of empathy can have a destructive impact on relationships, teams, and public perception, as illustrated by Oscar Munoz's failed attempts to address a crisis. For example, I've witnessed directors or partners push their teams to work long hours to prepare sales presentations or RFP responses. There would be groups of people working well into the evening. The directors or partners failed to consider that their team members may have had family obligations or that, by 9 p.m., having worked non-stop since lunch, their teams would have appreciated a break for food and drink. A lack of empathy in these situations created uncomfortable moments and feelings of frustration and resentment. As leaders, we must strive to be mindful of the feelings and needs of our team members and colleagues. This is particularly important when facing times of crisis, or in high-pressure situations, when providing reassurance, support and kindness will be that much more appreciated.

Client relationships will also benefit when we are able to put ourselves in our clients' shoes. Too often, client conversations tend to take a distinct, formal, rigid, and cold tone. This is usually not intentional but rather a by-product of junior consultants wanting to make a professional impression or senior consultants not being confident in the subject matter or nervous in their delivery. Yet, the most successful client relationships are those where both parties acknowledge each other as human beings and strive to understand each other's points of view.

Genuinely listening to clients rather than trying to impress them with our latest methodology and tools is a great start. Striving to understand our clients as human beings is the natural next step. Often, this is facilitated by a change of physical environment to create space for relationships to develop beyond transactional, office-based interactions. Successful leaders create opportunities for these out-of-office interactions. It may be a lunch, a dinner, or an event that offers client teams and consulting teams an opportunity to venture outside of the office and discover one another as people.

By creating space for these interactions, we create an opportunity for relationships to grow beyond the transactional. These interactions offer an opportunity for consulting teams to understand the context of the client stakeholders better. Concurrently, as client stakeholders begin to view consultants as colleagues and partners, who have their best interests at heart, they will tend to be more understanding of the challenges that may arise during an engagement. That trust and understanding will go a long way to fostering a collaborative spirit where all parties feel that they are working together to solve a particular challenge or reach a desired objective.

Sarah McNabb, chief marketing officer at Gate 39 Media, articulated eight ways to better cultivate and express empathy:

### Understand their pain points

Show them, anecdotally, that you've been there and that you truly "get" them. Avoid expressing sympathy with phrases like "I know how you feel." Instead, show them that you have been in a similar situation before and tell them how it made you feel. Ask them if it's the same for them. Make a personal connection over a shared experience.

### Listen first

You'll never learn anything about somebody if you're the one doing all the talking. Stop selling and listen. Active listening goes beyond what you hear; it also takes body language, facial expressions, and other non-verbal signalling into account. You may have to take notes or provide feedback during your conversation. Your feedback—whether it's a nod, a smile, leaning in, or a verbal comment—should encourage the individual to keep talking.

**Learn how to read emotions**

Being able to recognise emotions in others will help direct the way forward. You'll know when you're on the right track or when to pivot. Learning how to respond appropriately is key.

For example, if the client is venting, he or she might just need to let off some steam. If you try to interject with a solution before they are done, it will be the equivalent of throwing gasoline on a fire.

**Put yourself in their shoes**

Even if you don't personally share your customer's perspective, putting yourself in their shoes will help you see the situation from where they stand. Only when you genuinely understand their point of view will you be able to offer a solution.

**Know their priorities**

Every client has a list of priorities. If you make them your priorities, your empathetic connection will be aligned. Listen to what they are and address them in the same order—essentially, you want to mirror them. This approach will reassure the client that you know what they want to accomplish and you're ready to help them make it happen.

**Accept their viewpoint**

Your client's interpretation of a situation might not be aligned with yours, but you don't have to agree with them to have empathy. Accepting their viewpoint changes your perspective and will, in all likelihood, help you make a more conscious assessment of the situation. The goal here is to come up with a solution, and this approach can help you see ways forward that you might otherwise overlook.

**Restate their problem**

Restating the client's problem ensures you are on the right track. It also reiterates that you have been actively listening.

You might open with "Let me see if I understand this correctly ..."
and finish by asking whether your interpretation was accurate.
This is critical, as you don't want to waste time (yours or your clients)
by offering solutions that don't align with their goals.

**Ask the client's permission before you proceed**
Asking permission to move ahead is a critical step, as it reaffirms
that you and the client are on the same page.
At this stage, they may invite you to move forward,
at which point you can present your ideas. If they need to
discuss the matter further, it may require a return to the
beginning of the conversation to realign and reconnect.[60]

Empathy plays a vital role in fostering relationships with our personal and
professional lives. Be it with clients, colleagues, friends, partners, or our
teams, the ability to put ourselves in the shoes of others in an honest effort
to understand their perspective allows for improved communication and,
over time, trust. As recounted by Stephen and Maria, acts of kindness can
have a profound impact on how we are perceived as people and as leaders.
Sometimes, a simple "thank you" can change someones day for the better.

# Embraces change

"In consulting we attract a lot of high-performing, ambitious people,"
Andrew Hogan observed, discussing the need to challenge people
to step outside of their comfort zone and embrace change. "To me,
the biggest attrition risk is when I can see people are just not challenged.
They're doing the same thing, in the same way, for a long period of time.
That's usually a signal to me; I can see they will probably not be here much
longer. Because they strive for stimulation, for a challenge. Part of the
leader's job is to help identify what is it in this given project, in this given
workstream, in this given performance year—whatever the metric is—what
are you going to do to stretch?"

"It's like when you go to the gym; if you work out a muscle, you have to work it to the point where it starts to break a little bit. Because then when you stop, you take the load off, it starts to heal, but it heals in a way that it's stronger than it was before. It's the same thing in professional skills, you gotta take it to that point. Now, there are some people who take it too far and you see lots of cases of mental wellness, and stress, and burnout, that's not good. But if you don't have it far enough, if people get bored, that's almost as bad."

Andrew concluded, "If you end up in the hospital and need an operation because you worked out too hard, you're no better off; you're worse off. If you go and you keep doing light repetitions at the weight you mastered two years ago, you're not gonna get any stronger. It is finding a balance. Part of leadership is helping find your own balance but also finding your team's balance."

Personal and professional growth requires us to step outside of our comfort zone and keep challenging ourselves, which in turn will allow us to better embrace the changes happening all around us.

**Outside of your comfort zone**

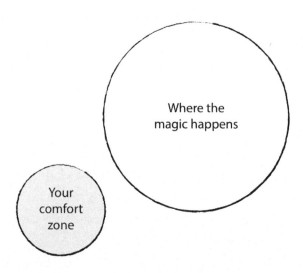

Jeremy Dalton overcame his insecurity and improved his public speaking skills by consistently challenging himself, stepping outside of his comfort zone a little bit more each time to keep incrementally enhancing his skills and gaining confidence while doing so. As for Anatoly Roytman, moving to a different country with $1,000 in his pocket placed him well outside of his comfort zone, but he would not have achieved all that he has if it were not for that bravery. Meanwhile, Andrew stepped outside of his comfort zone to pursue an MBA, which in turn helped him make lifelong friendships and propelled his career in a new direction.

According to Alan Henry and Rebecca Fishbein, writing for *Lifehacker*, "Outside your comfort zone can be a good place to be, as long as you don't tip the scales too far. It's important to remember there's a difference between the kind of controlled anxiety we're talking about and the very real anxiety that many people struggle with every day. Everyone's comfort zone is different, and what may expand your horizons may paralyze someone else. Remember, optimal anxiety can bring out your best, but too much is a bad thing."[61]

According to Alan and Rebecca, there are a few ways to break out of (and by proxy, expand) your comfort zone without going too far:

**Do everyday things differently**
Take a different route to work, go vegetarian for a week, try a new restaurant, challenge yourself to do more public speaking, or join a new club or society. Don't be discouraged if things don't go the way you planned. Embrace the different perspectives and experiences.

**Take your time making decisions**
Sometimes slowing down is all it takes to make you uncomfortable. Slow down, observe what's going on, take your time to interpret what you see, and then intervene. Sometimes just defending your right to make an educated decision can push you out of your comfort zone. Think; don't just react.

**Trust yourself and make snap decisions**

Alan and Rebecca purposefully contradict themselves, and for a good reason. Just as there are people who thrive on snap decisions, others are more comfortable weighing all of the possible options over, and over, and over again. Sometimes making a snap call is in order, just to get things moving. Doing so can help you kickstart your projects and teach you to trust your judgement.

**Do it in small steps**

It takes a lot of courage to break out of your comfort zone. You get the same benefits whether you go in with both feet or start slow, so don't be afraid to start slow. If you're socially anxious, don't assume you have to muster the courage to ask your crush on a date right away; just say hello to them and see where you can go from there. Identify your fears, and then face them step by step.

To effectively embrace the rapidly changing world around us, we must endeavour to continuously evolve and adapt, seeking out new opportunities for self-improvement. We will need to overcome our anxieties as best we can and persistently challenge ourselves to step outside of our comfort zone, even if only by small steps at first. After all, even small steps in the right direction signify progress.

# Mentors

Throughout our careers, we will make many decisions that will have a significant impact on our career trajectory and our professional and personal development. In most scenarios, we will use our experience, education, knowledge, and instinct to guide our thinking to select what we believe to be the best alternative. However, there will be many times when we would benefit from discussing the different options available or having someone else ask us the right questions.

Our friends or parents will always have the best intentions. Unfortunately, they may be biased in their opinions, lack the professional context or experience necessary to provide us with the insights we require. That is why identifying a mentor—a person who may have travelled a similar career path before us, someone who will be more objective in their assessments of our situation, and someone who will not be afraid to ask challenging questions or sharing hard truths—is so critical.

"I think I've been very, very fortunate to have a couple of very good mentors," Andrew Hogan admitted. "The one at CIBC was by far the one who had the most profound effect on me and probably gave me the model of what good mentoring looks like, that I've tried to aspire to as well. The thing with him, but with all the mentors I've had, is that they make you uncomfortable sometimes. They can be your friend, but they're not; their primary role and purpose isn't to be your friend, it's to be your conscience."

When he was at CIBC, Andrew worked with Bob, who had also become the mentor of whom he spoke so highly. He recalled, "Bob wouldn't let me get complacent. If I'd achieved something and he was like, 'Okay, well done, but nobody's gonna remember what you did yesterday, it's what you're gonna do next.' Pushing me to strive for more and to try to achieve more, but also to try to learn more. I think in a good mentoring relationship, there's a bit of grit. It's not just back slaps and beers all the time. It can be uncomfortable sometimes, and if the relationship is solid enough, that's okay. They're there and you know why they're doing it. They're doing it because they have your best interest at heart, but sometimes it can be uncomfortable."

"I think that a fundamentally important part of the mentoring relationship is the challenge and the holding to accountability. One of the things that I found worked with me and I try to do it with those I mentor, is you've got to get the ambition and the vision and the dreams on the table. What is it you want to achieve? That's not just a kind of off the top of your head kind of conversation."

"It requires some serious and deep thinking about, 'Where do I want to be?', whether it's in six months' time or six years' time or 16 years' time. Being brave enough to say it out loud to your mentor is one thing, but then as the mentor, it's listening to that and challenging, 'You know, have they really thought it through? Have they thought of it from all the different angles? And then what are you doing to make that vision come real? Because saying it is the first step, but you need to follow the talk with action.' I think sometimes we're all guilty of procrastination; we're all guilty of doing the easy things first. Sometimes, what a mentor can do is act as a conscience and say, 'Have you really started to put into action a plan that will make some of that vision come to life?' So, I try to do that. I think it is about being clear on where you want to end up, and that is in professional terms, in personal terms, and all the different dimensions of a person's life, because they're all interconnected."

"Sometimes it's a mistake to think of your career in some sort of vacuum, some sort of isolation, but it's not right. It's part of a bigger thing called your whole life. So, you've got to think through things like your health, your family, your relationships, your faith if that's a factor; all of those things. Having a broad idea of what big-ticket items you want to work towards. Whether it's career development, promotion, whether it's marriage, whether it's children, whatever it is, and then thinking back, 'Okay, what do I need to start doing today?' It's like the farmers that want a crop in September. When you're sitting there in March, you're not gonna have a crop unless you start tilling the soil, unless you start planting the seeds, unless you start watering and tending to the ground. Then, eventually, if you do all those things, then you have a crop."

Working backwards from an objective and clearly articulating what steps need to be taken to achieve that objective is an approach we've noted in a previous chapter. In projects, as in life, it is a valuable tool to acknowledge the time and effort required while preventing the optimistic bias that we are all prone to.

As mentors and leaders, we play an important role in challenging our mentees, asking the right questions, and guiding them to find their own answers. While some mentor relationships develop naturally due to circumstance, proximity, and timing as they did for Andrew, others may require a more direct and deliberate approach. Melissa Max-Macarthy, for example, did not have a mentor but knew that she wanted one. Her approach was simple and inspired.

She recalled, "I went online, went on to LinkedIn, and decided at that point I wanted to speak to someone that was a product manager for a voice system. I found this amazing lady called Marwa. I reached out to her on LinkedIn just being like, 'Hey! I've seen your profile, would you like to mentor me?' I needed someone on the inside, someone that could help. I needed someone that was a few years ahead of me, that kind of got it and also worked with the products that I liked at the time. So yeah, I was just like, 'Hey, this is who I am, this is what I'm interested in, I've looked you up, I've done some research, and you just seem incredible.'"

"She took ages to get back to me, and when I say ages, she took seven days," Melissa laughed. "I remember the first day I was like, 'It's cool'. The second day, I was like, 'She's probably busy.' Then on the third day, I was looking at her profile; had she been online, has she changed the profile, nothing." At that point, Melissa began to get increasingly nervous. While her brother reassured her that she needed to be patient, her mother suggested she look to someone else as her mentor in an attempt to lift her spirits.

"I was like, 'Oh Mom, you just don't get it. Marwa is the right person; I just know it. I'm gonna wait, and I'm gonna give it a week,' and Marwa came back to me on the seventh day. She was like, 'Sorry Mel. I was in Seattle. Let's meet up.' We spoke, and we just really got on. She gave me exercises to do and just really got me to home in on those raw skills that I had and that I needed to refine. I remember her telling me to use the same approach I used with her to reach out directly to people on LinkedIn, so I did."

Following the advice, Melissa reached out to several people from companies she was interested in, which eventually led her to secure an interview with Accenture. Melissa did not have a mentor, but knew she wanted one. She actively sought one out, being very brave and direct, in the industry she was interested in. Consequently, with the mentor's guidance, she took active steps to improve and refine her skills while successfully seeking out a role for herself at one of the world's top consultancies.

Be it through good fortune, a robust network, a dogged determination, or all of the above, there are many avenues we can pursue in order to find a mentor. The value of having a good mentor, regardless of how the connection is made, is significant. According to statistics compiled by Nicola Cronin for Guider, 87% of mentors and mentees felt empowered by their mentoring relationships and had developed greater confidence. Mentees were promoted five times more often than those without mentors, and mentors themselves were six times more likely to be promoted. 71% of Fortune 500 companies stated they had mentoring programs, making it easier for mentors and mentees to connect. Yet, surprisingly, only 37% of professionals surveyed stated they had a mentor.[62]

Interestingly, according to those statistics, 89% of those who had been mentored stated they would go on to mentor others. The value of identifying an individual or individuals to provide guidance as mentors along our career paths is undeniable. Andrew has remained thankful for the time and advice that Bob provided him throughout the years. He went on to pay it forward by providing guidance and mentoring to many others throughout his career and, in a beautifully poetic continuity, mentored Bob's son when he needed it. Finding the right mentor to help us is the first step of the journey, but we must also remain mindful to pay back their kindness by mentoring and supporting others when they need it down the line.

# Culture

At a high level, company culture can be defined as a set of shared values, goals, attitudes, and practices that characterise an organisation. It's a shared ethos of an organisation. It is the way people feel about the work they do, the values they believe in, where they see the company going, and how they are going to get it there. Collectively, these traits represent the personality, or culture, of an organisation.

As leaders, we have a mandate to consider what sort of culture we wish to establish. We must take into account how our actions, the actions of our teams and the policies and practices of the organisation all contribute to that culture. When I was at PwC, James Easterbrook led the charge in articulating and agreeing upon the shared values of our practice. He believed, rightly, that one element of building the culture within our part of the organisation was to align with the values in which we believed. Rather than hoping that team members would recognise implied values, it was essential for them to be explicitly stated and agreed upon.

Unfortunately, there are many leaders and organisations that will proudly state their values without doing the hard work required to align themselves behind them. James agreed, "I think culture is an interesting one, and there are a number of factors that feed into culture. First is the real clarity of the proposition. What are we here to do? So, you know, one of the leading consultancies was 'Build trust in society and solve important problems.' And you're like, 'Well, that's just totally unrealistic.' I mean, you help people avoid billions of pounds in tax. That's not building trust in society. You wouldn't do that if that's what you actually believed in. So, you've got misalignment in the purpose and the activity. That's a problem. The other thing is when you say, 'Well, we want to behave as one firm,' but all your incentives are about personal gain. That doesn't work."

"They pay lip service to all of that, but they don't actually want it and are not actually interested in having that kind of good culture. They think culture is about letting people have beers at four o'clock on a Friday. You know, if you treat them like a [#@*%] the rest of the week, then some beers on a Friday doesn't make any difference."

One of the ways we build trust as leaders is by saying what we will do and then following through. Similarly, to foster a positive company culture, the organisation needs to align itself to and adhere to the values it claims to espouse. Not doing so will result in any claims of values to ring hollow.

"I think that there is a lot of that," James confirmed, "there is a lot of like, 'Oh, I can paper over the cracks with some culture things,' which are, 'Oh, I'll do a newsletter.' You know, it has to be a real commitment. You have to really believe it. You can't fake authenticity."

A lack of investment in building a positive company culture or lack of alignment with their values has significant consequences for organisations. In the book *Corporate Culture and Performance*, authors James Heskett and John Kotter identified that companies that had the best corporate cultures— that encouraged all-around leadership initiatives and that highly appreciated their employees, customers, and owners—grew 682% in revenue over 11 years. During the same period of evaluation, companies without a thriving company culture grew only 166% in revenue. A thriving company culture led to more than four times higher revenue growth. Additionally, 47% of people actively looking for a new job pointed to company culture as the main reason for wanting to leave their organisation, meaning if our aim is to increase both employee retention and profitability, improving company culture should be one of our priorities.[63]

James Easterbrook warned that it was up to all leaders within an organisation to hold themselves and others accountable when it came to adhering to organisational values.

He cautioned, "I've seen behaviours that I thought were totally unacceptable. Partners and directors balling out teams, junior people, in front of a client because they didn't like something or when they were exposed by the client. It doesn't even matter if it was that team's fault or if they got it wrong; you don't do that. That's not acceptable. You know, there's a collective accountability there. I thought that was really disappointing. Also, by and large, that went unchallenged because those people made money. It was as if, as long as you could make the cash, it didn't really matter if you behaved in whatever way you wanted to behave."

"It sends a message that you can be a senior person, progress, do well in an organisation, and exhibit bad behaviour. I think, therefore, you immediately legitimise it and that's toxic. That's cancer because you're saying it's okay to be like that. I do think there's a long-term impact. It chips away at the sustainability. You chip, chip, chip away and then eventually it will come around and bite you because you won't have the fellowship. You won't have the people willing to put in the hours for you. You won't have that kind of intangible connection that you're trying to achieve. That can be really difficult to see early. Over time it erodes. Say you're standing on a pillar of rock that's being eroded, and it feels pretty solid until the point that it's not right, and then you're in trouble."

Sadly, I've also witnessed situations where the behaviour of directors and partners did not reflect the values that their organisation claimed to hold. That disconnect resulted in, as James put it, the gradual chipping away at the foundation of trust within the organisation and, on a number of unfortunate occasions, taking a sledge hammer to it.

According to a survey commissioned by Deloitte, 94% of executives and 88% of employees believe a distinct corporate culture is important to a business's success.[64] Deloitte's survey also found that there is a strong correlation between employees who claim to feel happy and valued at work and those who say their company has a strong culture.

Alan Kohll, a corporate wellness expert, identified eight ways in which leaders can help shape positive corporate culture:

### Focus on wellness

No organisation can expect to foster a positive culture without healthy employees. Employees need to feel their best—physically, mentally, and emotionally—to contribute to a positive culture.

### Grow off your current culture

Evolve the culture you have by asking what your teams like and don't like about their current culture and work environment.

### Provide meaning

Create a mission statement and core values and communicate these to your teams. Give people specific examples of how their roles positively impact the company and its clients.

### Create goals

Leaders should gather with their team to create goals and objectives that everyone can work towards. Creating a company goal brings employees together and gives everyone something specific to work towards.

### Encourage positivity

Lead by example by expressing gratitude, celebrating success, and empowering others.

### Foster social connections

Provide opportunities for inclusive social interaction during regular work hours to make it easy for everyone to take part without having to sacrifice personal time or time with family.

### Listen

Being a good listener is one of the easiest ways employers can start to build a positive culture. Listen to your team and make sure they feel their voices are heard and valued.

### Empower culture champions

Culture champions are people who embody the values and mission of a company. They are excited to promote a company's aspirations and encourage others to do the same.[65]

Alan concluded, "One of the most important roles a leader has is creating a positive culture. Be sure to cultivate a positive culture that enhances the talent, diversity, and happiness of your workforce. Building a unique, positive culture is one of the best—and simplest—ways to get your employees to invest their talent and future with your company."

As leaders, it is our responsibility to help shape the culture of the organisations and teams within which we operate. That, on its own, is a considerable undertaking. However, beyond striving to exemplify the values we consider important, we must also be brave and vigilant in calling out bad behaviour when we see it. If we don't, we risk these bad behaviours chipping away at our culture, rotting the cohesion of our organisations from the inside out.

# Needs

In the 1960s, two decades after Maslow's hierarchy of needs was first proposed, David McClelland introduced a motivational model that attempted to explain how the needs for achievement, affiliation, and power affected the actions of people. Known as the "Need Theory" or "Three Needs Theory," it stated that we all have three types of motivations regardless of age, sex, race, or culture.[66]

These three needs are defined as:

### Need for achievement
Motivated by accomplishment and feedback in the workplace.

### Need for affiliation
Enjoy being a part of groups and have a desire to feel loved and accepted.

### Need for power
Need status recognition, winning arguments, competition, and influencing others.

McClelland's research indicated that 86% of the population are dominant in one, two, or all three of these three types of needs. By being honest with ourselves and introspective, we will be able to identify what our balance is. We will then be able to communicate these needs to others and take steps to ensure that the needs are satisfied in our professional and personal lives. As with most things, balance is essential, meaning it's vital to be mindful that one dimension does not become overly dominant. For example, winning arguments or being competitive may adversely impact relationships if taken too far, as anyone who has ever played *Monopoly* against me will surely attest to.

Concurrently, it's essential to take the needs of those around us into account. It is only when we acknowledge the needs of others that we will be better able to tailor our leadership approach and our communications. On a larger scale, we have an opportunity to create a culture that takes the needs of our team members into account, instituting feedback sessions, team building events or recognition structures that will attempt to satisfy the needs of our colleagues or teams.

When I was at PwC, I volunteered to take over running a monthly event for our practice. With the support of several colleagues, we turned "Final Thursday/Friday" into a fun, informal, TED-style town hall jumble of activities fuelled by copious amounts of snacks. Each session would feature team-building activities, presentations from team members on recent projects or exciting topics, celebrations of recent wins, speeches from the partners, and the "Chair of Truth," whereby a selected team member would answer questions from the audience about themselves. The event was held during afternoon work hours to make it convenient for everyone to attend without infringing on their other obligations while giving those who wanted to the opportunity to later reconvene at a local pub. To their credit, the partners and directors all made a concerted effort to participate, leading by example, providing updates on happenings from around the firm, and even allocating some budget to the snack and drink fund.

If we examine the recurring event through the lens of the Need Theory, we can identify how all three needs may have been addressed. The event created an opportunity to celebrate achievement, as we celebrated wins and spotlighted individuals who had gone above and beyond. It created space to network and brought the team closer together, aiming to address the need for affiliation. Finally, by offering team members the opportunity to speak about their projects, we attempted to address the need for power and recognition. Of course, this is not to say that one monthly event satisfies all the needs of a team or all the individual members in it, but it was a step in the right direction.

The way we engage with our teams will change depending on our organisations, team cultures, and immediate objectives. When Richard Murton of Ogilvy and formerly of Accenture wanted to form a closer bond with his team, acknowledging his teams and his own need for affiliation, he turned to the great unifier: food.

He reminisced, "What I did when I was in Amsterdam, every week on a Wednesday, I invited six people to my own flat and we had sushi. I have to tell you, to get through a team of 60, it took about three months. Every Wednesday, having these six different people, as I mixed the teams up, and we just sat there; we had drinks, it was paid for, and it was amazing. What was so amazing is that people went back to work and they're like, 'Oh my God, I've been to the boss's house. Richard's house is amazing! We had such a good laugh!' The halo and knock-on effects of that were really, really interesting. I think people then just see you as a human being, as somebody who's a bit messy in their flat, perhaps. We sort of pull covers over ourselves when we're leaders to try and make ourselves perfect. You have a bit of a laugh, it's a few drinks, and they just loved it. They really loved it."

By acknowledging the needs of our teams, we take an essential step in making them more engaged; more emotionally committed both to the organisation and to our shared objectives. As our teams become more engaged, they also become more effective. According to a Gallup meta-analysis conducted in 2012, the businesses that scored the highest on employee engagement showed 21% higher profitability and 17% higher productivity.[67] It is yet another example of where doing the right thing is also a sound business strategy.

# Inspires

"How do you inspire teams?" Andy Woodfield repeated to himself as he pondered the question. As a PwC Partner, a vocal leader, and contributor to numerous communities, Andy was undoubtedly looked up to by many. He considered the question a moment longer and replied, "Always do what you said you were going to do. Show people who you are. Be a human being, have people's backs, and be there to support people. Grab hold of every moment and opportunity to demonstrate your values, what you believe in, so that your words and your actions are in line, so that your values come to life in your actions."

"So, when you tell people that you care and there's a moment where you can demonstrate that, you better demonstrate it. I think just in general, be very conscious about the alignment of your words and your actions. I think when you say great things, make sure you do great things. Then you can shine a light on those great things. If you just say great things and never deliver on them with your actions you start to look and feel inauthentic and people don't follow inauthentic leaders."

"Make sure you tell your story; support and share other people's stories too. It's important to use your platform to do something good, sometimes that means being courageous. You should support and amplify the voices of others, especially those who you feel might not be heard. That means you also need to develop your own great listening and hearing skills. I think it's important to step up and speak up when stuff doesn't feel right, silence is collusion so you risk being just as bad as the terrible thing you just heard if you don't speak up. It's not easy, for sure, but it's important."

He continued, "There's a great phrase that I love and it feels super relevant to the ideas of 'authenticity' and 'purpose', which is, 'You can't fatten a pig on market day'. Just because you've now decided that you need to demonstrate your values, just because you've now decided that it's fashionable to be authentic, or you've decided it's important to have your authentic voice on social media, you can't just turn that on and expect people to believe you. It needs to be real, it really needs to be you; you can't fatten a pig on market day. You need to feed that authentic, purposeful, vulnerable little pig every single day and, eventually, it will get fat, or authentic and purposeful in this case."

Andy touched upon several traits that inspirational leaders embody, from empowering others to building trust, listening, being authentic and calling out bad behaviour when the situation warrants it. When it comes to inspiring others, Andy also noted one other important trait of effective leaders: consistency.

In an increasingly fast-paced, at times unpredictable world, our teams will look to us to provide them with a sense of stability and continuity. They will look to us to set the tone, to consistently demonstrate the values and authenticity we ask them to exhibit themselves. Our teams will understand we are human; they will understand when we make mistakes, as long as we are willing to acknowledge them and continue to strive to be a better version of ourselves. Consider the inspiring leaders that you've encountered or read about. They may have flaws; they may have made mistakes. Yet, they remained consistent in their efforts to live by and extol specific values they believed in to lift others up, to be authentic, and to make the world just a bit better. That is one of the reasons that genuinely inspiring leaders are so rare. Not only do they display long lists of admirable traits, but they do so consistently and persistently.

Anyone who has ever resolved to start going to the gym and watch their diet can attest that doing so for a single day or a week is much easier than doing so consistently and over the long term. Every January, most gyms are full of people in newly acquired exercise apparel, only for them to abandon their resolutions before the end of the month. However, perhaps even frustratingly, to truly realise the benefits of going to the gym and a balanced diet, there are no shortcuts. In the same way as you can't fatten a pig on market day, you won't get fit and healthy in a day, nor will you become an inspirational leader in a day. It will take dedication, consistency, and perseverance.

As we strive to improve ourselves as leaders, we can take some immediate steps to inspire our teams. Dede Henley, the founder of the Henley Leadership Group, compiled a list of seven ways by which to do just that:

**Get better at asking good questions**
The design firm IDEO encourages teams to begin with,
"How might we…?" For example, "How might we improve X?",
or "How might we completely reimagine Y?", or "How
might we find a new way to accomplish Z?"

**Change the way you meet**
In addition to regularly scheduled meetings, try short, fast stand-up meetings, like huddles, to keep the energy high.

**Ditch diplomacy**
Let people say what they feel. Encourage your team members to say what they are really thinking.

**Put your people first**
As Andy advised, support your team and be there for them when they need it. Go out of your way to make them feel valued.

**Inspire responsibility and provide autonomy**
Hold people accountable to big expectations and give them the autonomy to make their own decisions, much in the way Stephen was given the freedom to pursue the opportunity in Germany.

**Make it safe to fail**
The fear of failure cripples creativity and hamstrings the flow of ideas and, ultimately, productivity.

**Have some fun**
Too often is having fun or organising fun activities dismissed as frivolous, yet it is what creates opportunities for teams to bond. If people aren't having any fun, they aren't going to be inspired or creative.[68]

Anatoly Roytman wholeheartedly agreed as to the role that having fun plays in inspired teams. Having spent over a decade in a leadership role at Accenture Interactive, he noted the importance of fun, saying, "People being rewarded by simply having fun with other people; that is very hard to implement, but it does happen on occasion."

He continued, "It's not about money, but being proud of what you do, feeling good about doing it with other people, and creating a sense of community. That required spending lots of hours and building the fun part of the organisation. What's very troubling right now is that many of those things have become more and more formal. That kills all the fun. When you make fun formal, it kills it. Unfortunately, the modern organisational design is more about KPIs and formal management. This formality, I think, kills all the fun, especially the bigger the organisation, the more KPIs and more data-driven they become; it takes the human part out of that."

The most effective, authentic leaders I've spoken with were diligent in their efforts to improve themselves continuously. They consistently endeavoured to work on their complex mix of positive traits to be better as individuals and better at empowering others. Through their efforts, they led by example, displaying the types of values that others would look up to and subsequently exhibit themselves.

It is up to us to help shape the culture and values of our organisations. We can create a positive and supportive environment by leading by example, being brave in calling out bad behaviour, and being consistent in our words and actions. Working with our teams, we can identify what works, what doesn't, and how we can continue to improve our organisations over time. Finally, as Anatoly highlighted, we must also remember to have fun. A highly underrated aspect of professional lives, having fun builds rapport within teams, helps create a more positive culture and effectively sets us up for success. As Dale Carnegie so eloquently stated, "People rarely succeed unless they have fun in what they are doing."

"Failure is an important part of your growth and developing resilience. Don't be afraid to fail."

Michelle Obama

# Failure

Andy King could not remember the last time he was so tired. The previous weeks had been a whirlwind of activity, with a seemingly endless barrage of fires to put out every single day. When he did find a moment for himself amidst the chaos, the frantic phone calls, and high-intensity meetings, he took a deep breath and thought to himself, "How did I get here?"

In his late-50s, Andy had the fortune of looking like a much younger man. Polished, with a neatly coiffed head of silver-white hair, he had the look of a man who had spent the better part of his life in branding, events, and campaigns. He thought back to all his success stories, to all of the brands he had helped along the way, and even to the cookbook he published. It was a varied career, with many highs and lows, but he was proud of all he had accomplished.

He thought back to this latest project and how the allure of creating a brand-new destination music festival on a beautiful tropical island had drawn him in.

He recalled how the charismatic Billy McFarland had pitched the idea to him and how they had taken over social media soon thereafter, with famous models and influencers posting photos online and inviting others to the event.

He thought back to how increasingly difficult the project had become, mainly as most of those involved had never set up events of this scale before. He was worried that, with very little time left before guests started arriving, they wouldn't be able to get everything finished on time. Even though he and the crew had been working around the clock for weeks, the guest tents weren't ready, the facilities were not set up, and the musical acts had started, one by one, cancelling their appearances.

He took a deep breath and allowed himself a hint of a smile. He had been in challenging situations before, and he had always found a way to work things out. Here, he was hopeful that the stars would align once again and that all the elements would fall into place. He was going to make this a success.

Just then, in a rare moment of cautious optimism, his mobile phone began to buzz.

"Hello?" he answered.

"Hi Andy, it's Billy," replied the voice on the other side of the call.
Billy had been calling with increased frequency over the last few days, and it was never good news.

Andy braced himself for the worst and replied, "Hi Billy, what's wrong this time?"

"Andy, we have an issue with the water bottles. They are stuck at customs, and they won't release them," Billy replied.

Andy knew exactly what water bottled he was talking about. He had meetings in Bermuda the previous week for the America's Cup and had missed the meeting with Cunningham, the customs representative, about the water bottle shipment. Cunningham had informed Billy and his team that they would have to pay $175,000 USD to release the water shipment.

Billy didn't wait for a response and continued, "Andy, we need you to take one big thing for the team."

"Oh my gosh, I've been taking something for the team every day!" Andy replied, exasperated.

"Well, you're our wonderful gay leader," Billy continued, without acknowledging Andy's objection, "and we need you to go down... will you..."

There was a pause on the line before Billy slowly finished his question.

"Suck...d*ck...to fix this water problem?"

Andy wasn't sure he had heard it right. "Billy, what?!"

"Andy, if you will go down and suck Cunningham's d*ck and get him to clear all of the containers with water, you will save this festival."

In all his career, he had never found himself in this type of situation. They finished the call, and Andy sat there for a moment, debating what to do next in his head. Then he drove home, took a shower, and used some mouthwash. He got into his car to drive across town to Cunningham's office, fully prepared to, as Andy recollected, "suck his d*ck".

Andy recalled what happened next: "But he couldn't have been nicer," he said, referring to Cunningham, the customs manager.

"And he's like, 'Andy, listen, I will release all the water; I will let you serve it, but I want to be one of the first people to be paid this import fee for what you're doing.'"

"'Okay, great,' and I got back, and I had all the water that we needed. Can you imagine? In my 30-year career, that this is what I was going to do? I was going to do that, honestly, to save the festival."

Andy King recounted his story in the popular Netflix documentary *FYRE: The Greatest Party That Never Happened.*

It was the story of how Billy McFarland, with the support of rapper Ja Rule, attempted to launch the Fyre Festival, a luxury music festival on Great Exuma island in the Bahamas. The event, scheduled to take place in April and May of 2017, was abruptly cancelled after attendees had already begun arriving due to problems with security, food, logistics, understaffing, and musical acts cancelling their appearances en masse.

In May 2017, McFarland and Ja Rule were sued for $100 million USD in a class-action lawsuit on behalf of Fyre Festival attendees. The following month, McFarland was arrested and charged with wire fraud in Manhattan federal court for his role in the organisation of the festival. After pleading guilty to two counts of wire fraud in March 2018, he was sentenced to six years in federal prison. The Fyre Festival became synonymous with failure; its name mockingly evoked to bemoan other organisations and events when they spectacularly failed to plan and execute.

Yet, regardless of how much fun it may be to mock the Fyre Festival organisers, there are valuable lessons to be learned from their failure that are very much applicable to the world of consulting.

After all, consulting projects also fail at a spectacularly embarrassing rate, but thankfully to, in most cases, much less public scrutiny and far fewer requests to perform fellatio to release detained water shipments.

First, we need to consider the warning signs that were summarily ignored along the way. Second, why those involved may not have come forward to voice their concerns. Third, we need to consider what steps we can take to reduce the probability of failing in our own endeavours.

# Canary in the coalmine

The term "canary in the coalmine" refers to caged birds that miners would carry down into the mine tunnels with them. If dangerous gases such as carbon monoxide collected in the mine, the gases would kill the canary before killing the miners, thus providing a warning to exit the tunnels immediately.

History is littered with countless examples of failed projects, both big and small, that did not take heed of early warning signs. They ignored the proverbial canary and just kept digging towards their ruin. Individuals that raised concerns would be removed, data suggesting unfavourable outcomes would be quashed, and years of experience would be ignored in favour of a naïve belief that "this time it would be different."

As per a 2020 KPMG Project Management Survey, 75% of projects were not delivered successfully, 60% were over budget, 58% suffered delays, and 49% did not meet the original goal or business intent.[69] Ultimately, only 52% of projects in question were delivered to stakeholder satisfaction.

Typically, projects do not fail dramatically or all at once. Instead, most projects will see a steady decline whereby early warning signs are ignored, performance indicators not tracked, and changing circumstances not communicated amongst teams or stakeholders.

According to research by the Project Management Institute, 55% of project managers agree that effective communication to all stakeholders is the most critical success factor in project management.[70] The research indicated that high-performing organisations are better at communicating key project topic areas, including objectives, budget, schedule, scope, outcomes, and the project's business benefit.

Additionally, high-performing organisations are notably better at delivering project communications promptly, providing sufficient clarity and detail, using non-technical language, and choosing appropriate settings or media for the delivery. High-performing organisations use formal communications plans more frequently and more effectively compared to low-performing organisations.

In the case of the Fyre Festival, countless early signs foreshadowed the tragic conclusion. The documentary features numerous individuals, from promoters to bookers, to logistic experts who, with the benefit of hindsight, talk at length about the warning signs that were ignored along the way. Yet, not many of them were able to point to moments when they stood up and raised the alarm.

After all, it is one thing to think to yourself that things are not right, but an entirely different one to give voice to your concerns. In the same way that standing up against inappropriate behaviour requires bravery, so does being the one to voice concerns when a project or programme is showing warning signs. However, we need to be mindful of how we approach the situation. Being the bearer of bad news, even with the clear intentions of benefiting the organisation, will not always be met with the acceptance and praise we'd hope for.

# Shooting the messenger

Throughout history and literature, being the bearer of bad news was never an enviable position to find oneself in. An early citing of "shooting the messenger" can be found in Plutarch's *Lives of the Noble Greeks and Romans*: "The first messenger, that gave notice of Lucullus' coming was so far from pleasing Tigranes that he had his head cut off for his pains; and no man dared to bring further information. Without any intelligence at all, Tigranes sat while war was already blazing around him, giving ear only to those who flattered him."

I vividly remember the sting of being shot as the messenger on one of my projects, and it was not a very pleasant experience. At the time, I was working on an internal project to develop a platform tailored specifically to local government councils. The rationale for the platform was sound, as each local council largely needed the same things from their online portal; give their citizens access to information and the ability to report issues. For example, a typical online query may be to find out when rubbish is being collected and a report may involve an abandoned car.

The partner leading the initiative, an energetic and enthusiastic man, was able to convince several senior partners that this was the right course of action, even though it was a vast departure from the standard consulting business model and represented a considerable risk for the firm. He understood the Audacity Ratio and put in extraordinary efforts to make sure everyone was bought into the plan. He put together a team of experienced consultants from across internal teams to drive the initiative forward while concurrently working to identify the first potential client.

I was asked to review the progress that was made on requirement gathering for the platform. As I familiarised myself with the state of the programme, alarm bells began to ring in my head.

Even though we had a large team of consultants on the project, doing the best they could, there was a significant shortage of individuals with platform development experience. The lack of experience meant that the requirement definitions for pieces of functionality were vague or riddled with inconsistencies. We were a few weeks into development and already behind schedule. With the requirements not well defined, a lot of re-work was required. Our local contractors also took issue with the code quality of the third-party developer, meaning more time was lost on endless calls and yet more re-work. Undaunted, the sales team and partner continued to push forward, making promises and setting expectations that would ultimately prove impossible to meet.

In previous engagements, I had learned how important it was to call out potential issues early, ensuring that stakeholders from all sides understood the implications and agreed to a revised, more realistic scope and timeframe if necessary. That transparency would go a long way in preventing uncomfortable conversations from happening in the future. As issues continued to compound, I asked our developers to look at our development backlog and estimate how long each piece of functionality would take to develop, considering the uncertainty and everything we had learned to that point. The high-level estimates began coming in a few days later and painted a rather dire picture. Based on their estimates, not only was there no way we would hit any of the milestones that were promised, but we would also miss them by some margin.

At the next team call, I raised my concerns. I presented the forecasts that were provided, which clearly indicated that we would not be able to hit our targets and that we would need to take appropriate action immediately. I also presented a number of steps that could be taken to gain better insight into the size of the challenge ahead. There were some questions on the call, but overall, everyone seemed to agree that it was an issue that needed to be addressed.

Not five minutes after the team call concluded, I was contacted by the lead director responsible for the development. He was not happy. He told me that development would sort itself out, that there were no issues, and that I was only fear-mongering. I provided him and others with the data, but it seemed no one wanted to hear it. Shortly thereafter, I was asked to step away from the project.

While being moved off a project is never a glamorous affair, and I was disappointed to take a step away, it was a real-world example of what happens to bearers of bad news if they are not strategic enough. I was young, I was too blunt, and I was foolish to think that my unfavourable assessments would be welcomed by all who heard them with open arms. Inevitably, the project did fall further behind, deadlines were missed, and potential clients were lost. It was a disappointing conclusion but hardly the first or last endeavour to suffer a similar fate.

Based on their own client partnerships and over 800 survey responses, Boston Consulting Group (BCG) concluded that only 30% of digital transformations worldwide are actually successful.[71] They identified six factors that need to be addressed to improve this percentage, including clear objectives, buy-in from leadership, modular technology, high-calibre talent, agile governance, and, unsurprisingly, effective monitoring of progress towards defined outcomes. When significant risks begin to appear, it is important to speak up, but it is equally important how that message is delivered, and by whom. Being the sole voice yelling that the sky is falling, even when it actually may be, is hardly an effective strategy. We need to build a coalition that aligns on the metrics we use, acknowledges the risks, and will collectively agree on the way forward.

"You need to, unfortunately, you need to get allies; you can't be the lone voice. That never works," Tor Gisvold, formerly of PwC, confessed as we discussed the need for building a coalition.

He continued, "You need to get someone to work with you. You need to convince someone that what you do is going to be the right thing, because you're a madman if you stand completely on your own. Then you need to spend enough time, with enough people, to get some momentum behind what you're saying."

"You need to convince more people and you need to keep on communicating at all levels within the organisation constantly. It's the most underrated talent. Engineers think it's enough to be right because their world is zeros and ones; you're either wrong or you're right. You're not just spending your own political capital, in that you need to spend it wisely. None of that happens without experience and without having failed a few times."

There is power in numbers. Forming a coalition of like-minded individuals is equally beneficial whether we are championing a new initiative or when we need to acknowledge that our proverbial canary had seen better days. We must be diligent in identifying risks and brave in calling them out, but also strategic enough so that we do not lose our heads in the process.

# Complexity

Projects rarely fail due to only one factor, but rather suffer a steady decline based on several factors that were not addressed with enough consideration. In the example of the Fyre Festival, there were a myriad of factors ranging from poor planning and lack of experience to unrealistic timelines and nonexistence of contingency plans that all contributed to the debacle that followed.

At the Project Management Institute Global Congress in 2007, Richard Discenza and James Forman presented what they identified as seven causes for project failure and articulated key actions to address them:

## Focus on business value, not only technical detail

This involves establishing a clear link between the project and the organisation's key strategic practices. The project plan needs to cover the planned delivery, the business change required, and the means of benefits realisation.

## Articulate clear accountability for measured results

There must be clear view of the interdependencies between the projects, the benefits, and the criteria against which success will be judged. It is necessary to establish a reasonably stable requirement baseline before any other work goes forward.

## Establish processes for managing unambiguous checkpoints

Successful large projects typically have software-measurement programs for capturing productivity and quality historical data that can be used to compare it against similar projects to judge the validity of schedules, costs, quality, and other project-related factors.

## Develop a methodology for planning and executing projects

There should be a detailed plan developed before any release date of a project is announced. Inadequate planning is one of the major reasons why projects spin out of control.

## Ensure that client stakeholders are engaged in all steps

Include the client at the beginning of the project and continually involve them as things change so that the required adjustments can be made together. Projects are less likely to fail if there are informed client stakeholders giving meaningful input during every phase of requirements elicitation, product description, and implementation.

### Manage and motivate people

This involves managing and retaining the most highly skilled and productive people. Knowledge is money. A project team made up of higher paid people with the right specialised skills is worth more per dollar than a group of lower cost people who need weeks or months of training before they can start to be productive.

### Provide the project team with the tools and techniques they need

The project team must be skilled and experienced with clearly defined roles and responsibilities. If not, there must be access to expertise that can benefit those fulfilling the requisite roles.[72]

Had we been more vigilant in identifying checkpoints, accountability, and ensuring we had the right level of experience when building the platform, chances are the risk of project delays would have been reduced. Sadly, it is often only in hindsight that we are best able to identify risks that were missed or necessary actions that were not taken.

Unfortunately, when it comes to learning from their mistakes, most consulting organisations simply do not have sufficient processes in place to adequately capture learnings to prevent the same mistakes from being committed time and time again. When a project fails, consultants will quickly move on to other engagements in an effort to redeem themselves, save face, and maintain their high chargeable rates. There is no built-in incentive structure to document why projects failed and certainly no perceived personal brand-building benefit to explaining what had gone wrong to others.

Therefore, unless something is fundamentally changed in the way consultants are incentivised or how their performance is measured, there is little hope that learnings will be documented or shared with others. The learnings will remain in the heads the consultants that were a part of the failed project, and even then, only as a fractional view of the whole.

Consultants will rarely have the opportunity to share their experiences with others who were on the same failed project, as others will also have quickly moved on, meaning there is no opportunity to compare notes and examine a holistic view of the events leading up to the failure from different perspectives.

If we cannot gain a holistic view of the risks, challenges, and failures at the end of the engagement, we must consider a different time to achieve that view. One of the ways in which a holistic view of risks can be attained is not to wait until the project has kicked off or already begun to drift. Instead, allocating time before project kick-off to review potential challenges will offer an opportunity to share learnings, discuss risks, and orchestrate contingency plans. Through a premortem exercise, we can better anticipate challenges and ensure that we implement the appropriate strategies to avoid potential pitfalls.

## Premortem

"Projects fail at a spectacular rate," Gary Klein wrote for the *Harvard Business Review*. "One reason is that too many people are reluctant to speak up about their reservations during the all-important planning phase. By making it safe for dissenters who are knowledgeable about the undertaking and worried about its weaknesses to speak up, you can improve a project's chances of success."[73]

Research conducted in 1989 by Deborah Mitchell, of the Wharton School; Jay Russo, of Cornell; and Nancy Pennington, of the University of Colorado, found that prospective hindsight—imagining that an event has already occurred—increases the ability to correctly identify reasons for future outcomes by 30%. They used prospective hindsight to devise a method called a premortem, which helps teams identify risks at the outset.

As often presented on television and in movies, a post-mortem focuses on the examination of a dead body to determine the cause of death. Trained professionals will take time, employing a multitude of tools and techniques, to thoroughly examine the deceased to understand all the factors involved. The exercise offers insights that would have otherwise been undiscovered, helping investigators understand the root causes of the untimely demise. As the name implies, a premortem is the hypothetical opposite of a post-mortem.

The premortem is a managerial strategy in which a project team imagines that a project or organization has already failed. It encourages the team to consider all of the possible causes for the failure before any work on the project has begun. One of the ways to approach the activity is to ask each of the stakeholders to write down one way the project could fail on a small piece of paper or Post-it Note. For example, stakeholders may write down "lack of sponsorship from management", "not enough time for activities", "global pandemic slowing implementation", or "alien invasion." Each of the possible causes for project failure is then placed on a matrix, with the likeliness of the event along the X-axis and the size of the risk on the Y-axis. The more likely an event, the further it will be placed to the right on the X-axis. The larger or more significant the risk, the higher it will be moved on the Y-axis. It may be argued by some that the event of an alien invasion, for example, should be categorised as a large risk and therefore be placed higher up on the Y-axis. Conversely, the likeliness of an alien invasion is considered very low by most people, meaning it would be placed to the far left on the X-axis.

Once each potential point of project failure is placed on the matrix based on their likeliness and size of the risk, an additional step may be required to group suggestions that are similar to others already submitted. When the grouping is complete, the focus needs to be placed on the items that occupy the top-right area of the matrix, as they will be the most likely and most significant risks.

## What could go wrong?

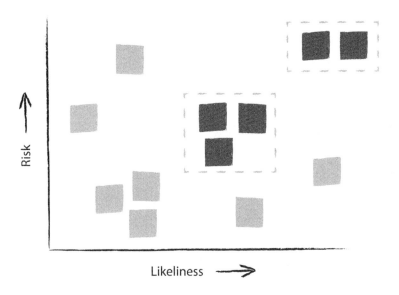

It's useful to review these risks with the stakeholders and subsequently identify the necessary steps to minimise them, ensuring to track them throughout the project's duration. It is not human nature to think about the things that may go wrong at the beginning of anything, be it a project or a planned holiday. No one wants to think about what could go wrong or the worst-case scenario, which is why so many tourist shops make a hefty business of selling umbrellas to the unprepared. Likewise, most stakeholders and project sponsors will be keen to jump into a project with an unmerited optimism; to get moving and start delivering without any hesitation. Any recommendation to take time to think about the worst-case scenarios will inevitably be met with resistance, as taking time to think about the worst-case scenarios requires acknowledgement that things may indeed not go to plan.

A premortem is an exceptionally useful method by which to force ourselves and our stakeholders to acknowledge that very fact; that not all things go to plan. It will also encourage everyone involved to discuss potential risks and subsequently take the necessary steps to address them. After all, it is much better to spend additional time at the beginning of a project considering the risks than to stand over the remnants of a failed endeavour, picking through the remains to identify reasons for its demise.

In the vast majority of cases, projects do not fail due to one single factor but to a multitude of contributing factors that were not addressed with enough care. The projects also do not, in most cases, fail suddenly. Instead, there is a steady downward spiral that may occur so gradually at first that the underlying factors are not noticed or given the consideration they require out of a misguided optimism that things will somehow improve on their own if ignored.

It is akin to the fable of the frog in the boiling water, an experiment I'd urge you not to try at home. According to the myth, if a frog were placed in a pot of boiling water, it would immediately jump out. However, if a frog were placed in tepid water, slowly brought to a boil, it would not perceive the danger and be cooked to death. Likewise, without the appropriate measures, checkpoints, and escalation plans, we may not know or be able to acknowledge a project is failing until it is too late.

Ensuring adequate time and attention is devoted before project kick-off to review and agree on the measures, processes, and contingency plans will significantly reduce the probability of project failure. Anticipatory exercises, such as the premortem, further reduce the risk. The team will have an opportunity to work together to brainstorm potential pitfalls and devise approaches to address them before they happen. While the risk of failure will never be reduced to zero, we will effectively set ourselves and our teams up for an increased probability of success by putting in the requisite time and effort to plan and anticipate.

"Plans are useless, but planning is indispensable."

Dwight D. Eisenhower

# Antoinette Kyuchukova

While some paths leading to a career in consulting are long and convoluted, others seem to have been predestined. These paths seem to map to an obvious, if not inevitable, series of events that lead from one step to the next, always on the path towards success in consulting. Looking at the career path Antoinette has taken that would certainly be the initial impression. Yet, recounting her experiences leading to a remarkably successful decade-long career with PwC, Antoinette admits that there were times where the path ahead was not as obvious as it would seem.

"I didn't plan to get into consulting, but I had always said that I'm going to make a difference," Antoinette admitted as we were sitting in one of the conference rooms in the PwC headquarters in London. She recalled one of her first experiences of making a difference when attending Oxford Brookes University.

"I was involved in student volunteering and was helping students navigate through their student life, so a number of people knew me," she continued. "Around the elections for president (of the University Student Union), a bunch of people ended up coming to me and saying, 'We think you should run for president.' I was like, 'You can't be serious! I am going to get a proper job!' But it wasn't one or two people; I had so many people who, within the space of a couple of weeks, came to talk to me and said, 'Why don't you run in the elections? You should seriously consider it; you'd make a great candidate.'"

She knew running for students' union president would not be easy. "I knew that the current president was rerunning for office. I was like, 'He will be a great president; he doesn't need competition.' But then I reflected on all the unexpected conversations I had and said to myself that I should consider it."

Antoinette took a pre-planned trip to France around this time to give herself time to clear her mind and consider what the next step was going to be. She knew that running for president would not be an easy undertaking and that if she chose to do it, she would have to do it right. She would have to mobilise many people to help her and put together a comprehensive strategy, a detailed action plan, and focus on executing that plan. By the end of that week-long trip, she went back to university with a decision, determined to run in the university's presidential elections as an international student.

"I put together a comprehensive campaign plan with the help of my friends and friends of friends, who made a fantastic campaign team. We had funny slogans, t-shirts, flyers. I attended every event you can think of that allowed me to introduce myself and have a conversation with someone new about student life, diversity, and elections. For example, I gathered the courage to ask for three-minute speaking slots at as many big lectures that I was able to attend. I knew that only a few people knew me, so I had to build much more support from the ground up. "

Antoinette understood the odds were stacked against her and what it would take to get more votes than the incumbent. She had a very ambitious objective and instinctively acknowledged the need to spend extraordinary efforts to make it happen in line with the Audacity Ratio. She took time to analyse the landscape, plan how she could gain an advantage and executed her plan with conviction and determination.

" I knew one of my strengths was that I was an international student, representing student groups that had not been actively represented before. I just had to figure out how to get more students to hear what I stood for and get to know me. I figured out if I turned up to the big get-togethers and parties happening within the period of two months, I stood a better chance. That meant I had to finish my assignments a hell of a lot earlier and take part-time work in the day to fund my social life. I finished all my academic submissions and assignments two months before the deadlines so I could have time to campaign. I made it to all those lectures, events, parties. I danced, went to gigs, and took every opportunity to meet students and simply chat."

"On the night of the election results, the university representative announced Tim's results, and the numbers looked significant. Everybody cheered with excitement. I just assumed Tim had won. Then they announced my votes, and the room erupted with mixed emotions, cheers from my supporters and some delayed confusion. Our results were so close that I had only won by a tiny margin of votes."

"It turns out that every conversation I had mattered, everything I did, every single contribution anyone made during the campaign, had made a difference." Antoinette became the first international female president in the history of Oxford Brookes University and paved the way for others to follow. She formulated a plan and executed it effectively with the support of a robust network, a skill that would serve her well throughout her career.

She took a one-year sabbatical to focus on her role as students' union president and the first few months were not easy. Not only did she have to contend with getting up to speed with all the responsibilities of the new role, but she also inherited a team of the former president's friends, who took some time to bring on-side. She recalled, "I remember the first three months were pretty rough. We disagreed on so many things. There were some hard feelings. After all, the elections were an emotionally charged period." The situation taught Antoinette a lot about navigating challenging politics, a skill that would also help her further on in her career. As consultants, there will be times when our ideas are challenged, and we must be able to adapt to the situation and build coalitions as needed. For Antoinette, that meant working with each member of her team individually.

Meeting with stakeholders individually may help uncover concerns or ideas that may not have been raised in a group setting. It will also help build rapport with stakeholders in a way that group meetings or update emails never could. While it is time-consuming and, at times, a logistical challenge, these one-to-one sessions serve a valuable purpose and will reduce the risk of friction within the group. As Antoinette built those relationships, the entire team began to be more cohesive, focusing their attention on the projects they wanted to carry out.

"I finished the role with the students' union and was now going into the big world," Antoinette recalled. "I knew I wanted to help organisations and people in the way we did at the students' union." In the wake of the 2008 financial crisis, she had sent out close to 80 applications, with PwC being the first and the one she wanted the most. After attending the assessment centre and completing a gruelling series of interviews and group sessions, she was made an offer in 2009. She concluded, "Ten years on, I never thought I'd be enjoying my chosen career path as much as I have. I feel a real sense of pride to have done so many things that have resonated with my beliefs and aspirations."

Antoinette's career has been exemplary of continuous learning and personal development. She has learned about herself and being confident in her authenticity, about empathy and working with others, and about being a better manager and leader. The combination of personal drive to improve in conjunction with an outstanding work ethic has propelled Antoinette from consultant to senior manager to director. Undoubtedly, these admirable qualities will continue to serve her well in the years to come.

"It's very important to have a feedback loop,
where you're constantly thinking about what you've done
and how you could be doing it better."

Elon Musk

# Feedback

As the story goes, an automotive executive responsible for the production of a new model was walking around the plant with his directors. He looked across the production line, examining the different machines, stopping to discuss each with the director responsible for that part of the assembly. Each director detailed how their respective area functioned as the group navigated the assembly line.

At the end of the tour, all the directors were called into a meeting room, where the executive thanked them for their efforts. He reminded them of the strict deadline that was fast approaching and the importance of being ready in time. He then went around the room, asking each director, one by one, if they believed that they would all be prepared to meet the deadline. One by one, the directors responded in the affirmative, confidently stating that they would, in fact, be ready. Around the same time as this was happening, an anonymous survey was taken of the workers in that production plant.

One of the survey questions asked if the workers believed that the production line would be ready by the aforementioned deadline. The results of the survey painted a much different picture, as the vast majority of workers stated they did not believe that the deadline would be met. Inevitably, as the deadline approached, the executive called the directors into his office, wanting to know why the project was so far behind schedule. He was only ever presented positive information by his directors, who, in turn, were only ever told good news by their teams rather than what was actually happening within their departments. It was a classic breakdown in communication and feedback.

When Richard Discenza and James Forman conducted an anonymous survey amongst a large group of professional project managers, they discovered that 43% of project managers surveyed responded that project communications factors were a key factor in the failure of projects, while 42% responded that process factors were critical, and only 32% responded that people were a crucial factor in the failure of projects.[74]

Open and honest communication, alongside frequent opportunities for two-sided feedback, within our team or with our stakeholders is essential in understanding where the areas of improvement may reside or what the risk and issues are. However, it will only be possible if the team members feel genuinely empowered to have their voices heard. If not in a group setting, they may feel more comfortable sharing in individual sessions. If not in individual sessions, they may feel more comfortable submitting anonymous feedback. Whatever approach is taken, it must give team members a voice to provide invaluable insights.

Furthermore, we must strive to create an environment where feedback goes both ways. On the one hand, we need to be mindful of how we receive and process feedback. On the other hand, we need to consider how we provide feedback to others, the approach we take and the frequency by which we provide it.

# Receiving

Receiving positive feedback can be a very gratifying experience. An acknowledgement by others of our efforts can motivate and encourage, instigating a feeling of pride in our achievements. Positive feedback can make us feel like we are on top of the world. On the flip side, negative feedback can be highly destructive, particularly when delivered poorly or with iniquitous intentions.

Antoinette recalled when she received negative feedback from a senior colleague that she suspected was delivered with the wrong intentions. "I really, really struggled to process it. It affected me, both mentally and on a personal level, because the feedback did not feel right. It didn't feel like that was me. It didn't seem grounded in facts. It didn't feel like it was meant to help me either." She continued, "If your feedback is intended to help someone grow and it's delivered with that kindness and intention for growth, then that's great. Give that feedback. If your feedback is intended to be delivered because of frustration or because of that little niggling thought, 'I'm going to teach you the lesson. Let me tell you what I think of you,' you probably shouldn't be giving that feedback before you overcome your own frustrations and ask yourself, 'Why do I feel this way?'"

"Receiving feedback that you can't relate to begs a number of questions: Are you self-aware aware enough? Or is that feedback actually a projection of the person that you're speaking to? If it's a projection and therefore not really about you, that feedback is actually about the feedback giver and speaks volumes. In my case, it really threw me off for a while. I'm lucky to have the support network around me to also check in with, to use different perspectives, to validate and crosscheck my data, to just see how much of something might be true. It also comes with the nature of what we do; the further you go, the more you expose yourself, the more you grow, the more you will also experience the rewarding conversations. Sometimes you will feel hurt, and you need to be prepared and work with it."

Being honest with ourselves and introspective, particularly regarding our strengths and weaknesses, is a necessary precursor exercise to allow ourselves to receive and adequately process feedback. Being oblivious to our shortcomings or, worse yet, thinking we don't have any will effectively prevent us from acknowledging any constructive feedback we receive.

*American Idol*, a television series where hopeful singers perform to a panel of judges in the hopes of advancing in the competition, initially aired in 2002 became one of the longest-running US television shows. Every season, the first few episodes showcase auditions from around the USA. Some of the auditions are phenomenal, where genuinely talented people are able to captivate the judges from the very first note they sing. Other auditions, however, do not go that well. The aspiring "singers" aren't able to sing in key, their tone is dreadful, or they pick songs that are entirely wrong for their range and audience. Their performances are usually cut short by the judges who deliver the bad news, namely that they are terrible singers and have no place in the competition.

What happens next is fascinating to watch. As the cameras follow the castoffs out of the audition space, their response to rejection typically follows a similar pattern as they shout at the camera, "The judges have no idea what they are talking about! I am an amazing singer! They don't know the opportunity they have missed! They will see me again!" Of course, the judges are industry experts, and anyone listening would objectively agree, without needing to be in the industry, that these "singers" are terrible. Everyone seems to know and acknowledge the same objective truth, except for the singers themselves.

In the case of the *American Idol* rejects, it was quite obvious that they did not have the self-awareness necessary to acknowledge how poor their singing truly was. Worse yet, those around them did not help them with that realisation either. In a misguided effort to be supportive, those close to them may not have shared the truth in an effort to spare their feelings.

Self-awareness, whether in acknowledging our singing skills or lack thereof, is no different than acknowledging our strengths or weaknesses in the world of consulting. After all, only when we acknowledge that there is room for improvement can we take the necessary steps to improve. Antoinette looked to her network, some of whom may have had entirely different personalities or working styles, to validate the feedback received.

She continued, "That's the whole point around introspection and self-awareness; you build that over time. We tend to surround ourselves with like-minded people. The danger is that it reinforces one side of who you are but doesn't give you the richness of perspective you need to grow. The first point of advice is when you reflect back on the feedback you've been given, reflect and check-in with yourself. Do you have perspectives coming from different sources, different to your natural state of play? I have consciously been working on building my relationships and network with a diverse group of people, who make me think in a very different way."

By calibrating her perception with that of her network, Antoinette put herself in a better position to gauge whether the feedback she received was in line with reality. If the feedback were constructive and helpful, she would be mindful to acknowledge it and to take steps to improve in that area. Conversely, if the feedback were given out of malice or spite, she would be better able to identify it as such and not let it get her down.

By augmenting our introspection and self-awareness with insights from trusted individuals within our network, we will form a solid foundation by which to keep ourselves grounded. We will be better able to understand where our areas of improvement lie, acknowledge and act on constructive feedback when we receive it while rejecting feedback that objectively misses the mark. At the very least, our self-awareness and support network will hopefully prevent us from going on an American Idol audition if our vocal talents are best reserved for the confines of the shower.

# Giving

"I have one rule," Antoinette admitted, "which is never give written feedback before you've had a proper conversation with someone. As a rule of thumb, I would never send feedback to someone if I haven't spoken to them first."

Antoinette described an example of a colleague missing a deadline. "It could be so many things, it could be incompetence, and maybe that's the first thing you're thinking about, but it could be family commitments, it could be a lack of confidence, it could be dysfunctional dynamics with others in the team, which made them hold back from contributing. You discover so much more when you give feedback if you do it through a conversation."

"The other thing is the power of questions. It doesn't mean you just talk; it's a lot about asking the questions to help you understand their perspective. Never wait until the end of the project to ask for feedback." Antoinette would ask questions at the beginning of any project, inquiring about the motivations of her team members; what it was they wanted to learn and accomplish. That way, she would be able to provide relevant feedback to her team based on each team member's wider context, personal ambitions, strengths, and areas of improvement.

According to Nora St-Aubin, of team engagement platform Officevibe, there is a lot of value in providing feedback, but that leaders need to do more to provide frequent and relevant feedback. According to her research, 23% of employees are unsatisfied with the frequency of feedback coming from their direct manager, 17% of employees feel that the feedback they get is not specific, and 28% of employees report that feedback is not frequent enough to help them understand how to improve.[75]

Regular check-ins are a great way for managers to calibrate the performance of their teams and for junior team members to understand if they are delivering according to expectations. These regular feedback sessions allow for incremental course correction throughout a project or performance period, meaning the probability of unpleasant surprises at the end of the engagement will be reduced.

According to the folks at Engagedly, there are five elements to consider when giving feedback:

**Lay a foundation**
Introduce the concept of check-ins and create a
framework that works with you or your team.

**Clarify goals**
Communicate your goals and vision and help everyone gain
a clear understanding of the purpose of the check-ins.

**Prioritise and make time**
It may be challenging to embed a new ritual, so make sure
to find the time and clearly communicate the benefits.

**Focus on self-improvement**
Check-ins should be more about self-improvement
opportunities rather than a wider team strategy.

**Keep it private**
Make check-ins a safe place to share ideas and concerns.
Keep your one-on-one conversations and all the forms and
data related to it secure and private.[76]

Giving feedback, as well as receiving it, is not easy. There is typically an emotional element that becomes intertwined with the objective basis of the discussion. It is essential to remember not to become defensive, as is our natural tendency when receiving constructive feedback. Instead, we should listen to the feedback, acknowledge it, and then take time for introspection and calibration with our network. That way, we give ourselves time to overcome the initial emotional reaction, process it, and determine whether there is merit to the feedback. If there is, it is incumbent on us to identify a structured approach for incremental improvement.

Perhaps the more challenging of the two, giving effective feedback requires the person providing the feedback first to ensure the feedback is given for a good reason and is not influenced by their own emotion. Having a bad day, for example, is no excuse to direct our own frustration onto someone else.

The feedback we provide needs to be structured, clear and delivered in a way that makes it easy for the recipient to understand and act on. We have little control over how the recipient will react upon hearing the feedback, but if we are mindful in our approach, we can minimise the risk of the recipient becoming overly defensive. Perhaps that level of responsibility and unpredictability is one of the reasons that feedback is not given nearly frequently enough. Yet, the majority of research indicates that communication and feedback are foundational elements of successful teams.

Therefore, as leaders, we must overcome our hesitation to provide and receive feedback. One of the ways in which we can accomplish that objective is by integrating feedback loops into our project plans and the rhythm by which we guide our teams.

# Rhythm

Every year, the Cambridge University Boat Club and the Oxford University Boat Club organise a series of races down the River Thames in London, England. Referred to as simply "the Boat Race," it is a tradition that traces its roots back to 1829. Over 250,000 people watch the race from the banks of the river each year. In 2009, a record 270,000 people watched the race live, and more than 15 million watched it on television.[77]

Watching the race live from the banks of the Thames on a rainy day in 2019, a friend turned to me and asked what the purpose of the ninth person in the boat was. In addition to the eight rowers, there was one person who was not rowing, facing the opposite direction of the eight rowers, and yelling out instructions. After a quick Google search on my phone, I confidently explained that, in a rowing crew, the ninth person is known as a coxswain, or "cox" or "coxie" for short. They are responsible for steering the boat and coordinating the power and rhythm of the rowers. Since the rowers sit with their backs to the direction of travel, the cox is responsible for setting the direction of travel. In some capacities, the coxswain is also responsible for implementing the training regimen or race plan. Most coaches cannot communicate with the boat or coxswain when they are on the water, so the coxswain is the "coach" in the boat.[78]

Our role, in some regards, is similar to that of the coxswain. By setting predictable, regularly scheduled meetings, we can establish a rhythm or drumbeat for our teams. By establishing regular feedback sessions, we can monitor the pulse to gauge progress, making the necessary adjustments along the way so that milestones are met on time. Regularly scheduled review sessions will help us understand where the areas of improvement lie and what corrective steps need to be taken. In my experience, regularly scheduled meetings and calls make it easier to plan around, as all team members know and will expect when the next session will occur.

The frequency of the calls and meetings will vary based on need, and it is essential to remember not to schedule too many back-to-back. Scheduling too many meetings or calls may not leave enough time for reflection or for actual work to take place, so finding the right balance between meetings, calls, and free time is an important consideration.

According to a 2019 survey by consulting firm Korn Ferry, more than two-thirds (67%) of respondents said that spending too much time in meetings and on calls distracts them from making an impact at work.[79] More than a third (34%) said they waste between two to five hours per week on calls or meetings that don't accomplish anything. Thirty-five percent said that they'd go to a meeting even if they knew it wasn't going to be productive, instead of declining the meeting.

"Too often, the answer to any work issue is 'let's meet.' While collaboration is absolutely what drives innovation and success in today's global marketplace, it's time to get creative with how we use our time together," said Korn Ferry senior client partner Cathi Rittelmann. "Meetings aren't necessarily bad, but the way we prep and lead them can sometimes derail productivity. The bottom line is this: clear objectives, an agenda, and identified roles never go out of style."[80]

Finding the right balance and frequency for check-in sessions, calls, and meetings will help maintain a predictable rhythm in a team, increasing overall efficiency and cohesion. Antoinette found a balance between providing in-the-moment feedback and a regularly scheduled, recurring structure to provide more in-depth coaching. She recommended that balance allows for small, incremental, course corrective advice to be provided when appropriate rather than building up to a big feedback session, saying, "You don't have to create this special *Oscars* moment to receive feedback or to give feedback. It creates so much intensity, and anticipation. Honestly, the less we create a big deal about speaking up about what works and what doesn't, the more useful that feedback becomes."

"At that moment, you have rich situational data that you can use to inform your coachee of what's going on, and then it's much more relatable because it has just happened. You've just reflected on it and it can give someone that really rich perspective, and at the same time, it can be both positive and developmental. Developmental is also positive. It's an opportunity to change or do something differently or continue to do what you're doing really well. For example, when you see someone struggling in a meeting and you want to really help them develop, you can catch that moment and say, 'I saw you lacking confidence in that conversation or the way you introduced yourself. You have so much more to bring into that elevator pitch of who you are, but it didn't come through. Why was that?'"

"That is very powerful because that opens something very important to talk about. You can help someone pick themselves up and regain their confidence, reflect on themselves, and think about how present they are in that particular situation or meeting; how focused or how clear are they of their personal value that they bring into an introduction."

The purpose of providing in-the-moment feedback is not to berate others about something that they have done incorrectly. As Antoinette noted, "If my intention is to create a confident, high-performing team that enjoys doing what they do, the way you give that feedback is very, very important." The language, the tone, the timing, and body language used when providing feedback will all be noticed by those on the receiving end. We need to be mindful that when feedback is provided shortly after an incident where the recipient may not have performed to expectation, they will be in a vulnerable emotional state to begin with.

"They've just beaten themselves up. They know coming out of that meeting, that they probably did not introduce the topic or themselves or do the presentation the way they could have. You have a choice as a leader to really magnify on the failure or use that as an opportunity for growth."

In an effort to set a predictable rhythm for her team, Antoinette would ensure that there was time set aside for coaching, saying, "I try and create a hold in my diary. Twice a week, I have an hour blocked in my diary for people time, which is non-commercial; not pressed by client meetings. In those moments, I can go a little bit deeper on a frequent basis. I take care to create a safe space for coaching, avoiding distractions that might come along the way."

According to the folks at Adobe, there are six key benefits of ensuring a good balance of one-on-one meetings:

### They strengthen relationships between leaders and their teams
People rely on the basic human need to feel validated. Face-to-face communication lets them know that their insights and concerns are appreciated and taken into consideration.

### They improve productivity
Weekly one-on-ones boost productivity and cut wasted time. Reduce the amount of generic emails in favour of tailored, brief, one-on-one sessions providing a high-level overview of current issues and progress.

### They build team loyalty
Employees trust your leadership if you meet with them regularly for one-on-one meetings. Loyalty requires frequent and consistent meaningful interactions.

### They benefit everyone
Not only will you have the opportunity to discuss needs, goals, and expectations, but you'll also give your team an advantage by providing your undivided attention.

**They deliver meaningful, personalised feedback**
Providing feedback for your team members can be uncomfortable, but one-on-one meetings offer the ideal opportunity to let your direct reports know how they're doing and what you expect from them moving forward.

**Clearly align on progress and next actions to attain goals**
It's in this meeting that you can do the necessary ongoing review of how your team member is performing in relation to their goals. It is here that you can give specific feedback on their progress and discuss next actions to hit the objective.[81]

Setting up a predictable rhythm to meetings and updates provides a steady drumbeat for our team. Through this rhythm, we can maintain and monitor the momentum of our teams. It also prevents us from avoiding or missing feedback sessions because they become ingrained within our rhythm. By ensuring regular opportunities for giving and receiving feedback, we can be much more incremental, which in turn will lessen the sting of constructive feedback. By taking a predictable, structured, incremental approach to the way we receive and give feedback, we can improve cohesion, loyalty, productivity, and the overall happiness of our teams.

# Reverse mentoring

As the name implies, reverse mentoring inverts the mentoring relationship, with the typically younger, junior team member providing insights to their more senior counterpart. Jason Wingard, professor of Human Capital Management at the School of Professional Studies at Columbia University, described one of the first large-scale implementations of reverse mentoring, writing in *Forbes*, "Jack Welch, the formidable, former CEO of General Electric [GE], popularized the concept of reverse mentoring in 1999. In his pilot project, he paired 500 senior and junior employees, in hopes the latter would teach the former about technological advances and tools."

"We tipped the organization upside down," Jack explained. "We now have the youngest and brightest teaching the oldest." Jason recounted that in the years since Jack's pioneering effort, many companies, including industry leaders such as Target, Cisco, UnitedHealthcare, and Fidelity have developed their own reverse mentoring programs. Although they vary in scale and scope, all share one common approach: coordinating shared learning between colleagues of diverse backgrounds to create symbiotic corporate learning.[82]

Jason continued, "While reverse mentoring has obvious benefits for the mentor and mentee. The approach can also instigate powerful results for the core organization. Beyond flipping the hierarchy and mobilizing non-traditional teams, it can also facilitate organizations achieving strategic goals such as increasing millennial retention, fostering inclusivity, and maintaining competitive advantage through technological advancements."

Reverse mentoring relationships help experienced professionals maintain a link to the motivations, attitudes, and drives of their younger counterparts. After all, the higher we move up in grades or in years, the more disconnected we become from those who typically represent one of the key target demographics of the organisations we work with. Reverse mentoring helps break down barriers in communication, creates an environment to solicit honest feedback, and presents an opportunity to expand our frame of reference.

"I have had a few reverse mentors and have also been one, myself." Antoinette recalled, "My reverse mentors have helped me truly step into their shoes. For example, they offered a different perspective and said, 'Hey, you know, that thing that we did? We got all the tasks started at 8:30 in the morning, well, perhaps you could have just checked in first if that worked for people, you know?'" Through the feedback she received, Antoinette was able to tailor her leadership approach to be better in tune with her team and create a better working environment.

According to Jennifer Jordan and Michael Sorell, writing for *Harvard Business Review*, there are four main benefits to reverse mentoring:

### Increased retention of young people
Reverse mentoring programs provide young people with the transparency and recognition that they're seeking from management.

### Sharing of digital skills
While digital skill development should not be the focus of a reverse mentoring program, understanding rapidly changing digital trends may play an important role.

### Driving culture change
Reverse mentoring offers an opportunity to identify new ideas or approaches.

### Promoting diversity
It is an opportunity to improve leaderships understanding of the challenges faced by people from different backgrounds.[83]

Jennifer and Michael also suggested there are three main considerations to reap the benefits of a reverse mentoring programme:

### The right match is crucial
Emphasise diversity, matching across region, department, and background. Also match for diverse personalities (for example, it is better to have an introvert paired with an extrovert than to pair two introverts).

### Address mentees' fear and distrust
Many executives are fearful of revealing their lack of knowledge to junior employees. But if the fears are addressed explicitly, open sharing can be incredibly rewarding.

**Ensure strong commitment from the mentees**
The number-one reason that reverse mentoring programs fail is that the executives don't prioritise the relationship; after a couple of cancelled sessions, the momentum quickly dwindles.

Successful leaders that I've spoken to never constrained themselves to only one channel by which to receive feedback. Instead, they sought out different perspectives from a wide variety of sources. Through reverse mentoring, for example, they were able to identify valuable insights and trends. Meanwhile, in their regular one-on-ones, they received and gave incremental feedback based on performance and objectives. With each conversation, each piece of feedback, they broadened and enriched their perspective, identifying new ways to better themselves and their teams.

"Everyone you meet is fighting a battle you know nothing about. Be kind. Always."

Brad Meltzer

# Mental health

As he looked out across the city bathed in the light of the setting sun, the scene was eerily peaceful. Standing on the rooftop terrace of the PwC London headquarters, looking over iconic landmarks such as the Tower of London and the adjacent Tower Bridge, he was high enough that the noise of the city became muted. The tourists and businesspeople milling around far below became an abstract composition of pixels moving across the riverfront promenade, in-between alleyways and down the busy streets.

The sprawling scene in front of him, complete with gleaming office buildings mixed amongst the historic landmarks, were quite unlike Guildford, a town of just over 80,000, where he had attended university. There he studied mathematics and was the third-team captain of the Surrey Spartans Hockey Club and an accomplished musician. Following the path of thousands of young, ambitious people before him, he joined the PwC graduate training programme after spending a year with the firm through his university work placement.

On the surface, everything appeared to be heading in the right direction. He was well-liked, had a great new job, and had his whole life in front of him. Yet, what a lot of his friends did not know, was that he was not in a good place.

A gambling addiction had led to tens of thousands of pounds of debt to banks, loan companies, family, and friends. He begged his parents not to tell PwC about his gambling. He led a double life. With his hockey and music friends, he was the life and soul of the party. On the inside, however, he struggled to cope.

Looking out on the city below him once again, he took a step forward, put his hand on the guard rail and lifted himself up and over, stepping out onto the ledge. Then he took one more, final step forward into the evening sun.

Josh was pronounced dead on the scene, steps away from the entrance of the PwC London headquarters, on July 30, 2015. The subsequent investigation brought to light his struggles with gambling and debt. In a statement to the Southwark Coroners Court, his father said, "This is such a waste of a young life with a promising future in front of him." He revealed his son had started taking out pay-day loans because his gambling was spiralling out of control. While his parents eventually took control of his money, giving him "a drip-feed" of cash to live on, they were unaware he continued to borrow from friends and banks.

The Surrey Spartans Hockey Club posted a note on Facebook: "A teammate to some. A great friend to many more. Gone too soon but will never be forgotten."

# Be kind

While I did not know Josh during my time at PwC, the makeshift memorial that formed on the sidewalk, filled with heartfelt notes from his friends and colleagues, was a moving testament to a young man full of promise whose life ended much too soon. Walking by the memorial every day stirred up a flood of emotion, as when I was in high school, a younger student, whose locker was next to mine, had also committed suicide. That event had stuck with me. Seeing the memorial outside of the PwC office reminded me of the frailty of life and the unseen struggles many of us face throughout our lives.

Conversations about the subjects of suicide, addiction, and mental health are never easy. Consequently, of all the chapters in this book, this one was by far the most difficult to write. In one edit, I wrote at length about the younger student's suicide in high school and how the unanswerable questions of whether I could have done more to prevent that tragic event plagued my mind. Yet, regardless of the challenge in confronting these subjects, I believe that there is value in having open and honest discussions about them. After all, we are all fighting our own battles, and there is comfort in the knowledge that we are not alone.

Consulting has never been an easy gig. Every day there are challenges from all sides. Tight deadlines, internal politics, shifting priorities, and ever-increasing client expectations create a remarkably high-pressure environment. No matter how resilient we are, prolonged periods in high-pressure environments in conjunction with long working hours and time away from our support structures will take a negative toll if we are not mindful of the risks.

Kapo Wong, Alan Chan, and S. C. Ngan conducted a meta-analysis whereby they synthesised 243 records from 46 papers published from 1998 to 2018 to examine the effect of long working hours on the occupational health of workers.

They identified a laundry list of correlations of long working hours to cardiovascular and cerebrovascular diseases, hypertension, diabetes mellitus, depression and anxiety, and health behaviours that include increased alcohol consumption and physical inactivity.[84]

Given the long working hours, time away from home, and considerable external pressures, some consultants face challenges ranging from depression and mental health issues to drug and alcohol abuse. Yet, many will hide their struggles to cope, putting on a brave face with colleagues and friends, not wanting to show vulnerability or being ashamed to admit they need help. Tragically, despite increased awareness of mental health conditions, more than 90% of people surveyed believe that admitting to a mental health condition could damage their career prospects, according to the Management Consultancies Association.[85]

The percentage of people unwilling to admit to mental health issues is worryingly high, and while most leading organisations have made positive strides in recent years to address the taboo surrounding mental health, there is still a long way to go. In order to overcome some of the challenges that a career in consulting may present, three themes emerged in the conversations I've had that may offer guidance:

> **Honesty** with yourself.
> **Empathy** for others.
> **Kindness**, always.

First, be honest with yourself. It is essential to take the necessary time and find the courage to be introspective; to identify what you are doing well and where you can improve. Consider what impact your actions are having on the perception others have of you and whether that is the perception you want them to have. Are you drinking more than you should? Are you not giving people enough time? Are you repeating the same mistakes time and time again? Have you been dishonest with yourself or others?

There are many questions to ask and only you will know the real answers. Being honest with yourself is the starting point of any personal growth journey. Speaking from personal experience, I know it is never easy to admit to personal failings, but the cost of not actively identifying these opportunities for self-improvement and taking active steps to address them will be much higher if nothing is done. I know that, through actions I have taken or not taken, I've missed out on opportunities and tarnished interpersonal relationships. While we will all make mistakes and learning from those mistakes is a fundamental part of life, repeating the same mistakes over and over again should not be. This is where honesty with ourselves and taking the right corrective steps is so important.

Second, find empathy for others. From our family to our friends, colleagues, or the man making your coffee at the local shop, everyone will have their own perspective on the world and will be fighting their own battles. Taking the time to understand people's perspectives and motivations will allow us to improve how we engage with them. We've discussed the importance of empathy when trying to understand how people interact with our organisations across user journeys. Understanding where a person is coming from, effectively putting ourselves in their shoes, presents an alternative viewpoint of any problem and helps us to understand why they are reacting or behaving in the way they are. Similar principles apply in everyday interactions, both personal and professional.

Empathy for others will not only make us better friends, better partners, and better people, but will also help ensure professional success within our own organisation and with external stakeholders. Entering any conversation with a client or colleague with the intent of understanding their point of view rather than only speaking of our own will effectively allow us to build bridges where there may not have been any before. In the 1981 book *Getting to Yes*, Roger Fisher and William Ury made the case that rather than only focusing on a problem or outcome, we need to acknowledge the humanity of the people behind the issue.

### Limits of our understanding

Someone's life

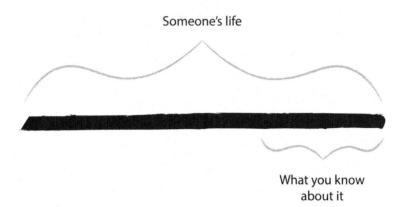

What you know
about it

Truly listening and taking the time to understand the values, cultural background, emotions, and points of view of others will enable us to better craft our own message. Roger and William wrote, "People listen better if they feel that you have understood them. They tend to think that those who understand them are intelligent and sympathetic people whose own opinions may be worth listening to. So, if you want the other side to appreciate your interests, begin by demonstrating that you appreciate theirs."[86]

Third, be kind to others and to yourself. There is a popular meme that has made its way across the internet with the slogan "life comes at you fast." A search for images bearing this slogan presents hundreds of examples of instances where life did not quite work out in the way the featured individual would have wanted. From sports professionals celebrating scoring in one frame juxta positioned against a photo of them inevitably losing the match, to aspiring influencers posing in the surf only to be subsequently knocked over by an incoming wave, the internet is a treasure trove of these types of memes. The meme serves as an excellent reminder that no matter how well we plan, life has a way of taking its own course.

The "life comes at you fast" meme is only the most recent iteration of a theme that can be found throughout history. For example, in 1785, Robert Burns wrote the Scots-language poem *To a mouse*, which featured the famous line "The best-laid schemes o' mice an' men, gang aft agley." There is an old Yiddish adage, "Mann Tracht, Un Gott Lacht," which translates to "Man Plans, and God Laughs." Even the Bible captures a similar sentiment in Proverbs 16:9, which states, "In their hearts humans plan their course, but the Lord establishes their steps." Regardless of the language or source, the message is the same: things will not always go according to our plan.

While we may not be able to control all of the chaotic elements that are a part of our lives or the inevitable missteps and tribulations we will encounter, we do have control over how we react to them. If we acknowledge that those around us are also facing their own challenges, we will be kinder, more patient, and more supportive of them when they need it. Concurrently, when we find time and space to be kind to ourselves, acknowledging our mistakes, learning from them, and moving forward with a determination to be better, we will continuously and incrementally improve as individuals, consultants, and leaders.

# Vice

"Everybody will react differently to different stimuli," Melville Carrie, formerly of Genpact, stated as we discussed the darker side of consulting. "Whether it's alcohol, whether it's sexual relations, or sexual attraction to other people, whether it's work itself, whether it's gambling, whether it's drugs; whatever it might be. People have got behavioural aspects, they'll have addictive characteristics, whether they're in consultancy or not. Being away from home, you're putting yourself in harm's way in many ways, because what you're doing is you're removing your support structures. Your support structure, other things that are around you, at home, they're also your barriers."

"So, for example, if you're sitting at home and drinking gallons of wine, or whiskey, or if you're addicted to strip clubs, or if you're having an illicit relationship. If you are at home, it's going to be a lot more difficult to fulfil all of those in the same levels than if you're away from home. Being away from home, as a result of being a consultant, enables you to fulfil those addictions easier. So yes, the two go hand in hand, but I don't think it's necessarily being a consultant that's the problem. You've got underlying issues, and it tends to be that you're also a consultant."

Scott Galloway, the blunt, fast-talking, thought-provoking professor and author of *The Four* and *The Algebra of Happiness*, has developed a reputation for always being incredibly honest about his failings.

He wrote of his experience with alcohol, "The Harvard Grant Study was the largest study on happiness, tracking 300 19-year-old men for 75 years and looking at what factors made them less or more happy. The presence of one thing in a man's life predicted unhappiness better than any other factor: alcohol. It led to failed marriages, careers coming off the tracks, and bad health."[87]

"When I was just out of college, living in NYC and working at Morgan Stanley, I'd go out every night and get sh*tty drunk at a very cool place with, what appeared to be, other successful people. It felt natural. I'm a better version of myself drunk. Sober, I'm intense and a bit boring. Drunk, I'm funny and optimistic. Also, I found it near impossible for me to meet women unless I was f*cked up. During the week, I found myself, in the middle of a workday, looking for empty conference rooms so I could nurse my hangover via a 60-minute nap under the table. Mornings were about Diet Cokes and greasy food so I could get to the afternoon where, for about an hour, I felt human again and would inevitably agree to meet a bunch of my friends from Salomon and some models at The Tunnel or Limelight, where we'd order $1,200 worth of vodka, and fun Scott would show up."

He concluded, "Not going to class nor learning much at UCLA made me a mediocre banker. However, alcohol made me a mediocre person. I'm lucky I don't have a physical addiction (I think), and when I moved to the West Coast, I didn't miss the sauce. Ask yourself, post-college, are substances getting in the way of your relationships, professional trajectory, or life? If yes, address it."

Having spent a portion of my own young adult life in beautiful venues surrounded by beautiful, sad people, all participating in a collective escape from reality fuelled by copious amounts of vodka, I can certainly relate to Scott's experiences. At the time, that escapism constituted an addiction in its own right, a siren call to lure me away from the pressures, challenges, drudgery, discontent, or anxieties of everyday life. Every weekend would turn into a blur of partying, drinking, and painful hangovers.

Being surrounded by other people doing the same, it wasn't easy to see the experience for what it truly was. Instead, it felt like we were the kings of the world, as we knew most of the promoters, bouncers, and bartenders at the better clubs in the city. We felt like we belonged. When something becomes a habit, an addiction, that has detrimental effects on health, well-being, and relationships, it is time to take a step back and reassess the situation. The most challenging part, of course, is that introspection and honesty with oneself are never easy, particularly in situations when we keep trying to convince ourselves that everything is "fine".

In a previous chapter, we discussed the need for feedback in a professional context, be it from colleagues, support networks, or mentors. In a professional context, our support structure can provide us with insight regarding our behaviour or force us to ask ourselves difficult questions. In that same way, we must look to our support structure to calibrate our behaviour when things aren't, in fact, "fine". We may find the support we need from our friends, our families, our spiritual advisors, professional counsellors, or anonymous support groups.

Whatever the options we choose, it is essential to talk through the underlying issues affecting us and their effects on our well-being and relationships. Keeping things bottled up, or hoping that something will change on its own, rarely works out and typically only prolongs any hope of getting back on track.

As Scott rightly highlights, the costs associated with addiction are high. There are financial implications to consider, professional ramifications to ponder, and reputational damage that may result, but more important are the personal relationships that will suffer along the way. We owe it to our loved ones, friends, colleagues, and ourselves to do whatever we can to identify positive steps we can take to become a better version of ourselves. For consultants, the challenge of dealing with high-stress situations and long hours are compounded by prolonged periods away from home. Travel takes us away from our support structures while simultaneously presenting ample opportunity to act on bad instincts. We must therefore be particularly mindful when travel for work is required.

# Travel

Sitting in the offices of KPMG, discussing the importance of work-life balance with David Fowler, he admitted, "I'm not sure I have done a great job of this, right? So, you know, being very honest, I'm divorced, right? My partner worked for Deloitte and basically, work-life balance, I think is probably the most significant factor in why we end up going in separate directions."

I was taken aback for a moment, as I hadn't expected that level of honesty. In the consulting world, there is a tendency to put on a brave face and never admit to moments of vulnerability or personal failings. I very much appreciated David sharing what was undoubtedly a difficult episode in his life as a cautionary tale for others who may find themselves in a similar situation.

He continued, "There was a time, for example, where she worked at Deloitte and I worked at Accenture and every Monday morning, joking aside, we'll travel to the airport together. London City Airport at 6 a.m. I'll fly one direction, she flies in the other. We would come back together on a Friday. Effectively would have Saturday, which was, sometimes one or both of us having to work. Sunday, you're back into doing all your chores, washing, packing your bags, getting an early night, and then Monday back on the road. The work-life balance thing, you know, it's tough. When I work on outside projects now, for example, I try to never do more than three nights away midweek. Now, it just depends on the client and sometimes you have to do more, but if you can do Monday, Tuesday, Wednesday night, come back Thursday; you're spending more nights at home than you are away. On the mental health perspective, candidly, that period of time, just after my divorce, I signed off work for two months. I don't think that was necessarily the divorce. I think I was probably burnt out."

David's experience, gut-wrenching in its authenticity, is unfortunately not unique in the world of consulting. Speaking with Jon Hughes, formerly of Genpact and Cognizant, he recalled a similar experience, saying, "I remember distinctly I used to go to Paris on a Sunday evening to do work in the south of Paris. I used to fly back on a Friday night and my wife would pick me up. I got into the car and within half an hour, we were arguing because we were still just married and didn't speak to each other for Saturday and Sunday. Then, by Sunday afternoon, we kind of got back to normal, and I was off on a plane again. I think that separation of some of your loved ones can be a real trial and something that people should understand."

Melville Carrie shared the impact that long durations away from his family had as he recalled, "I wasn't aware of just how incumbent on my life that would be. It really took a toll. It took a toll on my family. My daughter said, 'I really miss you Daddy, can you get another job?' That was after about six months. My son said, 'I no longer recognise you to miss you. You're not here enough that I'd actually miss you anymore.' I felt that."

Andrew Rundle, associate professor of Epidemiology it the Mailman School of Public Health at Columbia University, discussed the impacts of frequent travel in the *Harvard Business Review*. He wrote, "Compared to those who spent one to six nights a month away from home for business travel, those who spent 14 or more nights away from home per month had significantly higher body mass index scores and were significantly more likely to report the following: poor self-rated health; clinical symptoms of anxiety, depression and alcohol dependence; no physical activity or exercise; smoking; and trouble sleeping. The odds of being obese were 92% higher for those who travelled 21 or more nights per month compared to those who travelled only one to six nights per month, and this ultra-travelling group also had higher diastolic blood pressure and lower high-density lipoprotein (the good cholesterol)."[88]

The emotional and physical risks of frequent and long-term travel are substantial. Being aware of these risks allows us to develop mechanisms to deal with them effectively. For example, keeping a regular exercise regimen when travelling, opting for healthier food options from the room-service menu, or avoiding drinking during the week may all contribute to reducing the associated health risks.

Finding the right balance of travel for ourselves and our teams is also essential. "I try and make sure that there's a cycle of three projects," Jon Hughes advised. "This is in an ideal world. You know, one project you'll get within a reasonable distance of home, and you can get back most nights. That's the 'A' project. A 'B' project is something where you're going to travel for maybe an hour and a half to two, three hours early on a Monday morning or late on a Sunday night and get back late on Friday. Not ideal, but, you know, you can go to the gym, do your Masters or other things in the evening as well. Having some time to yourself can be a good thing. Then there's the third type of project, which is, the arse end of humanity Nova Scotia [no offence intended to our Canadian readers] for two months at a time."

"The idea, obviously, from a managerial point of view is you don't want to give a young consultant two type C projects in a row because they will leave unless they particularly like living in Nova Scotia. The idea is you're trying to get a mix of A's, B's, and C's."

"As a younger consultant, I would take the opportunity to travel and do as much as you possibly can, understanding that you probably don't have kids. So, you have a period of time to actually do those B and C projects and learn a bit. I learned a lot by working overseas, say Paris, Brussels, South Africa, and other places. It was difficult from a personal point of view because myself and my fiancé or girlfriend or wife, depending on what time period it was, struggled with that. But, I learned a lot about different cultures, how businesses work, and had some good times."

My personal experience had been similar to Jon's in the way that travel for work was exciting when I was younger, and in many ways life changing. However, it's important to choose your destinations carefully, because not everyone is lucky enough to be working in sunny Nova Scotia.

Places such as Stoke, Reading, Manchester, and Macclesfield in the UK are lovely, each with their own history and wonderful people, but may not offer the same experiences as working internationally in Paris, New York, or Warsaw. I've also enjoyed working in countries such as South Africa, Italy, Switzerland, Netherlands, and others; each country offering opportunities to truly experience their respective cultures, exploring new places, and meeting incredible people along the way. While I'm very thankful for these opportunities, there came a time when the prospect of living out of a suitcase for weeks, if not months at a time, became increasingly less appealing. Travel can be an exciting and enriching element of consulting life. However, it's essential to be mindful of the impact that work and travel may have on us and our relationships.

Acknowledging the risks and taking the appropriate steps to take care of ourselves and those close to us is essential in finding the right work-life balance. Setting clear expectations with our managers or with our teams will also serve to avoid uncomfortable situations where we are asked to travel for extended periods when we are unable, or unwilling, to do so.

# Big picture

"With a sixth of workers experiencing a mental health problem at any one time and stress, anxiety, and depression thought to be responsible for almost half of working days lost in Britain due to health issues, the relationship between mental health and the workplace is a complex one," stated Rebecca George OBE, vice chair and UK public sector leader at Deloitte in their *Mental Health and Employers* report published in January, 2020.[89]

According to the report, poor mental health among employees costs UK employers anywhere between £42 billion GBP and £45 billion GBP each year. This is made up of absence costs of around £7 billion GBP, presenteeism costs ranging from about £27 billion GBP to £29 billion GBP, and turnover costs of around £9 billion GBP.

While public attitudes towards mental health have been improving, and with more employers instituting programs to encourage discussion and self-care, there remains a lot more to be done. Approximately 14.7% of people experience mental health problems in the workplace, according to a report published by the Royal College of Psychiatrists, with depression being the predominantly stated factor. Evidence suggests that 12.7% of all sickness absence days in the UK can also be attributed to mental health conditions.[90]

"The reality for many employees is that they still don't feel able to talk about their mental health," noted Paul Farmer CBE, CEO at Mind, a mental health charity in England and Wales.[91]

He continued, "A recent Business in the Community 2019 Mental Health at Work report found that only 49% of employees felt comfortable talking to their line manager about their mental health, and 39% of employees surveyed said that work had affected their mental health over the past 12 months."

If you, or someone you know, needs additional support, please do not hesitate to reach out for help. "There is a wide range of treatment options, from talking to a counsellor or accessing mental health support online, to alternative therapies and medications," Kevin Fenton wrote for *Public Health Matters*. He continued, "Knowing more about mental health conditions can also encourage us to take better care of our own mental health and wellbeing."[92]

# Balance

Rabbi Harold Kushner is often credited with the quote, "Nobody on their deathbed has ever said, 'I wish I had spent more time at the office.'"

Yet, consultants spend an incredible amount of time at the office, travelling, or working from home. We tend to check and send emails incessantly, at all times of the day or night, including on the weekends. That compulsion does not leave much time to disconnect and truly focus on ourselves, our friends, or our families.

Finding the right work-life balance is not easy and will be different for each person. Everyone will have different circumstances that will dictate what priorities they set and how they arrange their days. That being said, the benefits of spending more time focused on ourselves or with those we care about, effectively disconnecting from our work tasks and devoting more time to ourselves, are universal.

While there is no one simple solution for finding the right work-life balance, there are several incremental steps we can take to be better to ourselves and those around us:

### Take care of yourself
Exercise and a balanced diet are a great start, but don't overdo it. You don't need to run a marathon straight out of the gate. If you don't exercise, start with an hour a week, then do more when you feel ready. Set objectives and work towards them.

### Make time for others
Sometimes, after a long day at work, the last thing you may feel like doing is playing with the kids, seeing friends, or calling your mother. Remember, you will never get this time back, so make time for others.

### Set expectations
Be transparent with your managers and colleagues about your schedule. The good ones will understand if you need to go to the gym at lunch or if you need to leave early to pick up the kids or be with your family.

### Learn to say no
Not an easy thing to do, particularly as an associate or junior consultant. However, you will do yourself and others a disservice if you take on too many things all at once. If your plate is full, let others know.

### Clear your head
It may be as simple as going for a walk or biking the long way home. Give yourself time to decompress throughout the day. Before you ask, no, going for a smoke does not count and you should quit immediately.

### Prioritise
No matter how much we'd like to think we have superpowers, we don't. We can't be everywhere at once or do everything at once; therefore some things will need to be set aside so that we can focus on others and give them the consideration they deserve.

### Impose boundaries
Don't check work emails at dinner and turn off work-related notifications in the evenings and on the weekends. Unless it is an emergency, replying to the late evening or weekend email can wait.

### Delegate
Doing household chores or grocery shopping can take up a lot of time that may be better spent relaxing. If you have the option, hire a cleaner to help around the house or order your weekly groceries online.

### Ask for help
If, at any point, you are feeling overwhelmed or have a stressful issue at work, don't hesitate to ask for help. Look to your team, to your mentor, or to your wider support structure.

### Find happiness in the little things
Life is short and unfortunately, unless the singularity happens, finite. Therefore, every single day is precious, and we should strive to find joy even in the smallest things.

I recall a day, many years ago, when I was driving with my mother sitting next to me in the passenger seat. Suddenly, she pointed at the car's digital clock and exclaimed, "Look! It's 11:11!" Without fail, she would always point out when it was that time, as the lines on the digital display formed an aesthetically pleasing, symmetrical form.

I must have been having a bad day, because my reply was a rather dismissive, "Oh Mom, why do you always make a big deal about that?"

Her reply, which I will never forget, was beautiful in its simplicity when she said, "If you can find happiness in this little thing, you can find happiness in everything."

Finding happiness in the little things, much like finding the right work-life balance, will differ for each person. Likewise, identifying the appropriate mechanisms by which to avoid some of the dangers we discussed in this chapter may also vary. Yet, as we set time aside to take care of ourselves and become better at finding happiness in the little things, we will be in a much better position to make time for and to take care of others, both in our professional and personal lives.

"There is always light.
If only we're brave enough to see it.
If only we're brave enough to be it."

Amanda Gorman

# Stephen Knight

"I came out of university with a crappy degree in 1994, in the middle of a recession. I'd really drunk my way and enjoyed my way through university. Therefore, my first job was in a call centre in the back-office, filing, which I started five hours after I finished my last exam," Stephen Knight recounted his triumphant entry into the workforce with characteristic nonchalance. Good humoured, with a healthy dose of cutting sarcasm when necessary, Stephen had come a long way since those early days, advancing to the role of managing director at Accenture.

"I've never had a day unemployed," he continued. "I realised that I was going to have to graft hard. I started at the call centre, answering calls and selling insurance on the phone. I then became a team leader. Then the call centre forecasting manager resigned. I'd done some analytics in my degree and had the call centre contact me to ask if I would want to take over."

"I said, 'Yeah, that sounds like a great job.' I had a week to learn because the forecasting manager was on a week's notice. I had to do the forecasting for three and a half thousand staff over three locations in an Excel model. I was 22. So, with the confidence of youth, I cracked in, and that took me on a journey of marketing. I moved to the headquarters of the direct insurance arm and got into marketing."

Early on in his career, Stephen recognised the value of hard work and of building out a robust network. When he became the team leader, he volunteered to take on additional hours and supported the agents in his firm with basic analysis and data-processing tasks. When the new role became available, his manager knew he could count on him. Putting in an extra bit of effort helped Stephen stand out from the crowd and gave his manager the opportunity to notice.

"I'm definitely not clever," Stephen openly admitted. "I'm not the most intellectually clever person I work with. There are people that are massively more intellectually clever than me all the time. But, I'll honestly outwork most people, and that comes from my dad. My dad is a mechanic. He used to get up for six in the morning, be at work at seven, work until five, and come home. He always worked outrageously hard all his life."

"I went to Eagle Star, now owned by Zurich, and I started to work in the marketing analytics team. We did stuff 20 years ago that people still think is cutting-edge now. I was using neural networks to do predictive modelling. I was on chat groups with Sergey Brin, the founder of Google because he was one of the leading proponents of neural networks in the world. We were doing incredible market analytic stuff and started to offer that as a service to our clients." Shortly thereafter, based on the success of the work his team were undertaking, it was agreed that the group would be spun out as a private company. Several of the senior leaders joined and established a marketing analytics agency called Profit Share.

"I lasted for six months," Stephen deadpanned.

"Take these big corporate leaders, put them in a small start-up business, and they'll tell you the first thing to do is to buy a company Jaguar. I used to have a countdown clock of how many days we had left. We took the cash we had in the bank, the revenue, and just worked it out. I used to update it every day, so that as we got new sales, we could see where we were."

"At one point, we had 140 days left, which isn't great. Now when we get a sale, it went up to just over a year. The behaviours and attitudes were terrible. So, I quit and went into a telco company called Plantronics."

Stephen worked with the marketing team, coordinating activities across European markets, learning valuable consulting skills along the way. Just as he was planning to move to California to join the head office, his wife became pregnant, quickly changing their plans. Looking for a new challenge, Stephen joined British Energy. He continued, "I'm now about 29 or 30, and I'm doing a job which is dead easy. I mean, like really easy. I could go to work at nine, and I could do most of my job by lunchtime. I used to work nine to five, but about two years in, and I got really, really bored."

Stephen negotiated with his boss to allow him to complete a part-time MBA programme, with the promise he would return with new ideas to improve the business. The company had been number one in company satisfaction for ten years, so when they dropped to number two for one quarter, it was the ideal opportunity to restructure, cut costs, and become more efficient. Stephen worked on that initiative, completed the MBA programme around the same time, and designed what he thought would be an ideal job for himself. He was hoping to be promoted based on the success of the restructuring and cost-cutting initiatives. Unfortunately, he was passed over for the role.

"I ended with virtually the job I had started out with two years previously. Then the guy that got the job I wanted asked me to lie in front of our board director; I didn't, and I, therefore, put him in a bad place." Not wanting to continue working in a toxic environment, Stephen knew it was time to move on.

"I went to work for Logica, which is now CGI, because that helped me with transformation. I went to work for people I trusted. That's probably the thing I would characterise my career in consulting as; I've worked for people I trust and the person I work for, I have to have a good strong relationship; I have to have to trust."

After two and a half years with Logica, Stephen was ready for a new challenge. "I started to interview; got three offers. One from Capgemini, one from a company called Vertex, and one from PwC. PwC was the lowest offer, but I met Steve Randall and just fell for a guy who I really got on with incredibly well, very quickly. It was a very complex process to go through; go in for the day and have an interview with the director, do two aptitude tests, have an interview with the partner, then meet HR, and then they'd take a couple of weeks to come back to you. I'm sat there with Steve Randall at the end of the meeting. We ran for two hours. He offered me the job in about 15 minutes. We talked salary. We talked how it could work. We talked about structuring and what would happen. I walked out of there, actually that was Thursday, and they phoned me up on Friday lunchtime and offered me the job with a full package in writing on Monday."

Throughout his career, Stephen continued to build strong networks within his organisations, and across the industries he worked with. He knew that he would be able to rely on his network for support, insights, and guidance. He was also able to look to his network when one of the lead partners stood in the way of his promotion at PwC and enabling him to quickly identify an opportunity with Accenture, going on to lead Transformation, Insight, and Growth for clients in the energy and utilities sectors.

Reflecting on his career, Stephen concluded, "A very odd sort of start to get into consulting, but then a classic entry. Do an MBA, become a consultant, which I think is about 90% of people that do MBAs end up as consultants. Just so they have something to say," Stephan joked. "That's how I ended up as a consultant. I've had ups and downs, great teams, terrible teams, amazing projects, horrible projects. You know, that's the career. I've managed to renovate a house, have three kids, do various mad things. All that."

"Courage starts with showing up and letting ourselves be seen."

Brené Brown

# Network

"So, when I was in the early part of my career, I was very much in the utility sector, I'd get lots of conferences, I used to speak quite a lot," Stephen Knight explained, "and that was helping me to raise my profile. With Mark, a good friend from CGI Logica, we wrote thought leadership papers and got those published. We wrote one very deliberately that was very, very controversial, which challenged the national grid view of the security of the nation's energy supply. We did a huge amount of work modelling and using their data to disprove one scenario, which got talked about in Parliament. So that helped raise my profile."

We were discussing the importance and challenges of building a personal profile and robust professional network. Stephen continued, "Having a profile is really important. I don't think too many people do that. I am very well known in the utilities industry, and I'm pretty well known in the customer consulting community. My LinkedIn profile is very prominent; I will often be pushing information out, sharing, and I deliberately do that as I've got a huge network on LinkedIn."

"LinkedIn is like having a fan club, and there are some that are not really connections, but there are a few that are very tight connections; the people that I'm really closest and connected to. I make sure to call those of my closest friends; I'll talk to them every six to eight weeks."

"There's a little group, in the utilities industry, where we have had Christmas dinner every year for 15 years. We always get together and have a beer to catch up. We gossip about the industry and we're very open with each other because we trust each other. So now I might come up against a situation that I don't know about, I can call, and you need some close friends that can give you a bit of advice."

Networking plays an important role in career and business development. A year-long survey of 3,000 people conducted by Lou Adler of Performance-based Hiring Learning Systems, in partnership with LinkedIn, revealed that 85% of critical jobs were filled through networking. Another study by Mark Granovetter found that we are more likely (58%) to get a job through acquaintances than friends.[93]

According to a LinkedIn survey, over 35% of the respondents said that casual conversations on LinkedIn Messaging had led to new opportunities. While the evidence suggests networking plays an essential role in our career development, it is not an easy skill to master.[94]

"I've definitely had a fear of networking in the past, and it's partly related to confidence and partly related to my personality," Jeremy Dalton admitted. "I don't, or at least I didn't, feel comfortable just reaching out to people randomly. But, in the same way that I talked about practising public speaking to make it as perfect as possible, the more you reach out, the easier it becomes, because you start to see the macro picture. People are reaching out to you; you're reaching out to other people. You help others, and others help you."

He concluded, "It is give and take. There's a balance to the universe, and you have to give up some of your time to help others and others should be willing to give up some of their time to help you."

Networking can be difficult for some, but as Jeremy pointed out, it is a skill like any other. The more we practice, the better we will become. What we must consider is where and to whom we devote our attention, what types of relationships we are aiming to build, and how to craft trusted, long-term, mutually beneficial relationships.

# Circles

Making new connections has never been easier. There's a multitude of online platforms and mobile applications that enable us to find individuals and groups with whom to connect. Thus, we can quickly grow the number of our connections from a few dozen to hundreds, if not thousands, with relative ease. Yet, as we subsequently discover, someone accepting an invitation to connect is not the equivalent of a relationship being formed. Instead, we realise the logistical challenge of proactively engaging with vast circles of tenuous connections. Meanwhile, as our closer relationships require a more personal touch, we find ourselves trying to balance the time we spend expanding our network versus nurturing the relationships we already have.

Robin Dunbar, a British anthropologist and evolutionary psychologist, used the correlation observed for non-human primates to predict a sustainable number of relationships, or social network size, for humans. Using a regression equation, he suggests a cognitive limit to the number of people with whom one can maintain stable social relationships. He defined relationships as ones where the individual knows who each person is and how each person relates to every other person. Using the average human brain size and extrapolating from the results of the primate studies, he proposed that humans can comfortably maintain approximately 150 stable relationships.

Dunbar explained it informally as "the number of people you would not feel embarrassed about joining uninvited for a drink if you happened to bump into them in a bar."

"Dunbar's number" is by no means an exact figure after which close relationships become untenable, nor should we entirely ignore the inexact method by which Dunbar arrived at the number itself. Rather, the number is a suggestion that, regardless of the technological advancements and the thousands of connections we may have on social networks, there is a much smaller number with whom we share a closer connection. It is important to maintain the wider "fan club", as described by Stephen, while simultaneously ensuring that attention and care is devoted to those who make it into our closer inner circle.

According to Dunbar's circles of acquaintanceship, the large number of tenuous online connections belong to the outer layers or so-called "weak tie" connections. As there is virtually no cost of connecting, there is no emotion or time invested by either party. Yet, information may be exchanged between weak tie connections dependent, of course, on what items the social network algorithms deem worthy. Therefore, these outer layers have a role to play, not only for personal brand building and information sharing purposes but also for the fact that they may become helpful at one point or another throughout our careers.

Mark Granovetter, the American sociologist and professor at Stanford University, discussed the importance of these weak ties in his aptly named paper *The Strength of Weak Ties* (1973).[95] He makes a basic distinction between the respective functions of strong and weak ties and points specifically to the importance of the latter, stating that weak ties are "an important resource in making possible mobility opportunity" by facilitating information flow.

## Dunbar's hierarchically inclusive levels of acquaintanceship

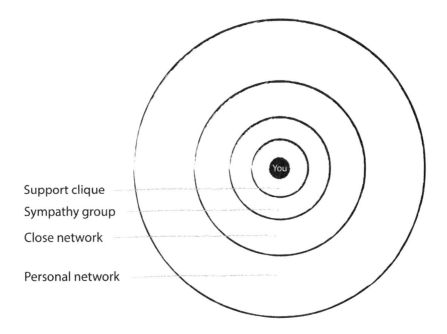

Support clique
Sympathy group
Close network

Personal network

According to Mark, these bridges play an essential role in the process of diffusion of new ideas or concepts, as they allow for the spread of an idea from one group to another. He presents a set of studies that demonstrate how new ideas spread (most rapidly) through people with few strong connections but numerous weak tie connections.

When Mark first published his paper in 1973, he probably never dreamt of a world that is as interconnected as the one we live in now. The internet is undeniably one of the most transformative and fast-growing technologies in human civilisation. In 2019, for example, there were over 7.7 billion people in the world, with 4.3 billion, over 50%, having access to the internet. Of those, approximately 3.5 billion were active social media users, spending an average of 144 minutes on social media sites per day.

The staggering growth of social media has resulted in, on average, Facebook users uploading 147,000 photos, Twitter gaining 319 new users, Instagram users posting 347,222 Stories, and YouTube creators uploading 500 hours of video every minute of every day.[96]

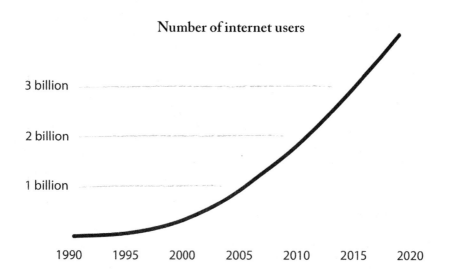

**Number of internet users**

With 2.3 billion users, Facebook is the most popular social network platform today. YouTube, Instagram, and WeChat follow, with more than a billion users each. Tumblr and TikTok come next, with over half a billion users.[97]

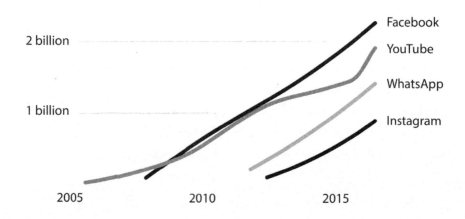

**Number of people using social platforms**

Yet, regardless of the progress that has been made since Mark published his paper, the basic premise he described is as true now as it was then. The weak ties he described are now ever-present in online social networks. While the number of these weak tie relationships may have numbered in the dozens in the 1970s, they now number in the hundreds, if not thousands.

Statistics from 2016 showed that 27% of LinkedIn users had between 500 to 999 first-degree connections. However, the label "first-degree connections" here is misleading, as most of these connections fall firmly into the weak tie category. The ease of adding someone as a connection and the inherent desire to accept connection requests results in a situation whereby LinkedIn users may have first-degree connections with whom they have never met or even exchanged any meaningful communication.[98]

**Number of first-level connections of LinkedIn users (March 2016)**

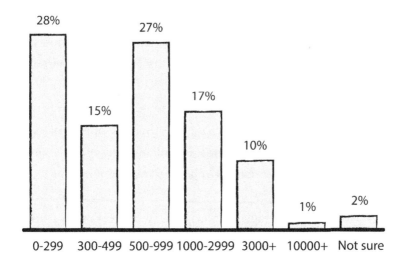

"You can get lost in the fog of thousands of LinkedIn contacts, and actually don't have that many," Richard Hepworth, formerly of KPMG and PwC, cautioned. "How many times have I heard a senior partner say they've got a fantastic relationship with this person, and they actually don't?"

He continued, "It's one of those interesting things. One of the things that I think everybody should do is really think about their clients as part of the team and part of their own network. The experience that you give them and the relationships that you build with them are as important as the internal relationships. You should stay in touch with people."

"The other reason why I built up that network and I keep in contact with people, one of the things I've missed the most about being a consultant, is seeing the end impact of the stuff that you do. Reconnecting with them a year or so after the project to see how it really went and understanding a bit more about it. Of all the stuff that you do, I still think only 10% makes a massive impact. So, trying to reconnect with that person to understand the impact they're having and how they're getting their career going is really important to me. It's that curiosity. Curiosity from a personal level, and then connecting and keeping the good relationships going. Secondly, from, well, did that stuff really work? We have to be very careful about understanding what we've actually achieved, what we've done, and the legacy that we're leaving. For me, keeping that network alive and coming at it from that lens of you and the impact that can have; I think it's incredibly important."

As our online networks grow, we need to be mindful to distinguish between the close and weak tie relationships, devoting the appropriate time to nurturing the close tie relationships and identifying effective means by which to maintain a connection with the weak tie relationships.

"My first consulting engagement at PwC was working for an energy company, and the lead engagement partner for Accenture was a guy called Martin," Stephen Knight recalled. "When I got approached about a job at Accenture, who was the first person I called? It was Martin. Since I first met him, I'd kept in touch and would probably see him once or twice a year, as we'd be at different industry events. I'd go over to the Accenture building and have coffee, or eat, or we'd just meet every now and again."

"I've probably got a dozen close connections now, and then there's probably 50 or 60 people that I will connect with through a year to make sure I keep in touch with and catch up with. Having that sort of light contact, it normally pays dividends."

For Stephen, maintaining two or three circles with varying degrees of contact frequency allowed him to ensure that he was able to make the necessary time and maintain those relationships in the long term. Maintaining the different types of relationships in the long term required focus, consistency, and the ability to prioritise.

"My system just naturally evolved over time. I didn't realise I did it. It was when the financial crash happened and I was at PwC. I hadn't been there long, maybe two or three years," Stephen recalled. There was a consulting group meeting from one of their projects and one of the partners stood up in front of the group and proclaimed, "We expect you to make three calls a week to people you haven't talked to."

The partner asked everyone in the room to stand up and said, "Okay, who hasn't made a single call this week to somebody they're not working with? Sit down." The consultants in the room looked around tentatively as a few colleagues sat down. He continued, "Who hasn't made two calls this week?" A few more consultants sat down. The partner repeated the process and, as the number of calls increased with each subsequent round, more and more of Stephen's colleagues would sit down, until he was one of the last remaining standing.

Stephen concluded, "It's a skill you see in the best partners at PwC. Like Charles Bowman. He was one of the senior audit partners; or Sir Charles Bowman, as he was the Mayor of London. Charles could call any of the board, any of the non-execs, and the chairman at the multinational energy company we were working with. He just had this great relationship with anyone. That's what I do with all my clients."

"I get to know them, I'll make sure we get on well, I'll take them for lunch, build a relationship. It's important for me as their auditor to be it for them, for them to trust me, for me to be able to call them at any time. Twenty years on, I've got all these relationships all over the city of London, which really helped. I think that young consultants don't invest in their relationships enough."

"Building relationships is not just a critical career skill but a critical life skill," confirmed Rebecca Zucker, partner at leadership development consultancy Next Step Partners.[99]

She offered several tips on building and maintaining professional relationships:

### Take a broad approach
"Never assume who will or won't be helpful," Rebecca said.
This mentality supports taking as broad an approach as possible
to building relationships by putting yourself out there.

### Momentum is multiplicative
"Whether you're looking for clients or a new job, if you get
introductions to new people, they can then introduce you to others,
and you're more likely to find what you're looking for. Getting one
ball rolling in your search leads to others," she added.

### Harness the strength of weak ties
Rebecca pointed to the previously mentioned research by Stanford
sociologist Mark Granovetter on the value of "weak ties";
reaching out to the wider network versus the people we know best.

### Don't be afraid to reconnect
It can be easy to talk yourself out of contacting those you've
lost touch with, even if they might be helpful to you today.

### Think beyond yourself

Ultimately, networking, like many other professional activities, is about looking beyond yourself. "It shouldn't be mostly about self-interest," Rebecca added. "It's thinking things like 'What can I do for this person? How can I help?'"

The most robust networks are formed when all participants are willing contributors, supporting one another and enabling further connections. One of the best things we can do, Rebecca suggested, is to build our network to be a connector for others: "Generosity is a critical part of networking—being able to offer something others find helpful."

# Reciprocity

"I distinguish transactional relationships from the sort of more long-term relationships. It's not to say the transactional relationships are bad; it's just they are what they are," Andrew Hogan noted as he reflected on reciprocity in relationships. "Sometimes you need something from somebody, or somebody needs something from you, you transact, and those things are usually done in a relatively short period of time. They are usually once and done, and then that's it. Sometimes there may be long periods of time between transactions. I have people in my network of relationships that it's nice to say I don't need, pejoratively; they're transactional relationships. Internally in the firm, externally with the market, in the clients."

Considering the research of Mark Granovetter, while it is necessary to distinguish between strong ties and weak ties, we should remain cognizant that there is inherent value in our weak tie relationships. Weak tie relationships may be transactional, they may share useful information, and they may connect us to people outside our immediate network. While they may not warrant the same attention and care as our inner circle or close tie relationships, they play an important role in our wider network.

In a similar way to how David Fowler described building his support structure through organic and structured means, Andrew Hogan does not consider taking a structured, pragmatic approach to networking as inherently negative. "I don't think that if something is deliberate and thought through, that it is necessarily manipulative or Machiavellian. People, in my experience, see through it. If you are being kind of a sneaky, strategic relationship builder, then people see through it and it doesn't work. I don't think that means that you wouldn't want, even in genuine and authentic relationship building, to have some deliberateness to it; some consciousness about it. It says you're thinking through who the people are that you want to form better and deeper relationships with and why. It does, I think fundamentally, and I don't apologise for it, come to reciprocity. My ability to give and to receive things from other people, but that's what makes the world go 'round. I mean, we are reciprocal beings; we are relational beings in our personal lives and in our professional lives. I don't think that's a bad thing, but it has to be done from the right intention, which is, 'I'm not in it to get the most for me and screw everybody else.' It has to be on the basis of true and honest reciprocity."

While there are different interpretations of the principle of karma, a popular interpretation suggests that the intent and actions of an individual influence the future of that individual. As a matter of cause and effect, good intent and good deeds contribute to good karma, while bad intent and bad deeds contribute to bad karma. I've always appreciated the simplicity of the equation, which suggests that what we get out of our relationships largely depends on what we invest into them.

Jennifer Spencer, CEO of Energent Media, noted four ways in which the law of reciprocity can be put into real-life practice:

### Start by building trust
Building trust with consumers, particularly those who
have never interacted with your brand before, is key.

This is why you see so many start-ups, particularly software as a service companies, offer free trials that allow users to try those companies' services before buying. It's why many industry authorities post a wealth of blog posts sharing actionable information or share free e-books with their users.

### Continually show appreciation

Building trust at the beginning of a customer relationship is vital. To continue to enjoy that strong relationship for many years, you must periodically show your appreciation. Satwick Saxena of EvaBot noted, "According to data from the U.S. Small Business Administration, 68% of customers end a business relationship because they don't feel appreciated or cared about. That's a lot more than the 14% who ditch a business because they don't like the product."[100]

### Incentivise your audience

Sometimes, you can be upfront with how you use the law of reciprocity and still go a long way toward strengthening your brand. As a case study reported on by Overthink Group revealed, Dropbox used its referral program to grow from 100,000 to four million users in a 15-month period by rewarding referrers with free storage.

### Give before you receive

At the end of the day, the most important element of the law of reciprocity is that you be willing to give away something of value without expecting something in return.[101]

Maria Axente echoed the importance of being there for others. "When someone asks for your help, I think it's really important to try to find a way to help them. Saying no, it's not just a 'no' to the person, it's 'no' to yourself, because it's another step in building a bridge in between yourself and the other."

Maria continued, "Even if you can't help, acknowledge your weakness and say, 'I'm sorry, this time, I cannot help you. But have you thought about this...', trying to give it a different perspective that potentially the other person wouldn't see. This openness, to help whenever help is solicited, I think, allows everyone to build good relationships. Healthy relationships are based on mutual interest, not on self-interest, that I can't stress enough. Just because your objective is to get promoted, you establish some very transactional relationship that's going to get you the promotion, but that doesn't mean that you are a connected individual."

Andrew added, "My experience is if you build relationships, if you sustain them over time, that takes deliberate effort and planning and thinking. There are the odd, serendipitous bump-ins when you see somebody in a tube station; that's fine too, that's good. But, I think if you're ever going to build and sustain a network, it doesn't happen by itself. The other analogy I always think of is to put it in a sports context. If you are in a sporting team, you have to have relationships with your teammates. You have to be able to trust them, that when you're on the attack, you're gonna have somebody who's staying back to defend. When you're in defence, people that are going to be ready for the counterattack. That understanding, that building of trust, and the coordination of different roles, it's a form of relationship. I see it similar in the business world. It's the kind of thing where you have to be able to have, especially in our business, good effective teammates that you can trust and that you can rely on. Not always within the context of a 60 or 90-minute game, but within the context of a career."

Being there for others is a great way to build trust and sustain relationships over time. It requires dedication and a willingness to put in the effort. When others see that you are willing to help, they will be that much more willing to help you in return. It's a virtuous circle that will continue to incrementally strengthen the bonds in our professional and personal lives.

Networking, much like any other skill, can be improved with practice. We can train ourselves to be better at networking, giving the appropriate level of care to our close and weak tie connections. However, it is only when we work on ourselves, becoming more comfortable in our own skin, more authentic in our approach, and more confident in what we have to say, that our networking will become that much more effective.

"All of us need to understand the importance of branding.
We are CEOs of our own companies: Me Inc. To be in business today,
our most important job is to be head marketer for the brand called You."

Tom Peters

# Brand

"I was delivering talks whenever I could, to whoever I could, on the subject of virtual reality (VR) and augmented reality (AR)," Jeremy Dalton shared as he described the experience of building his personal brand. "To begin with, find opportunities to give talks. It doesn't have to be anything significant. You can start off with low-risk casual meetups, expand to local conferences, and ultimately to international speaking opportunities, with larger audiences, more senior audiences, more knowledgeable audiences. Eventually, it not only helps your brand, but it helps you build your confidence. It's all about marketing yourself at the end of the day."

"The other aspect of brand building is signposting your expertise through whatever system or platform people search for you or come across you. In my case, I had 'VR/AR' in my e-mail signature and, as my portfolio of reports and projects grew, I also made those available as links there too. It helped because it gave people a signal, something to latch on to, that 'this guy is VR/AR.' It became clear that I was the guy to speak to if you wanted to know more about VR/AR."

"In the end, I had modified all my social media profiles and internal corporate networks to bolster the statement that 'Jeremy is VR/AR'. From a marketing standpoint, if people are getting hit constantly with all of these communications that 'Jeremy is VR/AR,' that key message is going to stick."

Creating a personal brand is not easy. First, we must overcome our insecurities or impostor syndrome, overpowering the fear that we are frauds and that our opinions and points of view are somehow not worth sharing with the world. An estimated 70% of people experience these impostor feelings at some point in their lives, meaning we are not alone in facing these anxieties. To overcome these fears, numerous people I've spoken with for this book suggested started small, sharing in smaller circles, practising, improving, and practising some more. Abigail Abrams wrote of overcoming impostor syndrome in *Time Magazine*, "It can also be helpful to share what you're feeling with trusted friends or mentors. People who have more experience can reassure you that what you're feeling is normal, and knowing others have been in your position can make it seem less scary."[104]

Second, you need to decide what it is that you want to be known for. This is not to say you aren't a multi-faceted, multi-dimensional, incredibly deep, unique snowflake of a human being. Of course, you are. However, in general, people have a short attention span and won't be able to grasp or process all of the nuanced awesomeness that makes you special. Therefore, we need to simplify, much like Jeremy did when 'this guy is VR/AR' became his strapline. Find the one or two things that you want to be known for and build your brand around them.

"Contrary to popular belief, there's nothing wrong with self-promotion. The key is honesty when you're doing it," wrote Gabrielle Lennox, a career coach at Korn Ferry Advance. Yet, she cautioned, "You cannot be an expert banjo player and an Olympic athlete and an award-winning opera singer and the CEO." You need to identify what you want to be known for and be consistent, confident, and concise when you introduce yourself as such.

Third, you need to craft an approach to building your personal brand. For example, writing articles, taking part in speaking engagements, sharing your portfolio, or adding your tagline everywhere are some of the ways to let others know who you are. However, your approach needs to be strategic and aligned with your objectives. Over time, your network will grow as you meet other like-minded individuals that share your interest and passion. As you successfully build your brand and network, your employer will benefit as well. One study found that an employee's brand message posted to social media is 24 times more likely to be reshared than when posted to the employer's social media account.[105]

Your brand can become a great way to build your network and expand your knowledge. It is also a powerful differentiator when exploring new opportunities. However, to be genuinely effective, building your brand will require focus, dedication, and consistency.

# Visual identity

"I think there's something about a consultant; you can be a bit of a chameleon, but also you can stand out. It's important to know when to stand down and to choose your moments," Stephen Knight commented as we were discussing visual identity as part of building our personal brand. "Physical personal image can be something that's very useful. We can go from proper suited and booted, white shirts, dark ties, crisp-looking shoes, to a pair of jeans and a t-shirt; and that's fine. We gauge the environment, the relationship we're in, and what's needed at that point in time."

Oscar Wilde is attributed with the quote, "You can never be overdressed or overeducated." I've found, however, that you can most definitely be underdressed. There was a time we were working on a strategy project for a luxury brand and headquartered ourselves in a meeting room located in their head office. It wasn't a very large room, but it was well-appointed, with a quality wooden table and modern chairs finished in pristine white leather.

As it was the kick-off stage of the project, we had spent several days in the room planning out the activities for the engagement. Given it was a luxury brand, I made an effort to pick out an outfit that could have been out of the pages of a men's fashion magazine: Shirt, tie, cashmere cardigan, fitted blazer, pocket square, classy indigo jeans, and smart shoes. It was, what I thought at the time, a classy outfit for a classy environment.

However, a day later, after we finished one of our first status updates for the client stakeholders, one of my colleagues approached me. He let me know that one of the executives had pulled him aside after the session and commented about jeans being inappropriate in the office. I was embarrassed to hear it but not nearly as embarrassed as I was once we made our way back to the room from which we had been working. There I discovered, to my dismay, that the white leather of the chair I had been sitting in had a slight blue discolouration compared to the other chairs. Apparently, the indigo ink of my jeans had transferred onto the immaculate white leather. We went on to great success with the project and expanded the account, but to this day, I don't know if anyone from the client side noticed I had accidentally ruined one of their chairs. Perhaps it's true that one can never be overdressed, but, as I learned the hard way, you can definitely be underdressed.

"One of the most powerful and impactful bits of career advice that I have ever received is the practice of treating every day at work as a job interview," wrote Bernie Klinder, an entrepreneur and consultant. "Whether you like it or not, you are constantly being evaluated and re-evaluated by everyone around you. How you dress at work sends a number of signals about how you view the environment, how much respect you have for your work and yourself, what groups you identify with, and where you think you belong. So if you dress more like the peer group you aspire to, and less like the one you are in, you are sending a powerful signal that you belong in that group. In addition, there is a common perception among management that if you can't handle the small things, you probably aren't well suited to handle larger responsibility."

He concluded, "Put simply: If you can't even dress yourself properly, you can't handle much else." [106] The amount of care we put into our image, be it our clothes, our hair, or even our posture, will be picked up on by others, consciously or subconsciously. While we may, on a philosophical level, disagree with the sometimes unfair emphasis on appearance, it does not change the fact that others will unconsciously pick up on visual cues we put forth. The clothes we wear and how we present ourselves play an important role in how others perceive us.

Interestingly, the clothes we wear may also have an impact on how we perceive ourselves. A study by Northwestern University in 2012 examined a concept called "enclothed cognition", which they defined as "the systematic influence that clothes have on the wearer's psychological processes." The researchers distributed standard white lab coats to participants, telling some that it was a doctor's coat and some that it was a painter's smock. All participants performed the same task, but those wearing the "doctor's coat" were more careful and attentive.[107]

Clearly, how we dress and present ourselves may not only impact our perception of ourselves, but also influence how we perform. Ultimately, the clothes we wear and how we present ourselves is an important element of our personal brand, meaning we need to be mindful that it is authentic and that we feel comfortable. Maria Axente spoke of finding her own style after years of toning down what she wore and the confidence it brought her, saying, "As a piece of advice, just try to be yourself; passionate, delicate, and elegant. Wear high heels and dresses and whatever makes you the woman you are, and don't hide it. Don't obstruct it. Just be yourself, and if the others have a problem with it, f*ck them."

The way we present and take care of ourselves will inevitably be noticed by others, which grants us a powerful opportunity to let others know who we are before we even say a single word.

# Behaviour

Social psychologist Paul Piff, standing on stage at the TEDxMarin event, introduced his topic by saying, "I want you to, for a moment, to think about playing a game of *Monopoly*. Except in this game, that combination of skill, talent, and luck that helped earn you success in games, as in life, has been rendered irrelevant, because this game's been rigged, and you've got the upper hand. You've got more money, more opportunities to move around the board, and more access to resources. And as you think about that experience, I want you to ask yourself: How might that experience of being a privileged player in a rigged game change the way you think about yourself and regard that other player?"[108]

Paul and his colleagues ran a study on the UC Berkeley campus, where they brought in more than 100 pairs of strangers into their lab. They randomly assigned one of the two to be the rich player in a rigged game with a flip of a coin. The rich player received two times as much money, they collected twice as much for passing Go, and they got to roll both dice instead of one, meaning they would move around the board faster. As Paul made his way across the stage, he showed short video clips of different pairs sitting down to play the game.

He continued, "As the game went on, one of the really interesting and dramatic patterns that we observed begin to emerge was that the rich players actually started to become ruder toward the other person—less and less sensitive to the plight of those poor, poor players, and more and more demonstrative of their material success; more likely to showcase how well they're doing." More video clips showed the rich players bragging about their wealth, making demands, and taunting the poor players. Paul noted, "Now, this game of *Monopoly* can be used as a metaphor for understanding society and its hierarchical structure, wherein some people have a lot of wealth and a lot of status, and a lot of people don't; they have a lot less wealth and a lot less status and a lot less access to valued resources."

"What my colleagues and I have been doing is studying the effects of these kinds of hierarchies. What we've been finding across dozens of studies and thousands of participants across this country is that as a person's levels of wealth increase, their feelings of compassion and empathy go down, and their feelings of entitlement, of deservingness, and their ideology of self-interest increase."

In another study, Paul and his team looked at whether drivers would stop for a pedestrian that they had posed waiting to cross at a crosswalk where it was the law for the cars to stop. They tracked cars for several days, and they noticed that as the price of the cars increased, so did the probability that the drivers would break the law. In the study, over 50% of expensive car drivers did not stop for the pedestrians at the crosswalk. They conducted several other studies, and what they found was that "the wealthier you are, the more likely you are to pursue a vision of personal success, of achievement and accomplishment, to the detriment of others around you." He continued, "We've been finding that the wealthier you are, the more entitled you feel to that wealth, and the more likely you are to prioritise your own interests above the interests of other people and be willing to do things to serve that self-interest."

The implications of these studies are significant, as they speak to how we identify ourselves, how we treat those around us, and our attitudes towards laws or regulations. As the *Monopoly* study suggests, we need to be mindful not to allow the advantages that we have been given in life to bequeath us with an unearned sense of superiority. We must remain humble, acknowledging that, much like in the *Monopoly* study, some of the advantages we have received were a matter of chance based on where we were born, when, or based on the circumstances of our parents. By equal measure, we must also be sensitive to the fact that there will be others that may not have had the advantages we had, and we must treat them with the appropriate respect they deserve.

Paulo Coelho, the Brazilian novelist, best known for *The Alchemist*, is credited with writing, "How people treat other people is a direct reflection of how they feel about themselves."

Finally, when Paul and his team studied the correlation of wealth to the probability of drivers stopping at a crosswalk, they uncovered an increased probability of ignoring laws or regulations amongst wealthier drivers. It was as if the laws did not apply beyond a certain income level or status. It is not an accident that every single consultancy has rigorous risk and regulation training, or that in many cases the training is an annual recurring requirement. After all, consulting organisations have a terrible track record when it comes to bending or breaking the rules, which is, at least in part, explained by the type of behaviours identified by the studies Paul and his team conducted.

Scanning headlines from 2020, McKinsey was to repay more than $40 million USD over a South African scandal, where there were allegations of irregularities in contracts the consultancy had with a local partner at government-owned companies. In Angola, Boston Consulting Group, McKinsey and PwC were implicated in helping Isabel dos Santos, daughter of the former president, become a billionaire by allegedly plundering state coffers. Meanwhile, an independent tribunal ordered Deloitte to pay £15 million GBP and a further £5.6 million GBP in legal fees after the firm was found to have broken the rules of the UK accounting watchdog.[109]

Each scandal was based, ultimately, on the actions of individuals. Just as in the study, where the richer, more privileged drivers broke the law more often, these consultants may have thought that the laws or regulations simply did not apply to them. Whatever their rationale, the outcome was the same, tarnishing their reputations and the reputations of the organisations they worked for. Therefore, the experiments Paul and his team conducted serve as a cautionary tale for us all.

On our way to becoming successful consultants and leaders, building personal brands that others will relate to, we must remain humble, keep our egos in check, consider our behaviour, and continue to always, always, stop our cars for pedestrians at crosswalks no matter how successful we may become.

# Authenticity

"I'm still amazed how many close good relationships, friendships, I developed with so many people in this field because all of us we have the same vision and mission," Maria commented as we spoke about the need for personal authenticity. "That's when the magic happens, in having that open mind and trying to understand each other. I feel like that's the secret; being yourself, being a decent human being, curious, and paying attention to what others are interested in and passionate about. Try to find a way in-between and you build a very strong relationship. You can pick up your phone and drop a message to people that otherwise would be inaccessible, and they reply in a second, because they know your good faith, because you do the same when they come to you with question or query."

Being genuinely authentic is not easy, particularly for new consultants entering the industry for the first time. There is typically a preconceived image of what a consultant should behave like, dress like, or speak like, that new consultants aim to aspire to, at the cost of being their authentic selves. For some, that challenge is compounded by the fact that they may not have yet truly figured themselves out. Questions of identity or sexuality are complex introspective journeys that may be complicated by the perceived behavioural requirements of the workplace. This preconception complicates the personal discovery journey, as there is a perceived pressure to act in a certain way that may not be authentic, consequently having a detrimental impact on our self-confidence and on the self-discovery journey itself.

I entered the world of consulting in my early 30s with, what I thought at the time, was a confidence of having worked in several industries, a recently completed MBA under my arm, and a clear understanding of who I was as a person. Yet, I still managed to make some of the classic new-consultant mistakes. One of these was thinking that big words and heap-loads of jargon would make me seem more serious and more competent.

I recall a social event with some of the directors and partners when someone called me out on it. One of the partners had asked me a question about a project I was working on, and I replied with a bunch of typical consulting gibberish. He turned to me and said, "I have no idea what you just said. Tell me again, in your own words." It turned out I didn't have to try to forcefully insert the word "leverage" into every second sentence in a misguided attempt to sound like what I thought a consultant should sound like.

Speaking with Richard Murton, he discussed his own struggle with being his true self. He joined Accenture straight out of the Royal Air Force, where he'd been a pilot. "When I went down for interviews to join the Air Force, I remember they asked two questions," Richard recalled, "and these were the two mandatory questions. There were three guys there on the panel, and one question was, 'Have you ever taken drugs?' and the other question was, 'Are you a homosexual?' Because it was illegal in those days to be homosexual in the Air Force. I remember looking at this guy's face going, 'My God, can you see through me?' Frankly, I put my sexuality to the back of my mind."

"The time I started to be myself coincided with the time that I came out to myself, really. I was about 31, 32, so quite, quite late. I think that was a big relief for me. Then, once I was more comfortable with myself, I just became more myself, and it was amazing." For Richard, coming to terms with his sexuality coincided with him gaining in confidence to be the authentic leader he wanted to be rather than the leaders he had read about and thought he had to mimic.

"I felt that I was always trying to be the person and the leader that I thought Accenture wanted me to be. I thought we needed drivers. I just was not myself, and I remember my dad used to read all these leadership books, and I was like, 'Oh, I can't think of anything worse. So boring.'"

"The day that I actually started to enjoy Accenture a bit better was when I just was actually honest with myself. I just sort of went, 'Stop trying to pretend to be a leader that you've read in a book and just be your own self.' And you know what? It was just the most incredible shift."

"When I was myself, I actually realised that, you know, you didn't need to be Einstein to lead. Actually, you needed to be a people person more than anything. I think leadership is more about retention and attraction of top talent, and I saw I was quite good at that people side of things. I was also digital and quite funky. Obviously, Accenture had gone into this funky new digital era. I think I was always seen as a bit of a funky outsider. So, I got given all these jobs; peripheral jobs to set up the digital floor and stuff. I really loved it because suddenly I was me. I think that for me, it was the thing that changed. I spent my eight years trying to be a leader that I thought I read in a book. I had to do this and that. The minute I started to go, 'Actually, just be yourself,' I realised that my leadership qualities are not what you read in the book. They're in you as a personality and as a good person. I did have leadership qualities, you know; I just didn't realise they were there."

Unfortunately, there is no magic bullet or spell by which we can snap our fingers to miraculously achieve an epiphany as to who we are, who we want to be, and gain mountains of confidence overnight. The path of self-discovery is a long and winding one, different for everyone. As Richard described, while the process itself may be prolonged, the reward of being comfortable in our own skin and the associated benefits are significant.

Michael Bianco-Splann, the author of *Conscious Leadership*, outlined five reasons why authenticity in business is important:

### Authenticity ignites human connection

You are never better, stronger, more creative, or compelling than when you are your true self. The energy you possess and emit connects you with your colleagues, clients, and those you care for. Authenticity opens the door to vulnerability and unity.

### Living in a way that's open and honest

Acknowledging your shortcomings and mistakes is life-affirming and builds unity. Great leaders show their humanness, dropping the corporate guard and standing with those being led.

### Authenticity allows you to learn about others

If you live your life on the fringes—always being afraid of opening up—you miss out on the wonderful experience of learning and knowing others on a deeper, more meaningful level. Being authentic creates room for others to do the same.

### Authenticity moves you into the present

When you decide to show up as the real you, you have consciously moved into the present, into a realm of real-time connections. Here, you are better able to make informed and enlightened choices that uplift you and others. When you live in the present, you experience one interaction at a time despite the disruptive nature of a rapidly evolving digital world.

### Authenticity changes your world perspective

When you no longer need to hide behind what others want you to be, say, or do, you put aside falseness and lies and open up to a world of endless and positive opportunities.[110]

How we go about finding our authentic selves will be different from person to person and will not happen overnight. Finding our true selves will help us become more confident and allow us to form more robust, more authentic relationships with our colleagues and clients.

In the conversations I've had, three common threads emerged that might help: First, take time to be introspective; learn what makes you tick, who you are, what your values are and who you want to become. Second, rely on your existing support structure or seek out support structures in which you can talk openly about your journey and learn from others. Third, books and the internet are a treasure trove of stories of people who may have been on a similar journey to yours. You can learn from them and be in a better place to reflect on your own journey.

Therefore, building an authentic, personal brand is inextricably connected to our introspective, personal development journey. It is a virtuous cycle, as the more comfortable we are in our own skin, the more confident and consistent we will become. The more confident and consistent we become, the more authentic we will allow ourselves to be. The more authentic we are, the better consultants and leaders we become, able to more effectively empower others along personal development journeys of their own.

"I had no idea that being your authentic self could make me as rich as I've become. If I had, I'd have done it a lot earlier."

Oprah Winfrey

# Richard Hepworth

"You're a bit of a disruptor, aren't you?" the psychometric test consultant stated, looking up from the report in his hands during a feedback session as part of an interview process.

Without missing a beat, Richard replied, "Do you know my wife?"

The year was 2008, and Richard was interviewing to join the Accenture marketing sciences team, as it was known at the time. The team occupied a small office in the middle of the fashionable Soho district in London, UK. The partner who ran the teams firmly believed that everyone who joined had to be psychometrically tested to identify cultural fit. Part of the process was to have a psychometric personality test completed. Upon receiving the results, the consultant called Richard into his office to review the results. "He unpacked my psychological profile, turned to me and said, 'Richard, you're made to be a consultant, not work in industry. I think once you've made the move into consultancy, never move back.'" Hearing these words must have been reassuring, as his transition to consulting was not easy.

He had come a long way from his first role in the energy sector in Southampton. After over 15 years in the private sector, he joined Accenture, moved to Capgemini, then to PwC. At the time of writing, he held the role of partner at KPMG. His rapid ascent through the ranks of the most renowned consulting organisations is a testament to his personality, wit, and ability to adapt.

A tall, boisterous man, Richard always reminded me of a football coach, yelling instructions across the pitch one moment, laughing and joking with his team at the pub in the next. In the times we worked together, I was impressed by his engaging personality and, at times, self-deprecating humour. He was never one to shy away from a joke and always in a good spirit. He also had an uncanny ability to forget the names of stakeholders, even though he may have been reminded of them numerous times before. While his easy-going approach helped to quickly put stakeholders at ease, he was also very structured and able to adapt to changing circumstances without ever losing his cool.

Richard joined British Gas straight out of university on a graduate programme after completing an engineering degree. "It was enjoyable times; I did lot's of diverse things," Richard recalled. He initially worked with commercial contracts before moving on to helping launch the first natural gas vehicle fleets, tackling a diverse set of challenges, including identifying engine manufacturers, bus manufacturers, and logistics, including how the fleet would be re-fuelled. He went on to work on new energy products, developing geo-fuel offerings, and running the pre-payment business. Around that time, there was a change of leadership. "It was at that stage that I really looked around, having probably done everything that the company could offer me. It was either doing more of the same or go and do something different. That's when I was approached by the former marketing director of British Gas who had joined Accenture. He said, 'You'd love this,' and that's when I moved into consultancy properly."

As someone who had spent his entire career until that point in the private sector, joining Accenture as a senior manager was not easy. He noted, "It's rapidly the most difficult and disorientating move that you'll ever make in your life."

"To go from 'this is your role', 'this is your place in the structure', 'this is what you do' and scope defined, into the wild west of consultancy. It's a very disorientating move," Richard reminisced. "I remember my first engagement because it was with an energy company in Ireland. I remember not realising the standard expected of consultancy deliverables. We had a stakeholder meeting, and I remember talking to my primary client contact saying, 'Look, we're not quite ready, are you comfortable if we just go with an early draft of thinking?'"

"My client contact said, 'Yes, no problem at all. That's fine. We'll go; this is a gatepost in the project. No problem at all.' Of course, we presented it, and the COO went ballistic due to the lack of quality of thinking. I was expecting my client to sort of come in and say, 'No, this is what we expected to do,' but there was just tumbleweed silence. You suddenly go, 'Oh, sh*t, this is one of those learnings as you're on the job, where you suddenly realise every single interaction has to be really high quality.' The pace of work and the rest of it has to be much higher for consultants, which takes a little bit of adjustment. So that was a bit of a learning curve. It only happened once, but that was the kick in the a** that you sort of get every now and then."

Aside from a few inevitable early stumbles, he adjusted to consulting life and grew into his role at Accenture, leading digital, operating model transformation and customer analytics projects. However, while he found the work engaging and rewarding, his previous life in industry did not prepare him for the intricacies of advancing within the consulting organisation structure.

Compared to many other industries, the way to progress from one grade to another is a lot more involved in consulting. It can be a very nuanced and complicated process, from the way we shape our stories, to our relationships with our people managers and partners, to the different performance indicators. It all culminates in a series of moderation sessions, typically held twice a year that are a ritual in their own right. It's a complex process and one that Richard was not exposed to in his previous life in industry.

After five and a half years with Accenture as a senior manager, he joined Capgemini for a brief stint before going onto PwC in 2014 as a director. In 2018 he was offered a partner role with KPMG, and, as he recalled, "When you get offered a partnership, it's tough to turn them down."

"I enjoy the pressure," Richard said, reflecting on his career in consulting and what kept him engaged. "You have to be leading edge in terms of your thought leadership; you're doing things that hadn't been done before. Because if you're bringing things that have already been done to clients, they're not particularly interested. I think all those sorts of things are really enjoyable. Working with really bright people; it's a really stimulating environment to be in. I've enjoyed the teams I've worked in, I like the variety and all that kept me refreshed and hungry, I suppose. You need to be fresh and hungry, I think, to survive in consultancy environments."

With his affable, good-humoured nature, Richard has successfully navigated the challenges of moving from industry to consulting, where he has achieved considerable success. In addition to working with an impressive list of global clients, he also makes sure to find time to help others navigate the often challenging waters of career progression.

"I am not a product of my circumstances.
I am a product of my decisions."

Stephen Covey

# Progression

As evidenced by the stories shared in this book, there is no definitive way by which to enter the world of consulting. Some people will join straight out of university. Others will work elsewhere before moving into consulting. Others still may go back to school to pursue an MBA before making the switch. While there are many avenues that lead to consulting, the choice to specialise and how to specialise are questions each consultant will need to consider, no matter their grade.

Jon Hughes, whose own career in consulting spans over two decades, received some excellent advice when he was starting out. "If you imagine a Rubik's cube," he said, "it's a three-dimensional cube of knowledge, and you look at all three dimensions. One dimension of the cube would be, 'What do you want to be?' Do you want to become an expert in procurement, finance, operations, or marketing, or sales, or whatever? The business process set you want to become part of; each of those represents one square in that dimension."

"Another dimension might be industry, so pharmaceuticals, financial services, government—God-forbid. So that would be the second dimension. Then the third dimension, which is around consulting again. Do you want to do organisational change? Do you want to do IT? Do you want to do performance management? If you combine those three axes together, you end up with the cube, and the choice you really have to make fairly early on is do you want to be a specialist in one single cube? So, for example, 'I want to be the number-one process expert in financial services for operations', or do you want to actually have a broader-based view of the world? The disadvantage of the former approach is that you tend to get pigeonholed quite easily, but it's relatively straightforward if you've chosen the right parameters to get a role somewhere, but it can be restricting."

## Illustrative facets of consulting focus

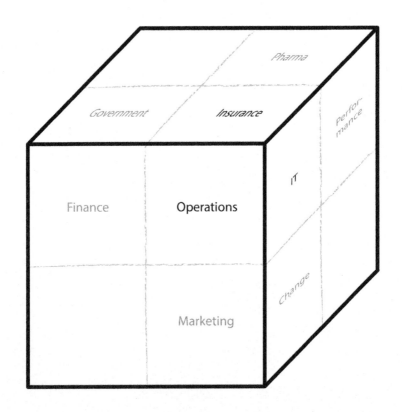

"My advice would be, from my own experience, to try and be as fungible as possible, but maybe stick to a couple of areas where you think you're going to have good traction," Jon suggested. Thinking of his own career, he took a similar approach. "Yeah, so, from a business point of view, it was really financial services of a vertical market where I spent a lot of time. Process re-engineering was an add-on to my IT skills, with a stretch being organisational change. From a business process point of view within the organisation, it was pretty generic; everything from strategy through to support services."

Possessing deep knowledge in a specific process or industry can be a useful differentiator, particularly when that process or industry is in high demand within client engagements. It may also serve as a branding opportunity, particularly early on in a consulting career, when being able to proclaim, "I am a blockchain expert," for example, may open doors and opportunities to network. In time, additional adjacent squares will begin to fill up, either through intentional upskilling or through exposure on client engagements.

"I was trying to add skills around things like change management and organisational design as the next step of filling up my cube," Jon recalled of his own endeavour to expand his knowledge base. He may have started his career with a narrow specialism, which served him well at the time, but over the course of his career he expanded his understanding. "I didn't understand enough about how businesses works. I knew how the IT function works. One of the big shortfalls I had in my IT career was I didn't really understand how to talk to an HR director or certain types of individuals in organisations because my knowledge of business wasn't good enough. One of the reasons I actually took my MBA was to broaden out my understanding of a business model."

"I think that as a foundation stone for a young consultant, understanding how business works and how the bits fit together is a really important thing. Again, it makes you more fungible."

"It also helps you if you're doing larger-scale transformation or re-engineering, which I tended to do, because I knew that if I couldn't solve a problem in IT, I might be able to solve it through some HR-related approach or vice versa. Understanding how business actually interconnects is really important, particularly now with digital transformation, because you are changing people, process and technology. You need to understand the ripple effect of that change on the rest of the organisation. So that fundamental understanding of how the business fits together is really important."

"I entered the world of consulting from a technical delivery side." Jon noted, "Interestingly, other areas of my cube began to materialise over time. For example, my focus shifted towards strategy, transformation, and innovation with an increased focus on human-centred experience design. When it came to industry alignment, my background had been in telecommunications, mobile, start-ups, and agencies. Through my work in consulting, new squares began to materialise on my proverbial cube as I worked in a variety of industries, from financial services and energy to hospitality and FMCG. When it came to digital skills, I began to expand my knowledge into automation, artificial intelligence, and architecture. Over time, I've simultaneously had some of the squares become a lot deeper, while others have begun to gradually materialise."

As consultants, we will never be experts at all things. However, we can be experts at a few things in a few industries and expand our understanding of associated topics over time. For new consultants, in particular, it's worth considering the industries that are of interest and what areas and functions of consulting are the most desirable. It is then a matter of taking the necessary steps to align ourselves there, build out our network, and deepen our knowledge in those areas and industries. They will open the door to new opportunities. In time, sometimes organically, other squares will begin to materialise, creating a potent mix of deep expert knowledge and holistic awareness.

# Moderation

"I would describe it as the religion of calibration, or moderation, or whatever the organisation calls it," Richard Hepworth noted, reflecting on the career progression system within most consulting organisations. "Where you are ranked and where you are rated, and how does that play out? When you start, you have this thing called a people manager (PM) or career counsellor. You think they are people to help you. What you don't realise is that eventually, your people managers are going to represent you in a moderation process. So, your relationship is not like a mentee; it's like a direct report relationship. That is not necessarily explained to you from the get-go. Again, when you first go into the moderation process, it is a complete eye-opener. It is completely unique."

"The first thing for people joining organisations is to understand the metrics of your grade properly. All right, how are you going to be assessed? Because, at the end of the day, I've worked there in Accenture, Capgemini, PwC, KPMG, and they all have essentially the same matrix; utilisation is number one. Number two, it's all about sales and understanding how you get sales credit changes significantly within different organisations. The third one is what I call the tiebreakers, which is practice development and, I call them hobbies, but what you're doing around thought leadership. Anybody joining a consultancy has to understand they have to work on all those three metrics. Obviously, the sales metrics become more important the more senior you get. So, when you first join, it is all about utilisation."

When I first joined Accenture many years ago, that was also one of the first valuable pieces of advice I received. Someone told me, "Just get on a project." Following the advice, I was fortunate to join an exciting project in London's Canary Wharf shortly after joining. There is an ever-present danger, however, that if new consultants do not actively seek out interesting projects to join, they will be put on projects that may not be aligned to their ambitions, in very far-flung, undesirable locations.

Richard continued, "You have to start thinking about what your story is going to be at the end of the year. How are you going to do that? I just talked to somebody the other day, where they were told that they could do this big BD [business development] project and it didn't work out. Then, at year-end, it's still all about utilisation, and they feel let down and all the rest of it. So, understanding the metrics, understanding where they're recorded, and understanding how your people manager is going to present you and how the league tables are going to run out. It's really important."

The advice that I've given to new consultants is that performing at grade level is never enough if the ambition is to be promoted. While at Genpact, one of the side-projects I took on was to lead the effort to define grade-level objectives for the newly formed digital team. As part of that exercise, the criteria for promotion were discussed at length. As Richard pointed out, factors such as utilisation and business development contributions were inescapable. Next were things such as personal and practice development, thought leadership contributions, and other ancillary contributions.

For all these considerations, the guidance became that as long as a candidate exhibited traits that were a level above their grade, they would be considered for promotion to that grade. Therefore, if promotion is the objective, we should introspectively consider how we are performing, our utilisation and business development metrics, and what traits we are exhibiting, not compared to others amongst our own grade, but with our colleagues a grade above us.

Regardless of grade level, there are five areas to keep in mind throughout the year when it comes to preparing for moderation:

### Grade-level objectives
Ensure that utilisation and business development targets are met or, ideally, exceeded.

### Ancillary contributions
Activities undertaken for the betterment of the organisation, personal development, and the development of others.

### Strong network
Regardless of industry or focus area, it always helps when people know who you are.

### Personal brand
In addition to knowing who you are, ensure your network knows what you are about and what knowledge or skills you contribute.

### Good story
There is not much time in moderation to review each candidate, so it's helpful to wrap all accomplishments into a compelling story or narrative.

"These organisations are relentless," Richard continued, "They give you fantastic opportunities, but the one thing that I think everybody struggles with in this place, is that people must have a career plan and vision about where they want to move their career to. Otherwise, you'll end up being a victim of the resourcing tombola. One of the things that breaks my heart, especially for the new graduates, is they do everything we just talked about, but because they get so fixated on that, they lose direction. If you know what direction you want to take, it gives you an option, and it gives you that conversation that says, 'Can I please go on that project because that's where I want to go.' There are occasional projects or clients that people don't want to work on, and you take one for the team, but you can say, 'Next time there is an opportunity, this is where I want my brand to go.' That's the way that people build their own brand and their own market positioning for their short, medium, and long term careers; so that they know where they're going."

"I think too often when graduates come in, they say, 'I don't know what I want to do, I'm just going to go through it and do those projects. My ambitions to be a senior manager or director in five years' time.' It's not good enough. I always ask that question, when people work for me, 'Where do you want to go?' Sometimes they don't know that. I'd also want to ask them about their broader life direction, 'Where is the balance between your home, your life, your family, your travel ambitions, your other ambitions?' and 'Where does work fit into that?' I don't think we talk enough about these things."

Richard cautioned that there are two things that people managers (PMs) need to look out for. "One, have really honest conversations. It's too easy to say, 'Oh, you're so close for promotion in this next year, you're a shoo-in for next round.' That always ends in disappointment. Stop that language and be honest. The second thing is the PM should have a more direct role or try and intervene to get them resourced on the right projects. I think there's a real obligation of these organisations and the PM to champion it, to make sure that their people are getting the right opportunities. If they're not being staffed on projects, find out why not, and make sure that you get an environment, a project, to get them on. A good PM should be giving them some resources."

The moderation season is one of the most nerve-wracking times of the year for all involved. For candidates hoping to gain promotion, for the people managers that represent them, and for the partners that fully acknowledge the ramifications of the decisions being made in the moderation sessions. In addition to meeting or exceeding the utilisation, business development targets, and ancillary contributions targets, both consultants and their people managers need to develop compelling stories that will help them stand out from the crowd. While success is never guaranteed, with a good story, hard work, effective networking, and a cohesive plan, the probability of success is dramatically increased.

# Promotion

"In consulting, you experience quite an accelerated career in general," commented Melissa Max-Macarthy of Accenture. "You are put under an immense amount of pressure, and it's generally seen as being more intense than a non-consultant role. You learn as you go. As a consultant, you must know things, and if you don't know, you need to learn it very, very quickly. One of the things that I think consulting firms do rightly or wrongly is to dangle promotion in front of you. The next level is always just in front of you, keeping you hungry for it. They built a culture that supports that. What we don't talk about enough is going for promotion and missing it; how that makes individuals feel and how those perceived failures can be the things that propel you in the future."

"I'd worked harder than I'd ever worked in my life. I had been dealing with the biggest projects and with really, really senior clients," Melissa recalled of a time when she was vying for a promotion to manager. Unfortunately, her people manager set unrealistic expectations, suggesting that her promotion was inevitable in that cycle. For Melissa, the promotion would mean the validation of her hard work, and the substantial salary increase would allow her to afford a flat in London.

"I was trying to be quite strategic," Melissa admitted. "I had this quite senior director who really didn't know me and didn't really understand what I did. I don't know how he represented me, but I don't feel that he managed my expectations properly. It shouldn't be a shock if you're not going to get promoted. You should have an understanding of that beforehand, just to manage expectations and good people managers need to do that. So, with my own people that I manage, they know where they are in the process and can appreciate that sometimes it's due to a variety of factors. Sometimes you probably have about six months more to learn and that's okay. At that point, I did have about six months more to learn, but that wasn't communicated in any way, shape or form. That was, I think, where the problem came in."

She continued, "I remember getting the call in November of 2015 and him saying, 'Really sorry, but you weren't successful, but don't worry, you're a slam dunk for mid-year.' Honestly, I just cried. I wanted to be strong on the phone, but it was like waterworks as soon as I put the phone down. I called my brother, and I was just like, 'I failed. I can't believe I failed. I don't fail. This is not right.' I was not in a good place. It was a failure, and I wasn't able to get past that. I had to do quite a bit mentally to get myself in the right place. There's one quote often attributed to Winston Churchill that I read that I really loved. It said, 'Success consists of going from failure to failure without loss of enthusiasm.' I remember taking that and telling myself that no one ever succeeded without failing first."

At the time, Melissa was understandably upset and reached to her mentor. Her mentor listened to her detail the situation, how low she felt and how she had considered leaving the organisation. Her mentor then took a pause and replied, "I'm sorry to hear this. It's really hard missing promotions. We've all been there. But one question before you make a dramatic decision: are you still learning? Because if you're still learning, you're still growing." Mel took a moment to consider the statement, realised she was still learning and decided to stay. She's used that as a barometer within her own life and with her mentees ever since. She acknowledged failure as part of her journey, reframing her approach to failure as not the opposite of success but rather as a part of it.

Regardless of the organisation or industry alignment, career progression within consulting is a complex and, at times, bewildering experience. However, by understanding the metrics, finding a good people manager, having a clear objective and telling a compelling story, we will be in a better position to succeed.

Melissa concluded, "I'm sure everyone says this, but it's a marathon, not a sprint. That has helped me frame my thinking as I've got up in the ranks."

"It's not what you achieve, it's what you overcome.
That's what defines your career."

Carlton Fisk

# Andy Woodfield

"If I wanted to be an actor, I would have tried my best to go to RADA," Andy confessed, referring to the Royal Academy of Dramatic Art as we were discussing the question of authenticity.

"I've never been very good at pretending to be someone or something I'm not. What I am is someone who is curious, able to bring people together, someone who can acquire new skills, who can listen, hear and understand people, someone who accepts that failure is part of not the opposite of success, and these things I've found help me to move teams, clients, organisations, projects, people, forwards, but we always do it together."

Andy grew up in Dorset, a picturesque county in southwest England. His family ran a car dealership, where he had his first experience of watching a business grow. His mother also bred German Shepherd dogs, meaning Andy has a lot of fond memories of being surrounded by puppies, chasing him and nibbling his ears.

Never deeply academic, he always found it difficult to focus at school. Thankfully, he knew how to make people laugh. Through laughter, he connected with others and discovered the power of human connection to drive change. He moved to Southampton, where he studied Computer Science for five years before the siren call of the big city became too alluring to ignore.

"I decided to move to London because if you're 'the only gay in the village', as I felt I was at the time, the only option back then was to move to the big city. I got a job with a small technology company in the City of London, which was very exciting. I loved it."

By 1998, Andy was ready for a new challenge. Having spent the first part of his working life with smaller organisations, he wanted to experience what it would be like to work for a big company and a big brand. He joined Price Waterhouse a few months prior to the merger with Coopers & Lybrand, giving him a front-row seat to one of the largest mergers in the industry at that time. He thrived in his newfound surroundings. The scale of PwC offered a never-ending series of new challenges and opportunities for personal growth. He concluded, "I realised that I was never getting bored because there was always a new client, a new project, a new problem to solve. I started to realise; this is what I love."

Reflecting on what made him successful over his 23-year long career with PwC, Andy noted, "If you can build relationships with your clients and your teams, if they all enjoy working with you, if together you can help your clients solve their problems, and build sustainable outcomes, then you're done, that's the job. Of course, you need to bring in revenue to the firm, that's a given, but that usually follows if you focus on helping to solve our client's important problem and creating an environment where people want to work with you".

Andy's career has been an interesting one as he's been with PwC for over 23 years, a long time to remain with one firm. Perhaps the reason he was able to build such a long-lasting, successful career within one organisation is that he has continued to challenge himself while always remaining true to who he is. Through that authenticity, he has made strong, trusted connections within the organisation, with his clients and within the many communities and individuals he supports. His willingness to go out of his way to help others, speak up for inclusion and diversity, and his straight-talking approach has endeared him to many who are quick to sing his praises. Through his tireless work ethic, high levels of self-confidence, and the expansive networks he's created, he continues to change the organisations he works with from within, all for the better.

"We need to resist the tyranny of low expectations. We need to open our eyes to the inequality that remains. We won't unlock the full potential of the workplace until we see how far from equality we really are."

Sheryl Sandberg

# Diversity

It was my first week at the consulting firm, and I was very excited. My new role was a significant step up the ladder from the previous organisation, and I was eager to make a great first impression. I reached out across the group, introduced myself to the partners and directors, and was on a mission to find my first project. It was then that I began speaking with one of the partners about a digital strategy piece of work for a renowned historical members club located in the centre of London. It was an exciting opportunity to make a name for myself, network within the group, and begin to collect precious chargeable hours. Success with the client could mean other workstreams of activity and an opportunity to build a team. It was also an illustrious, very high-profile members club, meaning the project would entail networking amongst some of the most successful people in the city. I couldn't wait to get started. Alongside the partner, another consultant and I visited the members club, made the introductions, and formulated a strategy for best achieving the client's objectives. It became apparent that, at least for the first phase of work, there was no room in the budget for two consultants.

The partner would have to choose between the other consultant and me. Without any bias, of course, I believed I was the right person for the job, as I had worked on similar engagements and understood the client. The partner considered both alternatives and called me into his office. He explained that both the other consultant and I were well suited for the project and evenly matched. However, because the client was very old-school English, he felt that the other consultant would be a better fit, as he was also very English, proper Queen's English accent and intonations included. I was taken aback for a moment, not fully processing what he had just said. Then it hit me. He simply didn't think I was "English enough" for the client. As I made my way back to my desk and had a chance to process the interaction further, I became increasingly uncomfortable with what had occurred. I was also faced with the daunting question of what to do next. Should I let it go? Should I say something? After all, I was still in my first weeks at the new company. Did I really want to rock the boat?

As I considered the options, I knew I had to say something. I wrote an email to the partner, making it very clear that I took objection to his rationale. Had the decision to choose the other consultant been made on merit, I was more than happy to accept the decision. However, I stated that my being English or not being English wouldn't play a role in my ability to effectively build relationships or deliver against the plan. Not five minutes passed after I sent the email before the partner replied with a one-line message to come and see him.

Back in his office, the partner danced around the subject and told me that I should come to him directly rather than send emails if I had issues with what he said. I suspect that his urging was primarily motivated by the fact that he realised what he had done and was nervous that the event would place him in a very unfavourable light if human resources were to become involved. It was infuriating, but at that time, not wanting to make more of an issue, I let it go and joined a different project. To the surprise of no one, the partner in question did not last long at the firm.

As an immigrant twice over, first to Germany and then to Canada at the age of nine, the incident brought back painful memories of when I had experienced xenophobia, classism, and bullying. Now I was dealing with a similar situation in a professional setting within the first weeks of joining a new firm that espoused the values of equality, tolerance, and acceptance. No matter how disappointing this particular incident was, I was also cognizant that my own experiences in dealing with prejudice paled in comparison to the experiences of some of my friends and colleagues.

Writing a chapter on inclusion and diversity as a white man becomes somewhat complicated by the fact that I am very aware of how privileged my life has been. Regardless of the challenges I've faced along the way, I'm conscious of how many situations I've encountered throughout my life where being a tall, white, reasonably decent looking (at least according to my mother) man has gotten me out of trouble or provided me with preferential treatment or opportunities that others may not have received. I'm also aware of the bigger picture relating to the gender pay gap, the race pay gap, and their historical and ongoing, systemic contributing factors.

For example, in 2019, CMI reported that eight out of 10 British companies paid men more than women.[111] Meanwhile, if pay growth continues for female executives at current rates, the gap between the earnings of female and male executives would not be closed until 2109. Another UK study found that the Big Four firms had an average racial pay gap of 13.4% and a bonus gap of 37.9%.[113] In addition to a slew of historical contributing factors, there are also many systemic challenges that need to be overcome in order to create a more equitable society. Prejudices exist in society, and while their effects may be experienced by some more than others, the fact that they exist at all is a detriment to the social fabric and our aspiration for a prosperous and just future. It also means that all of us, no matter our gender, identity or race, need to fight for that future. Even if we are not directly affected by a specific destructive "-ism", we need to be allies, supporters, and cheerleaders of those that are.

As Angela Davis, famed educator and activist, once said, "It is not enough to be non-racist, we must be anti-racist." In the same vein, we cannot only be non-sexist, we must be anti-sexist. We must be against all forms of prejudice and discrimination within ourselves and in vocal opposition when needed. As consultants, we must aspire to that ideal, as through it, we will improve our organisations and our communities. As leaders, we will be the ones that set the tone for our teams. They will look up to us and take cues from us based on what we say, how we act, and how we react.

Martin Luther King Jr. once said that "the arc of the moral universe is long, but it bends toward justice." It is up to us, collectively, to help guide that arc. In order to do so, it is essential to acknowledge the past and think about what steps we can take to create a more inclusive, diverse, and just society.

# Past

In the cinematic masterpiece *Back to the Future*, a young Marty McFly, played by the extraordinary Canadian actor Michael J. Fox, travels back in time to November 5, 1955, using a modified DeLorean. While the movie itself is thoroughly enjoyable, highlighting the cultural and technological differences between 1955 and Marty's original time in 1985, it conveniently glosses over some of the complexities Marty would have encountered. While 1955 was, relatively speaking, not a very long time ago, the world was a much different place then. In fact, the 1950s offer a convenient marker to gain a glimpse of where we've come from.

Cultural artefacts from the '50s, remind us how astonishingly sexist our entertainment and advertising industries were back then. A 1952 magazine ad for Chase & Sanborn coffee, for instance, shows a man preparing to spank a woman whom he's thrown across his lap. "If your husband ever finds out you're not 'store testing' for fresher coffee …" reads the ad copy, "woe be unto you."

In the UK, just 1.2% of women attended university in the 1950s, while in the US, women accounted for only about one-third of the total labour force.[114] Many teachers and parents would limit expectations for girls, suggesting their destiny be marriage, with work only as an interim measure between leaving school and walking down the aisle, rather than a career.

In 1954, in the landmark Brown v. Board of Education case, the US Supreme Court declared that "separate educational facilities" for Black children were "inherently unequal."[115] The ruling was not without opposition, with many Southern whites resisted the ruling. They withdrew their children from public schools and enrolled them in all-white "segregation academies," and they used violence and intimidation to prevent people of colour from asserting their rights. In 1956, more than 100 Southern congressmen even signed a "Southern Manifesto" declaring that they would do all they could to defend segregation.

Rampant racism was an ever-present part of life. In December of 1955, a Montgomery activist named Rosa Parks was arrested for refusing to give her seat on a city bus to a white person. This was at a time when the average African American household income was only 55% ($2,890) of that of white households ($5,228).[116] Meanwhile, in the UK, immigrants that arrived in the country could not find accommodation and were ineligible for council housing, as only those living in the UK for a minimum of five years qualified. At the time, there was no anti-discrimination legislation preventing landlords from refusing to accept tenants. Slum lords would take advantage, charging significantly more than they did white tenants, while offering extremely overcrowded, poorly maintained accommodation.[117]

In addition to sexism and racism, the 1950s were also notoriously hostile to the LGBT+ community. In 1952, Sir John Nott-Bower, commissioner of Scotland Yard, began to weed out homosexuals from the British Government at the same time as McCarthy was conducting a federal homosexual witch hunt in the US.

During the early 1950s, as many as 1,000 men were locked into Britain's prisons every year amid a widespread police clampdown on homosexual offences. In 1953, President Dwight Eisenhower signed Executive Order 10450, banning homosexuals from working for the federal government or any of its private contractors. The Order listed homosexuals as security risks, alongside alcoholics and neurotics. In 1954, Alan Turing, the English mathematician, logician, cryptanalyst and computer scientist, influential in the development of computer science, committed suicide. He had been given a course of female hormones (chemical castration) by doctors as an alternative to prison after being prosecuted by the police because of his homosexuality.[118]

Had the protagonist of *Back to the Future* been a woman, a person of colour, or a homosexual, it would have made for a much different and much more challenging movie. The world they would have encountered in 1955 would not have been the uncomplicated, filtered portrayal we saw in the movie, but a much more hostile and repressive place. Considerable progress has been made since, of course, but that progress has been hard-fought, fiercely opposed by some, and still ongoing.

Deep-rooted structural inequalities continue to reverberate for decades if not addressed through meaningful reform and restitution. Displacement, exclusion, and segregation have had profound and prolonged impacts on issues ranging from wealth inequality, housing, and healthcare, to education, employment and disparities in legal protection. Understanding the historical context of these issues will help us understand and appreciate their ongoing butterfly effects.

It is also worth noting that not all countries have seen the same progress in attitudes, policies, and laws as the US or the UK. Some countries continue to suffer racist violence, sexist laws, or repressive LBGT+ policies. Some politicians continue to use dangerous rhetoric when stoking fears or blaming "the other" for their own political gain. These are only further reasons why we must strive to set an example of why love trumps hate.

As the American poet Maya Angelou so eloquently stated, "I have great respect for the past. If you don't know where you've come from, you don't know where you're going." The same is true when discussing questions of diversity, inclusivity, and justice in relation to the world of consulting. Acknowledging the past allows us to understand the context of the present to be able to map out a better path forward.

# Progress

"I was born in Northern Ireland in 1977, when same-sex relationships were unlawful. One of the first political slogans that I can remember was 'Save Ulster from Sodomy.' It was not until 1982, after the European Court of Human Rights ruled against the UK that gay men were decriminalised across the whole of the UK," Steven Friel recounted of the shifts in public attitude towards LGBT+ over his lifetime and his personal experiences along the way in a blog post for PwC.[119]

Steven met his love in New York in July 2005, but at that time, marriage was not an option for them on either side of the Atlantic. By December 2005, the UK allowed LGBT+ couples to enter civil partnerships. It was not until 2014 that they were able to "upgrade" to marriage.

While significant progress has been made over the years, Stonewall research in the UK shows that nearly 50% of LGBT+ young people are bullied for being themselves at school, and 20% of LGBT+ people have reported being the victim of a hate crime or incident. Five percent of LGBT+ people have been pressured to access potentially harmful gay conversion "therapies" and services, and LGBT+ youth are at a significantly higher risk of suicide.

Likewise, while a lot has changed for the better in terms of diversity, consulting firms continue to be predominantly white and predominantly male. According to a report by DAMI, about 73% of consulting firms' employees are white, and so are 80% of their owners and partners.[120]

In the US, Black people account for approximately 12% of the population but occupy only 3.2% of the senior leadership roles at large companies and just 0.8% of all Fortune 500 CEO positions, according to CTI, a workplace think tank in New York City.[121] The study also found that about 65% of people of colour said they have to work harder to advance, compared to only 16% of white employees. Meanwhile, according to a Gallup poll on racial discrimination, Black and Hispanic employees were much more likely (24%) to state they felt discriminated against than the national average (18%).[122]

Meanwhile, a 2018 Fawcett Society study showed that one in three men and women are unaware that pay discrimination is illegal. The findings demonstrate that many UK men and women are oblivious to sex discrimination and equal pay discrepancies. In a sample of 81 US consulting firms, it was found that while female professionals accounted for 39% of the total workforce, female partners only accounted for 17% of total partners. According to a Pew Research Centre survey in 2017, about 42% of working women in the United States reported that they had faced discrimination on their job because of their gender.[123] While much progress has been made over the past decades, it is clear that more needs to be done in the name of diversity and inclusion within consulting organisations and society as a whole.

# Cover

"The journey to being an inclusive organisation feels like a 48,000-step program, it feels like we've made great progress at PwC, but we're really still just on step four," Andy Woodfield explained. "My biggest fear for many organisations is that they are starting to look more diverse, but if you're different and don't act like a heterosexual, white man, then you'll find it hard to be successful. We have to challenge ourselves to ensure we are not just coaching and mentoring diverse individuals to fit into the existing system; we need to listen to diverse individuals and learn from them how to change the system so they can be successful as themselves."

Legal scholar Kenji Yoshino described covering as any activity used "to tone down a disfavored identity to fit into the mainstream."[124] In a Deloitte study, 61% of respondents reported that they engaged in covering behaviour while at work. The study indicated that 83% of LBGT+ employees, 79% of Black employees, 66% of female employees, 63% of Hispanic employees, and 45% of straight white men reported engaging in covering behaviour.[125]

Kenji Yoshito described four common ways in which people would cover in the workplace:

### Appearance
Includes any activities that someone might take to appear "normal" or not stand out. For example, older people choosing to dye their hair regularly to blend in with their younger co-workers.

### Affiliation
Focuses on engaging in or refraining from behaviours specifically to avoid being labelled with common stereotypes. Consider a female employee who will avoid mentioning that she has children only to refrain from playing into the stereotype that she is less available than her single or childless co-workers.

### Advocacy
Relates to how vocal an employee might be when discussing a class or group to which they belong. For example, new parents being worried about proposing working from home or flexible working arrangements.

### Association
Manifested by an employee actively avoiding other members of their "group", such as when a gay employee avoids bringing their significant other to an after-hours work function to avoid appearing "too gay."

Authenticity is important, as it helps us be more comfortable and confident in our surroundings while allowing us to build closer, more trusted relationships. This is why it's important to create environments that reduce the likelihood that anyone will feel the need to engage in covering behaviour.

Dorie Clark and Christie Smith discussed five strategies to help people uncover in the *Harvard Business Review*:

### Shift the language

When corporations talk about "diversity," a significant chunk of the population tunes out. But if you introduce the concept of "covering"—downplaying or hiding certain aspects of yourself so as not to appear different—the conversations shift. Everyone can relate to the term because most people have done it at some point in their career, and it permits a new dialogue on your team about differences. It's a small but subtle change that ensures everyone recognizes they're a part of the discussion.

### Share your story

We know leaders set the tenor for an organization's culture. If you want your employees to feel safe sharing their stories, you have to step up and tell your own. Whether or not you're part of a traditional "minority" group, most of us have had experiences related to covering, whether we faced it ourselves or witnessed it in someone close to us. Start the dialogue and let others know it's OK to do the same.

### Embrace analytics

Companies could consider developing an Inclusion Index, as Deloitte has done. This tracks the hiring and promotion practices of each partner, across several specific slices of diversity. Tracking hard data holds departments, and the leaders in them, accountable for their actions when it comes to inclusion.

### Force the conversation

In the Deloitte Uncovering Talent study, 93% of professionals surveyed said their companies had stated a commitment to inclusion—but only 78% said their company lived up to it.[122] Making time for hard conversations now can help prevent serious reputation damage later.

### Look beyond the obvious

Conversations about "diversity" often focus on one element of a person—their race, their gender, their sexuality—to the exclusion of all else. But overwhelmingly, professionals don't want to be defined by a single dimension of their identity. Managers can help their employees "uncover" at work by recognizing that everyone has differences, and those differences represent only a part of who they are as individuals.[126]

Andy added, "Organisations need to review the way they recruit, and there's a lot of work that's been done in that space, and particularly in strength-based, capability-based recruitment, as opposed to trying to recruit people just like you. It tends to be more successful at the actual graduate and more junior grades. Most people recruit in their likeness, so unless you use a strengths approach and unless you have a diverse group of people involved in recruitment, you will probably just keep hiring the same kind of people, they might look different, but they will often think and behave in a consistent way. That's not diversity, and it's certainly not inclusion, it's sameness and conformity. All of that leads to an organisation that can become increasingly irrelevant in it's chosen market."

"Leaders really should be building networks of people that don't look like them and don't think like them, and then you can recruit from that network. The reality is that diverse candidates do exist; there are lots of very interesting and different candidates out there if you look in the right places. If you don't bother to look you won't find them."

Contrary to what we may have been taught in school, conformity is not conducive to success. According to a quote often misattributed to Albert Einstein, "Everyone is a genius. But if you judge a fish by its ability to climb a tree, it will live its whole life believing that it is stupid."

Every one of us has a myriad of strengths and areas of improvement, which is why diversity in teams is essential. Complementary skill sets, different backgrounds, and a multitude of insights will form more robust, more empowered, and more innovative teams. Effective leaders will strive to understand and embrace the differences amongst their teams. They will celebrate each team member's unique traits rather than focusing on their weaknesses. To put it in other words, they would never force a fish to climb a tree and criticise it when it failed but would instead identify and celebrate its incredible swimming abilities. It is up to all of us to create more inclusive organisations that allow people to be comfortable being themselves. Therefore, we should identify opportunities for improvement and apply pressure on leadership and hiring managers. Together, we will devise strategies that will result in more diverse and inclusive organisations wherein people don't feel pressured to cover up who they are.

# Future

All consulting organisations have made loud public claims regarding their inclusion and diversity initiatives. While commendable in their intentions, the sad fact is that there is a long way to go. In 2020, an investigation by *The Telegraph* in the UK found that just 11 of Big Four accounting firms' 3,000 partners were Black. Meanwhile, in 2019, the number of women in senior-vice-president positions was only approximately 28%, and 21% in the C-suite.[127] Though the numbers were progressing slightly upward, women remain dramatically underrepresented, especially women of colour. It is then unsurprising that a study from Boston Consulting Group found that nearly half of workers in Britain believed employers had not progressed on their Diversity and Inclusion (D&I) goals.[128]

As consultants and leaders, it is therefore incumbent on us to acknowledge that while progress has been made, there is more to be done. Those of us who are in positions of privilege have a moral obligation to do as much as we can to promote diversity and inclusion. We need to continue asking what we can we do to become more inclusive leaders.

As a vocal advocate for diversity and inclusion, Andy Woodfield compiled a list of 10 items for leaders to consider in their efforts to become more inclusive:

### You are going to get this wrong

That's okay, but you do need to accept that you will get this wrong and shouldn't pretend to have all the answers.

### You need to park your pride and your ego

Be prepared to listen, hear, and learn from others.

### Whatever you think you're doing, it's not enough

If you think you're doing more than anyone else, you're not. Even if you are, it doesn't matter; this isn't about you. It's about people who don't look and sound like you, so move the spotlight onto them and keep learning.

### You will need to take what feels like lots of risks and do things differently

Doing what you've always done hasn't worked for inclusion, so get used to feeling uncomfortable about recruitment, mobilising teams, performance management, and promotions. Know that the feeling of risk is there just because you're doing something that's different from before; it's all good.

**You will not be rewarded, nor should you be**

In all of your work to promote, mandate, speak up, and take action on inclusion, you are simply rebalancing a system that has been skewed for hundreds of years. Making sure everyone has a fair chance, fair access to work, and a fair opportunity in all respects is a fundamental human right. It's the absolute minimum you would expect for yourself; now it's just time you deliver it for others.

**It's your job to create the environment**

One conducive for those that are different from you to succeed, to enable the unlocking of their potential. It's not their job to come to you and perform for you against your processes and measures. These have all been designed to recognise, promote, and reward people who look and sound like you. Remember that what worked for you will most likely not work for people who are not like you.

**It's okay to feel uncomfortable about inclusion**

It's not okay to talk about your discomfort; you can't make this about you. Now it's time to use the platform you have to ensure the focus is on those who didn't have access to the things you had. Yes, you are privileged and that's okay; it's not your fault. It is your choice, however, to use that privilege for something that might make a difference; that might make you proud.

**You will need to find allies and coaches**

To give you strength on this journey and to challenge you, you need to connect with people that you trust, but not just people who are just like you. You can't do this with the same people you've always surrounded yourself with. Ask for help to find the right support system to keep you strong and focused. It's okay to ask for help; that's what great, inclusive leaders do.

### Share the story of what you've learned
Sharing what worked and what didn't will make a difference.
Being prepared to speak up and step in with support when you see others stumbling will make a difference; you will make a difference.

### You have the power to make a difference
Know that the single biggest factor in your success in driving inclusion will be your desire to make a difference; to make it happen.

Your job is not to explain the million reasons why it wasn't possible to make a difference, but to find the one reason it was possible. You have all the power in your hands.[129]

"First, listen and try to understand," added Jer Lau, formerly of PwC. "That might be you going out to ask the question first. That's kind of the first step of trying to understand some of the things or empathising with how people are feeling. Second one would be to educate yourself. If you haven't already educated yourself, go read an article, go read the books, Google a TED talk. There is lots of collateral out there that people don't tap into. There are loads of *Harvard Business Review* articles; so many *Forbes* articles, and everything about this topic of gender equality, diversity, and inclusion. I don't think ignorance is an excuse. You can't say in today's world you didn't know, because it should be your duty to know."

"The third step being after you've educated yourself, is to look into yourself and assess your own behaviours. Identify where you're projecting some unconscious bias and see where you're not being inclusive. Consider the values and ethos in the behaviours that you are demonstrating and role-modelling to others, because that is what people are watching. Fourth, work with the community to really think about some things that are going to make a difference to people."

"The 'ignorance is bliss' kind of attitude, where you just don't know you don't know, that is not good enough. Especially if you're a good leader wanting to be more inclusive, you can't just be inclusive by saying one day, 'I'm going to be inclusive.' No, you have to understand what that actually means. It could stem all the way from not having socials that are always drinks related, because not everyone drinks. It could be the references or the language that people use, the microaggressions. One of the things that I've heard that upsets one of my colleagues a lot is she, despite being in the team for five years, continuously gets called another Brown person's name by the partner."

As Andy highlighted, being an inclusive leader is not easy, but there are significant benefits to creating a more inclusive and diverse organisation. An environment where people feel more comfortable to be themselves is one where collaboration, networking, and the sharing of ideas is not hindered by perceived limits to expression.

A 2015 McKinsey report on 366 public companies found that those in the top quartile for ethnic and racial diversity in management were 35% more likely to have financial returns above their industry mean. Those in the top quartile for gender diversity were 15% more likely to have returns above the industry mean. Therefore, creating a more inclusive and diverse organisation is not only the right thing to do, but it is also a sound business strategy.[130]

"Your value will be not what you know; it will be what you share."

Ginni Rometty

# Dola Fashola

"I had just come back from my second maternity leave, and in the first week of my return, there was a project based in Scotland I was asked to join. I'm London based, so that would mean overnight stays throughout my time there. My first reaction was, 'Guys! Just chill! I just came back from maternity leave. I've got not one but two very young children at home and need to adjust to life with a new child in the mix while working full time. Best we all be practical and wait for a little longer than one week for longer commutes,'" Dola shared as she recounted her experience of trying to balance her home life with the demands of a life in consulting.

I had first met Dola when we were both at PwC. Personable, remarkably bright, insightful, and well-networked, Dola had quickly established herself within the customer experience team. Born in Lagos, Nigeria, she moved to the UK with her family when she was six. Even at a young age, she began showing high levels of aptitude, attaining one of the top A-Levels in the country. She developed an interest in computer science and management, prompting her to attend King's College in London.

She then joined the IBM graduate scheme, expanding her knowledge of consulting and business, before moving on to join PwC as a manager. Echoing a similar theme to other consultants I'd spoken with, Dola recounted that she too had to adjust to her new role and to the challenges of finding the right work-life balance. She recalled, "Early on in my consulting career, a group of us went out for after-work drinks. One member of the group was a male director who was also a father. One of the junior female consultants asked, 'Honestly, what do you think about having children as a consultant?' and he responded, 'To be really honest with you, I think it's impossible.' I thought that was a bit of a stupid thing to say. I remember her being so disappointed and deflated with that answer, and I'm sure it sowed the seed that led to her leaving consulting altogether after having her first child. I think she was looking for reassurance. I always remember that conversation."

"But then I did see one or two other females, either clients or partners and directors, who were doing it. I was like, 'Well, it's not impossible.' For me, finding that balance, it was a personal thing. I've got a village. I come from a Nigerian culture where you don't raise your children on your own. 'It takes a village' is a saying that's repeated in different cultures as well. It takes a village to raise a child, and I had to create a village for myself. That's really the only way I was able to do it. Having said that, though, when I had my first child, it was fine. When I had my second daughter, it was a bit trickier, and that was one of the reasons why I left consulting, because finding that balance for me was hard." Dola recalled the project in Scotland she had to turn down, "You've got billable hours, you're judged by your billable hours, and if you're turning down opportunities, those billable hours don't get made. I just felt I needed a break, and though a small factor, it did contribute to the reason why I took a break from consulting in the end. It was not the main reason, but it was one of the factors. The main reason was I just wanted to put myself in our client's shoes and work in the industry I regularly advised in."

As the pace of progress accelerates, being away from the day-to-day activities of a team or department for any period of time becomes increasingly more difficult. In fact, according to an Understanding Society study of more than 3,500 parents, only 28% of women remain in full-time or self-employment three years after childbirth, compared to 90% of new fathers. Additionally, while 26% of men have been promoted or moved to a better job in the five years following childbirth, the figure is just 13% for women.[131]

Forward-thinking organisations and governments are making significant investments in supporting the transition into parenthood. They offer paid maternity leave, paternity leave, flexible working and mechanisms by which to re-integrate new parents into teams they'd been away from. However, as most studies confirm, there is more that needs to be done to support women in particular. When asked what advice she would give to other women and new parents working in consulting, Dola advised that "If that's what you want for yourself, you can't let anybody dictate to you and say you can't do that. Don't listen to that bullsh*t."

"You've got to do it in a way that works for you. To be honest, you do need really good childcare. If you're going to leave a child and go to work, then you've got to make sure that you're comfortable with the childcare that you've got. With consulting, it's slightly different because you may be coming home slightly later, you're travelling from somewhere far, so you've got to make sure that you've almost got that 'round the clock childcare that you can rely on that's flexible. That's really hard. Having supportive partners, parents, whatever that may be, you've got to open that up. You've got to have multiple options as well. Multiple support groups and a tribe, a childcare tribe."

"The other thing I would say is to have those conversations and be the advocates for others. I have heard stories of a particular lady who was very hard on people who needed to leave early. She would say really horrible things to people or get them taken off of projects."

"So, when I heard those stories, I was like, 'You have to be the advocate in the room when other people are not being that advocate.' I think the more voices we have, that are united, the clearer the message is that there is a space for you. Otherwise, the message that you're sending out is that there's no space for you, and you will probably need to go look for another job. That's not the right message to present to anybody. Be the advocate for other people, if you see somebody who needs to leave early, absolutely support it, and shout it out and say it's okay."

"I think a lot of women try to hide and say, 'I've got an appointment, I've got to go' and not actually tell us why. We need to normalise the fact that she may need to leave early or may need to be flexible and come in later because she's got a child that needs to go to nursery slightly later. Whatever that may be, just normalise it because, with guys, if you've got football practice and you want to leave early, everybody knows about that, right? Sometimes they need to leave because of childcare issues, and I really respected the partners that made that really clear. Like, 'Sorry, guys, I can't have meetings between 8:30 and 9:30 because I've got to drop my kids to school.' So, whether female or male, normalise the fact that we have a life outside of work and we can speak openly and honestly about where our time has been spent. Just talk about it like it's normal, because it is normal."

"I've got one of my direct reports. When he started, during the first meeting he had with me, he said, 'Look, I've got a young daughter and I would like to work two days from home. I need to take her to nursery on to my mom's house.' I thought, 'Oh, wow, that's nice.' I was really happy that he was able to be really forthcoming with the reason why he needed to work from home two days a week. That was quite refreshing."

After a successful seven-year stint at PwC, during which Dola was promoted to senior manager and led a variety of customer-focused engagements, she accepted a role with HSBC.

She would go on to head up the Digital Customer Experience team within HSBC Digital Services, leading multi-disciplinary teams and advocating for human-centred design. The experience of operating on the consulting side and subsequently on the client-side offered her a unique perspective into how the relationship between clients and consulting organisations was changing.

"I think consulting is changing," Dola confirmed. "If I look at my time at HSBC and how we're using consulting now, I think it's more around a partnership. So yes, you are looking for somebody who has a proven track record, who's done it before, who can hold your hand."

"Also, you're looking for a partnership that can grow. I think gone are the days where I just needed somebody to come in and do a piece of work and go. I need a team of people that I can call on over a period of time, who are going to grow in my organisation, who understand what we're trying to do and the direction that we're trying to move into."

"Consulting is moving from that kind of 'One and done' activity and mindset to 'This is an account or a team that we work with over a period of time to achieve their goals.' That may be different stages of the journey, you know, it's not just about, 'I'm gonna come and present this really big idea, I'm going to give you a roadmap for how to do it, I'm gonna probably do the first two stages of the roadmap and stage three and four you got to do it yourself. Bye, bye, see you later.' It's going to be that relationship over time, it's about going on that journey together."

As consultancies acknowledge the need to integrate more tightly within the fabric of client organisations, they will also need to reconsider the method and structures by which they engage. Rather than focusing on single engagements, recurring revenue models will allow for long-term partnerships. Consulting organisations are beginning to realise the need to rethink old paradigms to adapt to a world of exponentially accelerating, perpetual transformation.

"I think that using the term digital isn't gonna mean anything to anybody anymore very soon because it's just going to be BAU [Business As Usual]," Dola continued. "We're not coming in to do a short sharp digital transformation piece, we're coming in to make the experience better. We're coming in to constantly innovate over time, to reach one of the bigger goals and to see how we can react to the shifts that are going on in society. It's just going to be that kind of constant partnership, to adjust, remodel, as time and as technology is changing, and shifting. I think it's going to be a combination of the experience that you as a consultant gives to your clients."

She continued, "What's the signature experience that I'm trying to create for you? If you go and stay in an Airbnb home versus a Hilton Hotel, you kind of know what to expect. I think it's that differentiator that we need to consider in consulting. That's going to help our clients decide if it is a PwC experience they want? Or is it a Deloitte experience? Or is it EY or a BCG experience? You know, I think that's going to be a game-changer. I think that's going to be really more pronounced in the coming years and, yeah, I think that's gonna be an interesting one."

Considering the ever-accelerating pace of change, there has never been a more exciting time to be in consulting. The myriad of new opportunities and emerging technologies to consider and make sense of, all while navigating the nuanced human interactions, represents an exhilarating cerebral challenge to undertake. It is perhaps no surprise that, after three and a half years at HSBC, Dola decided to reenter the fray, accepting a director role with PwC. Given her aptitude, excellent interpersonal skills, and broad-based experience, she will undoubtedly make a positive impact as the consulting world continues to evolve and change around her.

"Technology advances at exponential rates, and human institutions and societies do not. They adapt at much slower rates. Those gaps get wider and wider."

Mitch Kapor

# Exponential acceleration

While the exact origins of chess remain a matter of controversy, there is a legend that tells of its origins. As the story goes, a long time ago in a land far, far away, an inventor presented a new game to a great king. He wanted to demonstrate to the king that empires are not only formed of the royal family but of people of all kinds, with each playing an important role in the empire's success or failure. Thus, the game he invented represented the kingdom consisting of the king himself, his queen, rooks, bishops, knights, and pawns, all of which were important. The king was impressed.

"This is a wonderful game!" he exclaimed, "I shall see to it that you are rewarded handsomely! How much gold do you want for this invention?"

"None, your majesty," the inventor replied.

A stunned hush fell over the court.

"None?!" the king inquired, raising an eyebrow.

"None, your majesty," repeated the inventor in a calm tone.

"Bah, surely you must want something?" the king bellowed.

"Yes, your majesty," the inventor replied. "All that I ask is but a grain of wheat to be placed on the first square of the board. Then two grains of wheat to be placed on the next square, then four on the third, doubling every time for each square on the board."

The king laughed, as did most in the court. He proclaimed, "You are a very strange man!"

The king, baffled by such a seemingly small price for such a wonderful game, immediately agreed and ordered the treasurer to pay the agreed sum. "You shall have your wheat," he said as he looked over to his treasurer and continued, "Make sure this man receives his reward."

The inventor bowed his head and made his way out of the king's hall. The king was happy with his new game and invited all in his court to play. By the next week, everyone was playing the new game, so it took them by surprise when the inventor appeared in court with the treasurer in tow.

"Ahh, it is great to see you again," the king welcomed the inventor. "Have you created a new game for us to try already?"

"No, your highness, I'm afraid not," the inventor replied, "I have come regarding my reward."

"What about your reward?" the king inquired.

"I have not received it," the inventor admitted.

The king, taken aback by the accusation, turned to the treasurer. He pounded his fist against the arm of his throne and snarled, "What is the meaning of this?!"

The treasurer, shaking, stammered, "My king, I... I am terribly sorry, but the sum could not be paid. B... By the time we even got halfway through the chessboard, the amount of wheat required was more than the entire kingdom has in its possession."

The king considered the unsatisfactory information for a moment. Then he did the only rational thing a king could do in those circumstances; he had the inventor killed as an abject lesson in the perils of trying to outwit the king.

While the fable serves as a valuable lesson to not publicly embarrass people who have armies of trained killers at their disposal, it is also an important lesson in the power of exponential growth. From the one grain of wheat on the first square of the chessboard, the amounts increase slowly at first, doubling every time, meaning that by the time we arrive at square 64, there would be over 18 quintillion grains of wheat required.

# Hockey sticks

The reason the king did not understand or appreciate what reward he agreed to is the same reason that the future is so difficult to predict: Humans are terrible at understanding exponential growth and big numbers. Yet, we do a decent enough job of wrapping our heads around slow, gradual, linear growth. That is just the way our brains are wired. When early humans were roaming the plans of Africa or making their way across what would later be known as Europe, understanding exponential growth or large numbers was simply not necessary for their survival. For example, our primitive brains may have needed to count the members of another tribe or the number of animals in a herd, but that was about it.

For thousands of years, that was all our primitive brains needed to understand. Consequently, we are reasonably good at counting things but not very good at wrapping our heads around large numbers or exponential growth.

For example, we hear figures of $1 million, $1 billion, or $1 trillion being used on a regular basis when speaking of the economy or the astronomical wealth of Elon Musk or Jeff Bezos. We hear that these entrepreneurs have amassed a net worth of around $200 billion USD at the time of writing, each. Yet, our brains are simply ill-equipped to make sense of numbers this large. For reference, $1 million USD of $100 bills in a stack would be approximately the height of a chair (one metre or 3.3 feet). Meanwhile, $1 billion USD in $100 bills stacked up would be higher than the Burj Khalifa (approximately one kilometre or 0.63 miles). Much as our brains have a difficult time understanding large numbers, they have an even harder time understanding exponential growth.

**$1 million versus $1 billion USD** (not to scale, obviously)

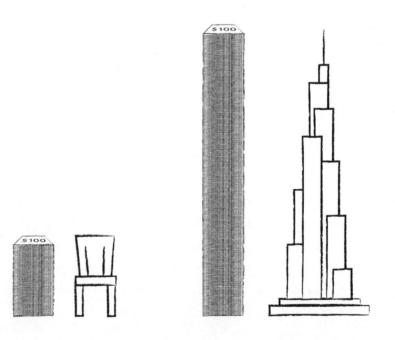

The easiest way to identify exponential growth when looking at a graph is to see if the increase in question is represented by a straight line or a curved one, like a hockey stick. While I'm sure we could also use other curved objects to illustrate this case, as I grew up in Canada, hockey sticks are all we knew. A straight line represents linear growth, where there is a steady, predictable, and constant increase over time. Exponential growth curves may start off looking linear, but as the numbers multiply repeatedly, they curve sharply upward, increasing dramatically over time. These types of curves can be found in many different scenarios, ranging from the human population from 2000 BC to 2000 AD, internet users from 1990 to 2010, and the number of Covid-19 cases as the virus swept across the world in 2020. In the same way, as the king failed to appreciate how many grains of wheat would be required, numerous politicians did not comprehend how quickly the Covid-19 virus would spread until it was too late.

### Total Covid-19 cases worldwide

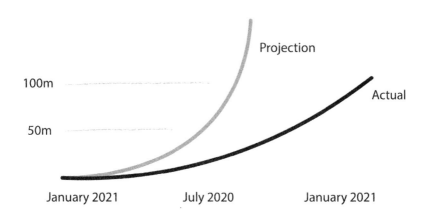

In the case of Covid-19, if no actions were taken to stop its spread, each contagious person would infect three other people on average. This is known as the R number. When the virus was first identified, there were some who made the case that the virus should not be taken seriously, perhaps because the R number was much lower than measles (12 to 18) or smallpox (5 to 7).[132]

These pundits did not fully comprehend how quickly small numbers become big numbers when they are multiplied over and over and over again. While some countries were quick to act, instituting policies to slow the spread, many other countries did not. The catastrophic failure to appreciate the exponential challenge ahead resulted in a tragic loss of life and significant economic losses as the virus surged.

Had nothing been done to limit the spread, the number of virus cases would continue to grow exponentially. In technology strategy, the "second half of the chessboard" is a phrase coined by Ray Kurzweil that refers to the point where an exponentially growing factor begins to have a significant economic impact on an organisation's overall business strategy. Much like governments that did not fully appreciate exponential growth, organisations that fail to appreciate the challenge and opportunity of exponential acceleration do so at their own peril.

# Faster and faster

The pace at which new technologies are developed and their subsequent adoption is accelerating at an exponential rate, representing incredible challenges and opportunities for organisations.

**Time to reach 50 million users**

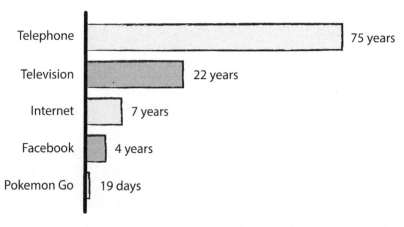

To put it into perspective, the telephone took approximately 75 years to reach 50 million users. Fast forward to when the television first became widely available, and it would only take 22 years for the same number of people to purchase a new television set for their home. Fast forward a little more, it only took seven years for the internet to reach 50 million users, four years for Facebook, and only 19 days for the immensely popular Pokémon Go mobile game. It would be fair to assume that, as Pokémon fans were out hunting for the elusive Charizard, they did not take time to fully appreciate and ponder the monumental feat that reaching 50 million users in 19 days represented. The incessant server issues that plagued the launch suggested that the team behind the game did not anticipate it either.[133]

The current pace of progress is simultaneously the fastest that it has ever been and the slowest it will ever be again. In 2001, American author, inventor, and futurist Ray Kurzweil wrote that every decade our overall rate of progress was doubling, "We won't experience 100 years of progress in the 21st century—it will be more like 20,000 years of progress (at today's rate)."[134]

He also made several predictions that, ultimately, proved to be eerily prognostic. In 1990 he predicted that a computer would beat a pro chess player by 1998, only for Garry Kasparov to lose to IBM's Deep Blue in 1997. Only two decades later, the Google AI Lab-built AlphaGo defeated Korean grandmaster Lee Sedol in a best-of-five series at the game of Go. To put the achievement into perspective, the 2,500-year-old game is played on a 19 by 19 board, meaning that in a game depth of 150 moves, there are about $250^{150}$, or $10^{360}$ possible moves. Yet, the computer defeated the grandmaster all the same.[135]

The pace of progress is staggering when we take a moment to appreciate it. For example, the iPhone was first unveiled in 2007, and now there are more than 3.8 billion smartphone users in the world, nearly half of the entire global population. [136]

We live in a world where the first human genome was sequenced in 2004 at the cost of hundreds of millions of dollars, and now machines can sequence more than 18,000 annually for less than $1,000 a genome. We see similarly rapid advances in all areas from big data and the Internet of Things (IoT) to machine learning, artificial intelligence, AR/VR, robotics, 3D printing, biotechnology, nanotechnology, renewable energy, drones, and satellites, to name a few. It is an incredibly exciting, if not slightly unsettling, time to be alive.

No matter the industry, emerging technologies are already having a fundamental impact on our lives. In radiology, for example, machine learning computers are already able to identify cancer lesions as effectively, if not more effectively, than groups of radiologists.[137] In a study from 2018, a group of radiologists with at least ten years of experience, reading more than 1,000 images annually, managed to find 80.7% of clinically significant cancer lesions in the study. The computer found 79.2%, a difference deemed statistically insignificant. In another few years, there will not be a radiologist alive that will be able to beat a computer.[138]

Consider, also, that using computer vision and machine learning to scan for cancer is only one narrow use case of the technology. By implementing computer vision and machine learning in vehicles, assisted and even autonomous driving becomes possible.

### Projected autonomous vehicle sales

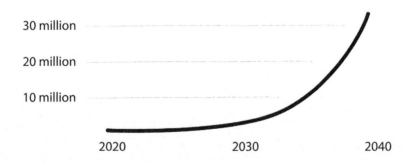

In time, fully autonomous vehicles that can interpret the environment, adapt, and operate themselves, will become the norm. According to a Deloitte report on autonomous driving, there will be an exponential increase in self-driving vehicles on the roads as the technology matures between 2030 and 2040.[139] In a world where numerous industries and millions of people rely on driving to generate their income, what happens when drivers are simply no longer required?

Meanwhile, forecasts suggest that by 2025 there will be more than 75 billion IoT connected devices in use, representing a nearly threefold increase from the IoT installed base in 2019. As all devices ranging from refrigerators to cars and industrial machines to streetlights become connected devices, they will gather incredible amounts of data. By 2025, the data volume created by IoT connections may reach a massive total of 79.4 zettabytes, and by 2023, global spending on IoT is projected to reach $1.1 trillion USD. [140] How will we ensure privacy and security for ourselves and our families in a world where every data point, movement, or action is tracked in real-time?

Blockchain is another example of a technology that has seen exponential growth, with the global blockchain market expected to expand from $3 billion USD in 2020 to $39.7 billion USD by 2025. Blockchain is a distributed ledger that contains the relevant details for every transaction that has ever been processed on the chain. The validity and authenticity of each transaction are protected by digital signatures. The decentralised, secure, scalable nature of blockchain technology makes it versatile and adaptable to many industries and applications.[141]

For example, as a complete record of transactions is stored on a blockchain, auditors will no longer need to request and wait for trading parties to provide data and documents. Blockchain will surpass the traditional audit sampling process and allow continuous audits for any "on-chain" transactions in any specific period. The adoption of blockchain will free up resources that were previously expended on evidence collection and verification.[142]

In the UK, 97% of audits of FTSE 350 companies were undertaken by the Big Four auditors, namely PwC, KPMG, Ernst & Young, and Deloitte. The process of completing an audit is immensely profitable. Between 2010 to 2016, audit fees increased steadily, climbing from £5.92 billion GBP in 2010 to £7.16 billion GBP in 2016.

While the need to audit may never be removed entirely, as any system involving humans will be prone to error, the adoption of blockchain will undoubtedly have a profound impact on how audits are conducted, how long they take, and how well organisations monetise them.[143]

While some ramifications—the butterfly effect—of the proliferation of automation, IoT, AI, blockchain, AR/VR, and other emerging technologies are challenging to predict, others are more evident. In our lifetime, for example, we will see hundreds of thousands of jobs simply disappear. The first jobs to disappear are ones that are easily automated, typically repetitive, low-paying jobs. These disappearing jobs disproportionately impact low-income families and significantly deepen the wealth gap. However, as AI capability improves, jobs will disappear in most, if not all, other sectors, from medicine, to transportation, to financial services and audit. How well or how poorly organisations and governments adapt will significantly impact matters ranging from quality of life and social security to domestic and foreign policy.

Barring any unforeseen global cataclysmic event, the pace of progress will only continue to increase. It will continue to change how we interact with others, how we learn, how we raise our children, and how we work, impacting every single facet of our lives. Back in 1970, Alvin Toffler predicted many of the challenges we now face in his book *Future Shock*. He wrote, "Future shock is the shattering stress and disorientation that we induce in individuals by subjecting them to too much change in too short a time." He went on to examine the potential impact that technology and progress would have on individuals, relationships, and society.

The challenges he described so presciently in 1970 have not changed but only, inevitably, escalated in their magnitude. As the pace of progress increases, we need to take steps in our own lives to accommodate the incessant bombardment of new information and to quickly and continuously adapt to the "new normal". Likewise, our organisations and those of our clients will need to take significant, drastic steps to adapt to an ever increasingly rapidly changing world at the risk of facing shocks of their own.

# Adapt or perish

"At its peak in the late '90s, Blockbuster owned over 9,000 video-rental stores in the United States, employed 84,000 people worldwide, and had 65 million registered customers. Once valued as a $3 billion company, in just one year, Blockbuster earned $800 million in late fees alone," Irene Kim of *Business Insider* explained.[144]

Given our current instant access to any movie or series through a plethora of streaming services, recounting the weekly ritual that hundreds of thousands of people undertook on a weekly basis sounds somewhat absurd in retrospect. Yet, for those who may never have had the privilege of meandering through a Blockbuster videotape rental establishment on a late Friday night, a short explanation may be in order. Blockbuster stores were large physical spaces filled with rows upon rows of videotapes (and later DVDs) for rent. People would physically make their way to these stores, browse the available selection of movies, buy ungodly amounts of snacks, and make their way home.

At home, they would put the tapes into a standalone VCR player and settle in to watch their movie. If, for whatever reason, they forgot to return the tapes on time, they would be charged significant late fees, meaning they'd have to drive to the local Blockbuster at least twice a week. For decades, this was the way of the world, with over 90% of US households owning a VCR towards the early 2000s.

Irene Kim continued, "In 1997, Reed Hastings founded Netflix, what at the time was a DVD-by-mail rental service, in part after being frustrated with a $40 late fee from Blockbuster. Two years later, having passed on an opportunity to buy Netflix for $50 million, Blockbuster teamed up with Enron (yes, that Enron) to create a video-on-demand service. In a deal that saw Enron do most of the work, a robust video-on-demand platform was successfully built and tested with customers. But it soon became clear to Enron that Blockbuster was so focused on its lucrative video stores that it had little time or commitment for the video-on-demand business. As a result, in 2001, Blockbuster walked away from the first major development of wide-scale movie streaming service."

"Blockbuster's troubles continued through the mid-2000s. After parting from Viacom and experimenting with in-store concepts such as DVD and game trading, Blockbuster was in the midst of an identity crisis. In 2009, Netflix posted earnings of $116 million. Meanwhile, Blockbuster, with its continuing business problems and legal battles, lost $518 million. On July 1st, 2010, Blockbuster was delisted from the New York Stock Exchange. Its foray into video-on-demand streaming came too late, and over the next three years, Blockbuster died a slow and painful death. DVD-by-mail services stopped, its various partnerships folded, and stores worldwide were rapidly plunged into administration."[145]

Netflix, meanwhile, continued its upward trajectory at an incredible rate by effectively shifting its business to streaming and original content. The company had a total net income of over $1.86 billion USD in 2019, whilst the company's annual revenue reached over $20 billion USD.[146] The number of Netflix's streaming subscribers has continued to grow in recent years, reaching 167 million in the fourth quarter of 2019 worldwide. Netflix has also invested heavily into original content, launching an estimated 2,769 hours of original movies, TV shows, and other productions in 2019 alone.[147]

Blockbuster may be the posterchild of squandering an outstanding opportunity, but they are by no means the only member of that tragic club. The dust heap of history is littered with the remnants of organisations that were unwilling or unable to acknowledge the need or the immediacy of the need for perpetual transformation.

The Kodak engineer Steve Sasson invented the first digital camera in 1975, at a time when Kodak was synonymous with photo camera film and photography. He recalled, "It was filmless photography, so management's reaction was, 'That's cute—but don't tell anyone about it.'" The leaders of Kodak failed to see digital photography as a disruptive technology. Don Strickland, a former Kodak vice-president, recounts, "We developed the world's first consumer digital camera, but we could not get approval to launch or sell it because of fear of the effects on the film market." Kodak filed for bankruptcy in 2012.[148]

"It's mobile prehistory at this point, but there was once a time when the ultimate smartphone you could get was a BlackBerry," Vlad Savov recounted in an article for *The Verge*. "Before Apple's iPhone arrived, Google's first Android prototypes were basically BlackBerry clones. It's easy to think of the stratospheric rise of Android and the iPhone over the past few years as inevitable, but we sometimes forget just what outsiders both of these platforms once were. Back in 2006, neither Apple nor Google had established relationships with carriers. Neither had a loyal following of business users to bolster its consumer proposition. And neither had the best text-input method ever devised for a pocketable device. BlackBerry, then known as Research In Motion, did."[149]

When the iPhone launched in 2007, BlackBerry did little to recognise the threat or to adjust their trajectory. BlackBerry co-CEO Jim Balsillie said "We're a very poorly diversified portfolio. It either goes to the moon or it crashes to earth. But it's making it to the moon pretty well, so we'll stick with it."

According to Jesse Hicks, who examined the rise and fall of BlackBerry, "That metaphor assumes gravity is the only challenge, and that no one else is aiming for the moon. Between 2006 and 2009, as the iPhone gained market share, Balsillie made three separate bids for professional hockey teams: first the Pittsburgh Penguins, then the Nashville Predators, and finally the Phoenix Coyotes. All the bids failed; in the case of the Coyotes, the bid went to court. In Balsillie's hockey dealings—coming at a crucial time for the company—critics see a lack of urgency. The iPhone had changed things, and RIM was too slow to respond."[150]

Steve Jobs, speaking in late 2010, said, "They must move beyond their comfort area into the unfamiliar territory in trying to become a software platform company. I think it's going to be a challenge for them to create a competitive platform and to convince developers to create apps for yet a third platform after iOS and Android. With 300,000 apps on Apple's app store, RIM has a high mountain ahead of them to climb." On June 20, 2008, RIM shares closed at $144.56 USD, and 49 months later to the day on July 20, 2012, it closed at $6.78 USD—a near 95% loss.[151]

MySpace, a social network predecessor to Facebook, came remarkably close to achieving the same level of success as Facebook. In 2004, Chris DeWolfe, the CEO of MySpace, met with Facebook founder Mark Zuckerberg to discuss a merger. Mark offered to sell Facebook to MySpace for $75 million USD, only to be rejected by Chris. More than a year after that talk, in the fall of 2005, after News Corp paid $580 million USD for MySpace, the two executives met again, and by that time Mark Zuckerberg had come up with a different price tag: $750 million USD. Again, he was rejected by Chris. Over the course of the following years, News Corp would disastrously mismanage their acquisition, all while Facebook continued to innovate and acquire more users.[152] By 2021, Facebook would go on to claim more than 2.5 billion users and a valuation of over $1 trillion USD.[153]

"MySpace failed to execute the product development," former Facebook president Sean Parker said in an interview. "They weren't successful in iterating and evolving the product enough; it was basically this junk heap of bad design that persisted for many, many years. There was a period of time where, if they had just copied Facebook rapidly, I think they would have been Facebook. The network effects; the scale effects were enormous. There was so much power there."

From Blockbuster and Kodak to Blackberry and MySpace, there are countless examples of organisations that did not acknowledge the need for change or did not adapt quickly enough to meet the demands of the market. With the ever-increasing pace of change, organisations are under more pressure than ever to keep up with the times. As a result, many organisations find themselves so focused on keeping up that they don't notice much of anything happening around them. They are running, stumbling, flailing forward to maintain momentum, at times not even looking up to see if they are still heading in the right direction. It is up to us, as consultants, to help guide our organisations and our clients in the right direction and, ideally, to implement changes that will allow them to become more adaptable and agile in order to keep ahead of the curve.

## Perpetual transformation

Perpetual organisational transformation, all happening at an ever-increasing pace, presents new challenges and opportunities for consulting firms and their clients. Consulting organisations, many of whom have grown organically and through acquisitions to become multi-national conglomerates, are facing increasing pressure to adapt to rapidly changing market demands. After all, the need for increased agility does not favour lumbering behemoths. Concurrently, demanding clients are forcing consulting organisations to rethink how they embed themselves within the fabric of their clients' perpetual transformation.

Increased agility is a multi-faceted challenge that includes how consultancies structure themselves internally, how they engage with clients and the methods by which they aspire to deliver incremental value. Rather than focusing on a project-based approach, perpetual transformation has prompted consulting organisations and their clients to increasingly shift towards an agile-based, iterative approach encompassing all aspects of the engagement.

Steve Denning wrote of the expanding role of agile in *Forbes*, stating, "Agile, which grew out of Lean, took off in software following the *Agile Manifesto* of 2001 and has since spread to all kinds of management challenges in every sector, not just software. We are now seeing Agile in manufacturing, Agile in retail, Agile in petroleum, Agile in strategy, Agile in human resources, Agile budgeting, Agile auditing, and Agile organizational culture. Agile arose as a response to massive, rapid change, growing complexity and the shift in power in the marketplace from the producer to the consumer. The Agile movement spread throughout the world because it enabled continuous improvement with disciplined execution—a challenge that 20th century bureaucratic management—also known in software development as 'waterfall'—had been unable to accomplish."[154]

"Agile has continued to evolve. It began first as a better way to run a single small team, then several teams, then many teams and then as a better way of managing whole organisations. In effect, it enables business agility," Steve concluded. Indeed, through various adaptations to better cater for larger teams and specific business needs, Agile has been effectively used by many leading organisations to better cope with the ever-increasing pace of change.

According to a 2017 report by CA Technologies, "Agile promises a range of benefits: faster time to market, increased productivity, fewer defects, cost savings and better employee engagement. Agile methods help you build and deliver products incrementally, get value to customers quickly and keep development work aligned with business needs."[155]

For decades, consulting organisations and their clients were happy to accept that every waterfall project had a beginning, middle, and an end. Considerable time and effort would be consumed to initiate a piece of work, to carry it out per specification, all without capturing any learnings. While this approach may have been sufficient a decade ago, the pace of change has increased to a velocity that has demonstrated severe limitations in its premise, forcing us to reconsider how we engage with our clients.

First, the time required to initiate any new piece of work is considerable, as there are typically internal bureaucratic hoops to jump through, approvals to obtain, team members to corral, and reviews to be had. The opportunity cost of any time spent ramping up is doing the things that actually deliver value. Consulting organisations that can significantly reduce mobilisation and analysis time to improve the "time to value" will be in an improved position to compete.

Second, as the project gets underway, there will inevitably be discoveries made, new ideas presented, and priorities shifted accordingly. At times, these discoveries or ideas may not be contained in the narrowly defined initial scoping document of a waterfall engagement, meaning the consultants or client stakeholders on the project will have absolutely no built-in incentive structure to capture or act on them. If the decision is made to pursue a new idea or priority, contractual amendments and other bureaucratic processes may be initiated, further disincentivising the identification of new opportunities. Consulting organisations that incentivise discovery and devise approaches to be agile enough to capitalise on new ideas and opportunities will benefit themselves and their clients.

Third, there are always noble intentions to capture the learnings and assets from the project to pass on to other teams. However, they rarely are, as team members quickly move on to other engagements.

Organisations need to devise persistent strategies by which to enable improved online collaboration, communication, and knowledge capture. While some consulting organisations do have knowledge management systems in place, they are usually cumbersome, archaic, underinvested and underused. Embracing platforms that enable easier communication and collaboration while serving as a searchable repository of curated, high-quality intelligence, modules, or contacts will improve operations and reduce rework. As these platforms are augmented by sophisticated algorithms to present the right information, to the right people, at the right time, they will yield significant financial and reputational benefits.

As the pace of change will only continue to increase, losing any percentage of a project's output to set up activities, bureaucracy, reinventing the wheel, or inability to adapt to changing dynamics is increasingly becoming unacceptable. Perpetual transformation, enabled by an agile approach, will allow consulting organisations to reconsider how they evolve their internal structures and how they interact with client organisations, effectively overcoming some of the limitations we've outlined.

Internally, consulting organisations need to embrace the flexibility and adaptability that an agile approach offers. For example, too often, consulting organisations do a stellar job of talking about improving the user experience with clients, but they don't do nearly enough to address the experience of their employees. Likewise, consulting organisations don't do nearly enough to address the legacy structural and technological deficiencies preventing them from embracing perpetual transformation. Part of the problem is captured in the expression, "The shoemaker always wears the worst shoes," suggesting that organisations are too busy working on behalf of their clients to work on themselves. However, in a world of accelerating perpetual transformation, organisations that do not devote adequate resources to restructure themselves internally in a way that is conducive to rapid change will face a significant and increasing disadvantage.

Project-based internal improvement initiatives need to be replaced with a more agile approach to deliver consistent, tangible value for employees. The flexibility of the approach will also empower employees by presenting them with a clear view of what new improvements are coming up next and allowing them to influence those priorities. After all, who better advise what incremental enhancements need to be made to the HR system, for example, than the people who spend every day working with it. The decentralisation and democratisation of the incremental improvement process will accelerate change initiatives while encouraging internal teams' engagement. While this trend may be counterintuitive for organisations based on hierarchical partnership models, these themes may very well prove necessary in challenging some of the short-term, tactical, profit-driven decisions partner groups tend to be prone to.

With client organisations demanding dramatically reduced "time to value", an agile approach offers numerous benefits. By running multiple work streams, consulting organisations can embed themselves within the fabric of client organisations, delivering consistent value with every cycle or sprint. Ideation, analysis, refinement, prototyping, testing, building, and deployment activities can be run concurrently, with each activity advancing incremental improvements. The approach is sometimes referred to as a "factory" or "engine", generating a predictable, consistent flow of incremental improvement and value. Granted, many client organisations are not yet used to buying consulting services in that manner, nor are many consulting organisations ready to step away from their waterfall, project-based approach. However, as history has taught us, organisations that do not adapt to change are sure to suffer dire consequences. Therefore, the question is not whether organisations will need to change. Instead, the question is whether organisations will adapt quickly enough. In an increasingly accelerating, perpetually transforming world, being agile enough to change with the times becomes a core organisational requirement. Our opportunity lies in identifying mechanisms by which to embrace change while delivering consistent, tangible value.

"The best way to predict the future is to invent it."

Alan Kay

# Future of consulting

"The only constant in life is change" is a quote commonly attributed to Heraclitus of Ephesus from approximately 500 BCE. He was one of the early pre-Socratic philosophers who would eventually influence the works of Plato and Aristotle, laying the foundation of Western philosophy.

According to Joshua Mark, director of the Ancient History Encyclopedia, "His central claim is summed up in the phrase Panta Rhei ('life is flux') recognising the essential, underlying essence of life as change. Nothing in life is permanent, nor can it be, because the very nature of existence is change. Change is not just a part of life in Heraclitus's view; it is life itself. All things, he claimed, are brought into and pass out of existence through a clash of opposites which continually create and destroy."[156]

As in life, the world of consulting continues to evolve, to adapt, to change. Consider that, as the pace of progress continues to accelerate exponentially, we will be inundated with new technologies at an ever-increasing rate.

Each new technology, in isolation, may spawn any number of butterfly effect inducing ramifications for how businesses operate or how people interact with those businesses. However, no new technology exists in isolation, as they are quickly combined with other technologies to create a dizzying array of potentially world-changing combinations. As with predicting the weather, predicting the future of consulting accurately is a complicated proposition. There are thousands, if not hundreds of thousands, of data points to consider, and their constant interplay and fluctuation mean that any prediction is only an educated guess.

Alvin Toffler perfectly captured this sentiment by stating, "No serious futurist deals in 'predictions'. These are left for television oracles and newspaper astrologers. No one even faintly familiar with the complexities of forecasting lays claim to absolute knowledge of tomorrow. In those deliciously ironic words purported to be a Chinese proverb: 'To prophesy is extremely difficult—especially with respect to the future.' This means that every statement about the future ought, by rights, be accompanied by a string of qualifiers—ifs, ands, buts, and on the other hands. Yet to enter every appropriate qualification in a book of this land would be to bury the reader under an avalanche of maybes."[157]

While we may never be able to predict the future with a great deal of certainty, what we can do is extrapolate trend lines, take inspiration from other industries, and consider emerging technologies to, at the very least, describe a hazy vision of what the future of consulting may be.

# Commoditisation

Of all predictions to be made regarding the future of consulting, perhaps one that is closest to being a certainty is that traditional consultancies will continue to face increasing pressure from all sides. Imagine a spectrum with traditional consulting organisations in the middle and potential competitors on either side.

On the left, imagine cloud-based hosting providers, software developers, IT outsourcing organisations, technical integrators, and platform providers. On the right, strategy houses and a wide array of communication, public relations, marketing, and creative agencies. Every single entity on that spectrum is, in one way or another, encroaching on the traditional consulting services carried out by traditional consulting organisations.

Take, for example, EPAM, Adobe, and Ogilvy. Each organisation is quite different from the others, as they all come from very different backgrounds and focus on different areas. Yet, each organisation is making increasingly bold inroads into offering traditional consulting services.

EPAM, founded in 1993, was originally a software engineering services company. The firm has grown by leaps and bounds, both organically and through acquisitions, to over 40,000 employees by 2020, across four continents. The portfolio of services offered by EPAM has grown to include a wide range of engineering, operations, and optimisation services. EPAM ranked as the top IT services company on *Fortune's 100 Fastest-Growing Companies* list as they rapidly expanded their integrated consulting capabilities.

Adobe, founded in 1982, originally focused on desktop publishing. As an interesting side note, Steve Jobs attempted to buy the company for $5 million USD in 1982, but the founders refused. According to Wikipedia, "Their investors urged them to work something out with Jobs, so they agreed to sell him shares worth 19% of the company. Jobs paid a five-times multiple of their company's valuation at the time, plus a five-year license fee for PostScript, in advance. The purchase and advance made Adobe the first company in the history of Silicon Valley to become profitable in its first year." Adobe grew to 21,000 employees by 2019. During their ascendency, they inevitably began offering consulting services alongside their suite of design, marketing, and collaboration platforms.

Ogilvy, an agency established in 1850, traditionally focused on advertising, marketing, and public relations. The company went through several iterations throughout the years and had 132 offices in 83 countries at the time of writing. As with the other examples, they unsurprisingly expanded their consulting offerings to include brand strategy, advertising, customer engagement and commerce, public relations and influence, digital transformation, and partnerships. In 2018 the company restructured again, absorbing all sub-brands into Ogilvy except for one: Ogilvy Consulting, which encompasses Growth & Innovation, Business Design, and Digital Transformation.

All the organisations on the spectrum will, in time, look to make a lateral move to diversify, increase revenue or build shareholder value. A company offering software development services will need to move towards either building out proprietary solutions or offering ancillary services, such as consulting, to boost revenue and create value. Agencies will inevitably move to provide more holistic, strategy and transformation consulting services to complement their core competencies. From EPAM, Adobe and Ogilvy to IBM, Apple and Canon, it would seem that all organisations are establishing or growing their consulting practices.

This trend, of course, is unsurprising. Traditional consulting organisations are, at their core, nothing more than groups of people with expert knowledge in specific areas. When clients were looking for advice to improve their customer experience, they would seek specialist advice from consultants. In turn, consulting organisations would either identify or hire people with the relevant knowledge to provide that advice. They would spend considerable time analysing the situation, identifying improvement areas, recommending a technology, and spending the next few months implementing and operationalising the new solution. The client would pay the fees, receive tangible value in return, and everyone was happy. However, as timelines shortened, budgets decreased, and expectations increased, friction began to occur.

That same client, being more aware of the choices they have in the market, may already know what platform or technology they want to implement. Rather than approaching a consultancy, they can look to the platform provider for advice. The platform provider, keen to secure the recurring revenue from their platform deployment, may severely undercut the consulting rates offered by providing their own advisors. They will also have expert knowledge of their platform that may far exceed that of their traditional consultant counterparts. Now the client is happy, the platform provider is happy, and the consulting organisation is left out in the cold. In time, building on their strong client relationship and insights into the client organisation, the platform provider may look to expand the scope of their consulting services, further encroaching on turf once held by traditional consulting organisations.

The above scenario, while admittedly a simplistic high-level view, has been occurring across the consulting world, in one form or another, at an ever-increasing rate. In a world where every organisation offers a layer of consulting services, consulting services themselves become commoditised. For traditional consultancies, this represents an existential threat to their core offering. James Chen, director of Trading and Investing Content at *Investopedia*, wrote, "Commoditization moreover often removes the individual, unique characteristics and brand identity of the product so that it becomes interchangeable with other products of the same type. Making commodities interchangeable allows competition with a basis of price only, and not on different characteristics."[158]

For traditional consulting organisations, being reduced to competing on price alone is untenable. While traditional consulting organisations continue to have strong relationships within client organisations, that will only take them so far. Given the cost and time pressures many of their clients are under; it will only be a matter of time before bigger and bigger chunks of traditional consulting business are distributed to more agile, cost-effective entities embedded alongside platform, software, or agency offerings.

One way that traditional consultancies have looked to maintain growth and shareholder value is to expand across the spectrum themselves. In March of 2021, Wipro announced the acquisition of Capco for $1.45 billion USD.[159] According to the press release, "This acquisition will make Wipro one of the largest end-to-end global consulting, technology, and transformation service providers to the banking and financial services industry. By combining Wipro's capabilities in strategic design, digital transformation, cloud, cybersecurity, IT, and operations services with Capco's domain and consulting strength, clients will gain access to a partner who can deliver integrated, bespoke solutions to help fuel growth and achieve their transformation objectives."

Accenture also saw the writing on the wall and went on a shopping spree on both ends of the spectrum. On the agency side, they acquired design giant Fjord in 2013, Karmarama in 2016, Matter in 2017, Droga5 and Bow & Arrow in 2019.[160] All told, over 30 acquisitions were made in a six-year period as Accenture expanded its media, digital, and creative credentials. On the other side of the spectrum, Accenture committed $3 billion USD and created a division called Accenture Cloud First in 2020. Fully aware that other organisations were encroaching on the traditional consulting space, Accenture made a conscious decision that their best course of action was to spread out laterally as well, diversifying revenue streams away from traditional core consulting and hoping that core consulting services would be integrated into up-stream and down-stream offerings.

On the surface, the strategy appears to have been an effective one, as the Accenture stock price has continued a steady climb. However, for Accenture, PwC, Wipro, or any of the other large consulting organisations, identifying synergies and proceeding with acquisitions may seem like a sound strategy in theory, but it is much more difficult in practice. Merging disparate corporate cultures, systems, and ways of working is not an easy undertaking. Only time will tell if the organisations are able to find the right integration of their increasing wide array of services and capabilities.

Meanwhile, according to Trefis, a data visualisation firm, the growing demand for digital transformation consulting has "blurred the line between pure-play technology and strategy consulting. This has led to large professional services firms increasingly becoming involved in this area. Large IT firms (Cognizant, Tata Consultancy Services, Wipro, Infosys, HCL, etc.), strategy consulting firms (BCG, McKenzie, Bain, AT Kearney, etc.) and the Big Four audit firms have all been trying to cater to the growing transformation opportunity."[161]

As organisations ranging from strategy houses and technology firms to platform providers and agencies all offer a growing variety of competing consulting services, with little in the way of differentiation, consulting services will become increasingly commoditised. Competing on price alone will not be sustainable unless firms drastically optimise their operations or find ways to stand out. Therefore, in order to be successful, consulting organisations will need to consider two interlinked themes: integration and differentiation.

# Integration

In a now-famous 2013 article in *GQ*, the Netflix chief content officer, Ted Sarandos, laid out the main challenge faced by the streaming company, saying, "The goal is to become HBO faster than HBO can become us."

The streaming wars are analogous to the world of consulting in that consulting engagements are akin to content, while platform providers are just that. The relationship between content providers and platforms in the streaming wars has shifted dramatically over the past decade, offering intriguing insights into organisational strategy and a cautionary tale for consulting organisations that do not adapt to changing client needs or the ever-increasing pace of change.

Netflix successfully evolved from sending DVDs by mail to becoming the preeminent online streaming platform. In February of 2013, they also began streaming their first original series, *House of Cards*. The series garnered overwhelmingly positive reviews and went on to become the first Primetime Emmy Award nominated series for original online-only web television for the 65th Primetime Emmy Awards.[162]

**Number of Netflix subscribers**

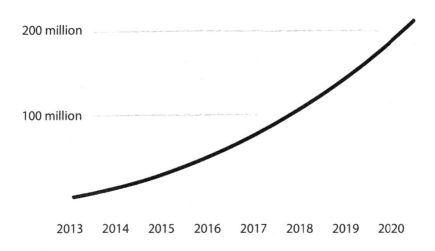

While Netflix traces its roots to content distribution through physical channels, HBO's origins trace back to December 1, 1965, when Charles Dolan was granted a franchise permit by the New York City Council to build a cable television system encompassing the Lower Manhattan section of New York City. By 1975, it had become the first American network to deliver its programming by satellite and thus became the first national cable channel. HBO focused on premium content, presenting movies, series, and sporting events. Beginning in the 1990s, HBO became more deeply involved in producing its own original programs. What followed was an impressive number of critically acclaimed series, including *The Sopranos* (1999–2007), *The Wire* (2002–2008), *Six Feet Under* (2001–2005), and *Game of Thrones* (2011–2019).

HBO understood the need to move into streaming services early on, launching HBO Go in 2010, which gave HBO subscribers access to HBO content on mobile devices. HBO Now followed in 2015, an over-the-top service that allowed access to HBO content without the need for a cable subscription. While HBO remained profitable, garnering $6 billion USD in revenue while allocating more than $2 billion USD per year to original programming, the rise of streaming services was impossible to ignore.

On October 10, 2018, a new streaming service was announced that would feature content from various WarnerMedia properties, including HBO, Turner, and Warner Bros. WarnerMedia would later announce that the service would be co-branded with HBO under the name HBO Max. The service, which was developed under a separate infrastructure from HBO's existing streaming platforms, HBO Go and HBO Now, would go on to replace those services.[163]

By the end of 2020, original programming helped drive HBO Max's activations to 17.2 million. It was reported that HBO and HBO Max had a combined 41.5 million domestic subscribers—up 20% from 34.6 million a year prior. These numbers may seem impressive until they are compared to Netflix, which surpassed 200 million paid subscribers and Disney+, which catapulted to over 73 million even though they had only launched their service in late 2019.[164] Meanwhile, Amazon Prime, the subscription service that includes faster shipping, music, and video streaming services from the ecommerce giant, announced it had surpassed 200 million subscribers in April, 2021.[165]

Each of the streaming services is also investing heavily into producing original content. Netflix spent approximately $15 billion USD on original content in 2019. Amazon Prime Video, meanwhile, spent approximately $6 billion USD, including $250 million for the rights to J.R.R. Tolkien's *Lord of the Rings*, planning to invest around $1 billion over five seasons, making it the most expensive television series in history.

In May 2021, Amazon also announced the acquisition of MGM Studios, a company formed in 1924, for $8.5 billion USD.[166] HBO Max was planning to spend approximately $3.5 billion, while Disney+ was looking to spend $2.5 billion. Other services such as Comcast's Peacock and ViacomCBS's CBS All Access services were also ramping up original content spend. The streaming wars had truly begun.[167]

Organisations that offer traditional consulting services are, in some ways, in a similar position that HBO was in the 1990s, but they are also much, much worse off. They also produce high-quality content, just like HBO did, in the form of consulting engagements, providing quality advisory services for their clients. However, unlike HBO, they will not own the intellectual property, as whatever they develop becomes their clients' property in the vast majority of cases. Furthermore, as most consulting engagements will typically have a technology or platform component, consultancies are building solutions on top of platforms owned by organisations that are increasingly becoming their direct competitors. HBO did the same when they produced quality content to be distributed on platforms that they would later compete against.

In the 1990s, HBO saw the writing on the wall and began to shift into streaming, developing their own platforms, but they were late to act, which allowed Netflix to dominate the space. Traditional consulting organisations may already be lagging too far behind most platform providers—be it Salesforce, Adobe, Google, Microsoft, SAP, or others—to develop new, competitive platforms from scratch. Without their own platforms or proprietary solutions, consulting organisations are similar to Disney, who continued to provide content to their future direct competitors well into the 2010s. However, when Disney realised their future lay in developing their own platform rather than only providing content to other providers, they made bold moves quickly, spending billions on technology, infrastructure, and content. The strategy was an effective one, propelling Disney+ to over 100 million subscribers just 16 months after its launch.[168]

**Total subscribers**

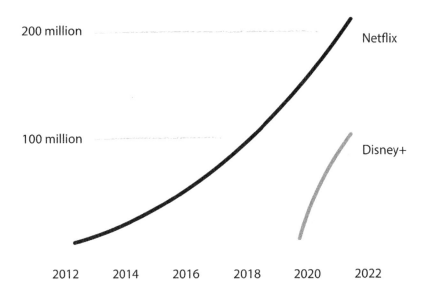

Without their own proprietary platforms or technologies, some consulting organisations have looked to establish progressively closer ties with platform and capability providers. For example, PwC has publicly touted its Salesforce and UiPath alliances. However, this approach is a temporary solution to a long-term strategic problem. Salesforce or UiPath are more than happy for PwC or any other consulting organisation to bring more customers onto their subscription-based platforms. In fact, it is in their interest to allow consulting organisations to lend their credibility and sales networks to support their cause of entrenching themselves into a broader client base.

However, their need for the same consulting organisations begins to diminish the moment they become entrenched, as they will often have their own consultants happy to support their new clients when they need it. To put this back into our streaming services context, it is as if Disney or HBO continued to funnel customers to Amazon Prime Video or Netflix long after realising that their competitors rapid growth and success presented a direct threat to their own long-term viability.

Additionally, Amazon has employed another rather dastardly tactic in their retail operation that should give consulting organisations pause, if not full-blown night terrors. Amazon has mastered the practice of identifying the most successful, commoditised, high-margin products on their ecommerce platform and then introduced their own carbon copy, private label products.

Thanks to the thousands of data points they have at their disposal, Amazon is able to identify regional shopping patterns and the most successful products. Once they introduce their own private label products, they undercut the prices of their competitors. From batteries and light bulbs to laptop bags and water filters, seemingly no product is safe from Amazon replication.

AmazonBasics was only the first foray into private label products by Amazon, as by mid-2020, Amazon offered 22,617 products from 111 of its own brands.[169] That means there are at least 22,617 products that were previously sold on Amazon by other brands, who now face stiff competition from the very platform they helped become successful in the first place.

Similarly, Google, Microsoft, SAP, Oracle, Facebook or Salesforce are more than happy to work with traditional consulting organisations for the time being, as long as it serves their own purposes. It is only a matter of time before they begin to offer lower-priced, competitive consulting services that they will inevitably give preferential treatment to. It may not happen overnight or for all services, just like it hasn't for Amazon. However, over time, little by little, traditional consulting organisations will see their services be usurped by the same platform and technology providers they helped make successful.

# Differentiation

In 2003, the prolific American author Seth Godin published *Purple Cow: Transform Your Business by Being Remarkable*. The *Wall Street Journal* and *Business Week* bestseller was summarised by a simple premise, "You're either a Purple Cow, or you're not. You're either remarkable or invisible. Make your choice." In a world of increasingly commoditised consulting offerings, the book serves as a valuable reminder of the importance of being recognised for something or not being remembered at all.

As an aside—and a valuable life lesson—I had the pleasure of meeting Seth Godin... almost. Allow me to explain. I was attending the TEDSummit in Edinburgh, Scotland. It was an incredible opportunity to spend a few days surrounded by inspirational, talented, and insightful individuals, each an expert in their respective fields. On the very first day, looking across the main hall, I noticed Seth Godin's unmistakable bald head. My initial reaction was somewhere in-between trying to be cool and that of a screaming Beatles fan in the audience of *The Ed Sullivan Show*. That being said, I did not want to interrupt the conversation he was having with another conference attendee. I made a pledge to myself that I would approach him at a later time. As luck would have it, however, I didn't see him at the conference again. Life lesson: When an opportunity presents itself, take it, as it may not present itself again. But I digress.

The basic premise of *Purple Cow* is that a brand needs to differentiate in order to truly garner attention and connect with clients. In the book, Seth tells the story of driving with his family in rural France. Driving along the picturesque farmland, his family notices a few cows grazing. The sight of the cows causes a commotion in the car, as everyone is excited by them. However, as they continue to drive, the sight of cows becomes less and less exciting. Godin's point is that a cow is just a cow after a while; that no matter how good-looking the cow, it will become boring, and boring things are easy to ignore.[170]

However, if his family saw a purple cow and it was the only purple cow, they would undoubtedly take notice. It would hold their attention; it would be newsworthy. They would stop to take pictures and be sure to tell all their friends. Seth explains and gives examples of how important it is for companies in the modern business world to identify what their purple cow is. It may be a remarkable idea, product, or service that will differentiate them from their competitors. However, it needs to be truly remarkable, not a thin layer of marketing fluff sprinkled on a generic offering. As consulting services become increasingly commoditised, organisations must identify their remarkable differentiators. They must then speak to them convincingly and emphatically and truly embrace them as part of their very being.

For example, the overall client experience is one differentiator many consulting organisations and consultants point to as their own. Yet, to truly deliver a differentiated client experience, the entire end-to-end client experience needs to be reviewed and improved. It would need to become truly remarkable. Even then, as every consulting organisation will undoubtedly claim that their client experience is the best, the words begin to lose meaning unless there is something to back them up.

Equally, when walking down Brick Lane in London, there are many Indian restaurants, each claiming to be "London's best". Seeing the first restaurant with that claim written in bold text across their façade, we may be tempted to walk inside. After all, who wouldn't want to try "London's best" Indian food? However, as we continue walking and notice every other restaurant making the same claim, the boast becomes meaningless. Similarly, if all consulting organisations claim to offer the best client experience, true differentiation will need to originate elsewhere. The story we tell as consultants must be consistent across every single touchpoint to be genuinely effective. Most importantly, as Seth has pointed out, no matter how good the story and how well the organisation carries through with their promise, our differentiation will only be effective if it is truly remarkable.

# Recurring revenue

"It's easy to forget now, but Amazon wasn't always the king of online shopping. In the fall of 2004, Jeff Bezos's company was still mostly selling just books and DVDs," noted Jason Del Rey, senior correspondent at *Recode*. In those years, Amazon faced threats from all sides, with Best Buy growing at 17% annually, Toys 'R' Us suing Amazon for violating an exclusivity agreement, and Amazon's website suffering repeat outages, which did not sit well with their customers. According to Jason, "Amazon was worth $18 billion USD at the time. Its online rival eBay, on the other hand, was an internet darling worth nearly $33 billion USD. If you were an outsider to both companies and had to pick one as the future Everything Store, it might have been hard to imagine Amazon as the victor."

He continued, "But 15 years later, Amazon is worth more than $900 billion, compared to just $33 billion for its old foe eBay, which spun off its (more valuable) payment division, PayPal. And the Amazon Prime membership program is perhaps the biggest reason why."[171]

Amazon Prime launched in February 2005. The offer was simple: Customers would pay a monthly fee in exchange for unlimited two-day delivery on orders. Fast forward to 2020, where Amazon Prime has expanded to offer a multitude of services, including same-day shipping options, the Amazon Prime Video streaming service, Prime Music, Prime Gaming, and Prime Reading, to name a few. The strategy of bundling the services into a subscription service has been incredibly successful, with Prime members typically placing twice as many orders as non-Prime customers. With over 200 million subscribers in 2021 and growing every year, Amazon Prime is the poster child for what has been branded as the recurring revenue bundle or, unfortunately, the "Rundle".[172] Terrible name aside, the trend to bundle products and/or services into subscription-based offerings has seen a significant uptick over the past decade.

For customers, it represents an easy, low-cost option to gain access to specific benefits of membership. For companies, it represents predictable revenue streams, increased customer loyalty, lower customer acquisition costs, and increased average per-customer revenue. Meanwhile, shareholders reward organisations that make a move towards subscription-based models by boosting the organisation's valuation.[173]

Walmart realised the power of recurring revenue at least 15 years too late. In late 2020, Walmart finally introduced its own service called "Walmart+" that would include same-day delivery, discounts on fuel at Walmart gas stations, and early access to product deals. Yet, as of December 31, 2020, Amazon was the leading retailer in the world with an estimated market capitalisation of $1.63 trillion USD, while Walmart was worth approximately $375 billion USD. [174] The power of the recurring revenue was evident as Amazon continued to outpace Walmart revenue growth, while Walmart was slow to act.[175]

**Market capitalisation in USD**

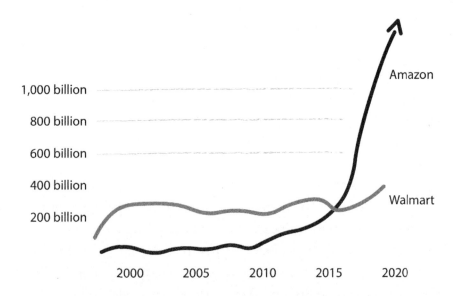

Realising the benefits of the recurring revenue model, organisations across industries began to introduce subscriptions or memberships of their own. Every company, from Google and Disney to Microsoft and Salesforce, have realised the benefits of the model and steadily shifted toward recurring as their primary source of revenue. In October of 2020, Apple launched a new subscription service branded Apple One that included Apple Music, Apple TV+, Apple Arcade, Apple News+, and Fitness+. Adobe moved away from selling one-time licenses to its Creative Cloud subscription service. Meanwhile, *The New York Times*, a company that traces its roots to 1851, passed the milestone of 6 million digital subscribers in 2020, while physical subscriptions and ad revenue continued to fall.[176]

In the automotive industry, the subscription services market size is set to surpass $40 billion USD by 2026. Zipcar, one of the leaders in the subscription car-sharing industry, was, as of 2018, present in 384 cities, operating more than 16,000 vehicles and serving more than one million members. There have been almost 1,000 cities that have added carsharing from 2016 to 2019, which is an increase of 47%. Forecasts by different consulting agencies such as Frost & Sullivan, McKinsey, and GMI all place the growth rate for subscription-based car sharing at 20%.[177]

In ecommerce, the subscription model continued its upward trajectory. According to a McKinsey report published in 2018, "The subscription e-commerce market has grown by more than 100% a year over the past five years. The largest such retailers generated more than $2.6 billion in sales in 2016, up from a mere $57.0 million in 2011. Fuelled by venture-capital investments, start-ups have launched these businesses in a wide range of categories, including beer and wine, child and baby items, contact lenses, cosmetics, feminine products, meal kits, pet food, razors, underwear, women's and men's apparel, video games, and vitamins."

For example, Michael Dubin and Mark Levine founded Dollar Shave Club in 2011, a subscription service that offered high-quality razors delivered directly to customers. In 2015, Dollar Shave claimed 48.6% of the online razor market, according to data from online retail consultancy Slice Intelligence. In July 2016, Unilever acquired Dollar Shave Club for $1 billion USD. Dubin told CNBC that he takes his cues from a variety of successful leaders, saying, "I don't think there's any one playbook out there in front of us that we should be following. You can take a little piece from Starbucks; you can take a little piece from Nike; you can take a little piece from Apple. You have to keep your eyes open, and you have to learn from others that have travelled the path before."

Dave Key, a cloud strategist, wrote of the appeal of recurring revenue, "To investors, the primary appeal of recurring revenue models is the value of predictable recurring revenue, particularly in comparison to one-time transactions. For example, a $20 million dollar company with 80% recurring revenue can count on $16 million dollars at the beginning of every year. That figure is stable and predictable. Management can plan and invest accordingly. The same cannot be said of a $20 million dollar business with no recurring revenue. That company has to start the year at zero. Of course, it can make some predictions based on past performance, but it doesn't have a contractually obligated revenue stream to base expansion plans around."[178]

## Adobe recurring revenue percentage of sales

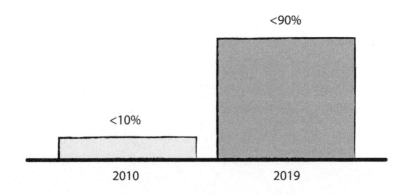

The trend to move to a recurring model has been a very effective strategy for organisations across a broad swath of industries, including those that offer consulting services. Adobe went from less than 10% of their revenue being generated from recurring sources in 2010 to over 90% of recurring revenue in 2019. Meanwhile, investors rewarded the shift, moving Adobe from a four times sales valuation to an 18 times sales valuation.[179]

Regardless of industry, service, or product, there has been a demonstrable rise in subscription-based offerings over the past decade, with the trend only increasing in velocity. The rationale for pursuing subscription-based offerings is clear, as subscriptions make it easier for customers to purchase while enabling lower acquisition costs and reduced churn. Investors see recurring revenue as a positive trait, rewarding organisations with recurring revenue strategies with substantial valuation increases compared to their competitors.

Leaders across industries are beginning to realise the potential of subscription-based business models, but many are struggling to adapt. In addition to internal challenges such as aligning stakeholders to the new strategy, which some may see as audacious, organisations in some industries will need to devote significant resources to change customer perception of the new offering.

Manifesto Growth Architect, a growth strategy consultancy, surveyed 504 senior business leaders in 2019 across the retail, finance, leisure, automotive, and utility industries. Even while 70% of leaders surveyed stated that they saw the value of the subscription model, only 24% were implementing it, and a mere 7% were generating significant revenue via membership. Another quarter of businesses were trying out membership models but were not sure how they would evolve, and 22% saw potential but were unsure how to proceed.[180]

While traditional consulting organisations have dabbled in offering managed services and risk share models, there is a case to be made why the future of consulting may very well be in offering subscription-based services. As the pace of change continues to accelerate exponentially, organisations are under increased pressure to deliver tangible value across customer journeys, while consulting organisations continue to be under increased pressure to deliver. The prospect of undertaking longwinded analysis projects may be viable for high-level strategy work, but not for organisations needing to demonstrate tangible value immediately. Therefore, consulting organisations that have been able to embed themselves within the fabric of their client organisations have a significant advantage. They will not require prolonged analysis to discover substantial opportunities, as they will be acutely aware of the challenges their clients face every day. For consulting organisations to truly embrace subscription models, three areas will need to be address based on the example of successful businesses in other industries.

First, the proposition needs to be easy to understand and easy to purchase. Our clients may not be used to buying consulting services in this way, meaning the onus will be on our organisations and us to make the experience an overwhelmingly positive one. By removing friction points and identifying opportunities to delight, consulting organisations can effectively shift clients onto a recurring model that delivers consistent, incremental value.

Second, to retain the subscription customer, consistent, measurable value will need to be delivered. As traditional consulting organisations become interwoven within the fabric of their client organisations, it will be increasingly easier to identify opportunities for improvement. However, one of the differentiators and measures of success will be the method by which these opportunities are identified, cut up into smaller elements, processed, prototyped, tested, refined, and deployed as iterative elements within the organisation.

The agile approach is akin to a factory or engine, supported by the consultants' expert knowledge in conjunction with the consultancy's proprietary technologies, algorithms, models, and processes. Whether that engine is a Ferrari, purring along, delivering consistent, measurable, substantial output, or a Yugo engine from 1983, breaking down regularly, all depends on that combination of factors. When the engine operates in a predictable rhythm, it will ingest opportunities for improvement on one end while delivering incremental, tangible value on the other. Even when relatively minor in isolation, the consistent, measurable value delivered within each cycle will form part of a more significant, incremental improvement over time. Tangible value, when effectively communicated and celebrated, will serve to build trust and effectively reduce the probability of churn. As they build trust within the client organisation, the consulting organisation will gain permission to discuss other tiers within the subscription model.

Third, it should be easy for clients to rapidly ramp up and ramp down their subscriptions based on their needs. Therefore, the challenge for consulting organisations will be to implement systems and procedures to identify promptly and onboard teams with specific skill sets when required and offboard them when they are not. Working with internal resources, smaller consultancies and pools of freelancers from around the globe, consultancies will need to ensure they always have the right teams, with the right skills, whenever they need them. The ability to quickly identify and onboard teams of freelancers and third-party agencies will allow consulting organisations to be more adaptable and agile, while reducing the need of maintaining large benches of consultants when they are not required.

"Rather than putting the focus of the business on the "product" or the "transaction", subscription economy companies live and die by their ability to focus on and serve the customer over time," Tien Tzuo, CEO of Zuora, stated in an interview for *Forbes*.[181]

By embracing subscription models, consulting organisations will be able to increase the value they deliver to their clients, reduce overhead costs, increase their valuations, and focus themselves on creating the best possible experience for their clients.

The shift to a recurring revenue model by consulting organisations will not be an easy one, as many have been selling consulting engagements in the same way for decades. Therefore, it's very likely that a portion of traditional consulting engagements will continue as it has, while we will see an increasing percentage of the client-consultancy relationships shift to recurring models. Ultimately, the increased pressures for clients and consultancies will drive the adoption. A more symbiotic relationship will allow both organisations to better adapt to the ever-accelerating pace of change and rapidly shifting market demands.

# Artificial intelligence

In any conversation regarding the future of consulting, we must consider the impact that artificial intelligence (AI) will have on all aspects of our professional and personal lives. However, before we can embark on any such examination, it may be helpful to disconnect our analysis from the popular culture portrayals of AI that may have influenced our thinking. From the apocalyptic vision of menacing intelligence called Skynet in the Terminator movies to the rogue programmes inhabiting The Matrix, AI has often been used as a compelling antagonist. While the probability of a superior intelligence decimating human civilisation will continue to be debated, for the purpose of this chapter, we will focus on the more immediate and benign applications.

In our broad definition, AI is a collective term for computer systems that can sense their environment, think, learn, and take action in response to what they're sensing and their objectives.

Maria Axente, who has been working with AI for over a decade, explained what we mean by AI by saying, "We look at AI as a combination of technologies, not just one, that allows us to replicate some of the traits of human intelligence. To sense the external environment, to reason, to think about it, to propose actions and then, in the end, to learn. So that next time, when you sense, it's based on the previous experience you have. Having this sensing, reasoning, thinking, acting, and learning is a straightforward way to define artificial intelligence and then, after that, you start aligning various technologies."

There are many areas of AI to explore, with each area continuously evolving and spawning new variations, combinations, and sub-sets. The most commonly mentioned sub-sets as they relate to consulting are:

### Machine learning

ML is a part of AI that enables computers to self-learn from information and apply that learning without human intercession. Massive datasets can be rapidly analysed and compared to vast historical records to identify patterns and anomalies. ML powers risk analysis, fraud detection, and portfolio management in financial services, GPS-based predictions in travel, and targeted marketing campaigns, to list a few examples.

### Robotics

Robotics encompasses technologies that deal with the design of virtual and physical robots enhanced by artificial intelligence. Robotic Process Automation (RPA) is the technology that allows computer software, or a "robot", to emulate and integrate the actions of a human interacting within digital systems to execute business processes. RPA has been used in order processing, call centre operations, claims administration, and expenses management.

### Natural language processing

NLP is a branch of artificial intelligence that deals with the interaction between computers and humans using natural language. The ultimate objective of NLP is to read or listen, decipher, understand, and practically make sense of human languages.

NLP has been applied to interpreting search queries, predictive text, translation, and smart assistants.

### Computer vision

Computer vision is an interdisciplinary scientific field that deals with how computers gain high-level understanding from digital images or videos. It seeks to understand and automate tasks that the human visual system can do, enabling autonomous vehicles, medical scan analysis, merchandising analysis, and crop management.

Each of these sub-sets of AI may be used in isolation or in any variety of combinations. They may also vary significantly in the degree to which human input or interaction will be required to complete their tasks. Automated intelligence, for example, is focused on the automation of functions and may not require human intervention. Assisted intelligence, meanwhile, is focused on helping people to perform tasks faster and better. Augmented intelligence focuses on assisting people in making better decisions, while Autonomous intelligence is focused on automating decision-making processes without human intervention.

Therefore, AI may be employed in different ways, utilising various technologies to achieve a particular task or set of tasks. We can already see many examples of these technologies taking on complex tasks in our everyday lives. Consider the way we receive insurance quotes, how our phones recognise our faces, and how our Google email predictive text seems to magically know exactly what it is we want to say next. AI is already playing an essential role in our day-to-day lives, even if we may not always be aware of it.

In the business world, AI has made a dramatic impact in a very short period of time. From eCommerce and financial services to HR and cybersecurity, every industry and function has, in one way or another, already been impacted by AI or will be soon. One of our challenges as consultants will be to identify new ways to employ AI while helping organisations embrace it, even as the pace of progress continues to accelerate exponentially.

As we discussed in a previous chapter, exponential acceleration is inevitable. In 1965, Gordon Moore predicted that the number of transistors fitting on a single chip would double every year. He amended that in 1974 to double every other year. His prediction became known as Moore's Law. According to a report produced by Stanford University, AI computational power is accelerating at a much higher rate than the development of processor chips. "Prior to 2012, AI results closely tracked Moore's Law, with compute doubling every two years," the authors of the report wrote. "Post-2012, compute has been doubling every 3.4 months."[182] In the fable of the invention of chess, the king did not appreciate how quickly the number of grains of wheat would reach staggering sums when multiplied over and over. Similarly, we are ill-equipped to fully appreciate how quickly AI capability will continue to accelerate in the coming years and what impact it will have on the world as we know it.

The impact of AI within disparate industries has already become evident, giving us a glimpse of what's to come. Within advertising, for example, the way that advertising is tailored and targeted used to require teams of people with specific skill sets. Today, sophisticated algorithms consider incredible amounts of data points to show us tailored advertising optimised for conversion. In the future, the algorithms and automation capabilities will only become more sophisticated, further eliminating the need for human intervention across all stages of ad creation and placement. After all, why would companies pay humans to design and tailor campaigns when AI can craft thousands of personalised micro-campaigns based on hundreds of thousands of data points within seconds?

In financial markets, humans are increasingly being replaced by sophisticated AI entities that are able to trade faster, smarter, and without the need for expense accounts or bonuses. High-frequency AI trading already represents about 50% of trading volume in US equity markets.[183] In the early 2010s, a new 6021-kilometre underwater fibreoptic link was deployed between North America and London at an estimated cost of over $300 million USD.[184] The objective of this massive undertaking? To allow computers to complete financial transactions five milliseconds faster. In the future, AI trading will become faster and more complex, further removing the need for human participation. In trading and financial services, as with all other industries, human participation in day-to-day activities will continue to be diminished, while the organisations with the best AI will be at an increasingly significant advantage. According to PwC research, global GDP could be up to 14% higher in 2030 as a result of AI – the equivalent of an additional $15.7 trillion USD – making it the biggest commercial opportunity in today's fast-changing economy.[185]

In 1947, before there were computers in the way we know them today, Alan Turing designed the first program to play chess and tested it with paper and pencil using himself as the computer. Two years later, Claude Shannon studied two different strategies for building "search trees". The Type A strategy considered all possible moves to a fixed depth, and the Type B strategy used chess knowledge to explore the more promising lines to a greater depth. With the rise of AI, a new Type C has emerged, where humans and algorithms work in a symbiotic relationship, with humans guiding powerful algorithms that may employ Type A and Type B strategies.[186]

On May 11, 1997, IBM's Deep Blue became the first AI to beat a human World Chess Champion, Garry Kasparov. In 1998, Garry hosted the world's first game of "Centaur Chess". Akin to how the mythological centaur was half-human, half-horse, these centaurs were teams that were half-human, half-AI.

They invited all kinds of contestants, supercomputers, grandmasters, and mixed teams of humans and AIs to compete for a grand prize. Unsurprisingly, a Human+AI Centaur beat the solo human contestants. But, more importantly, the Human+AI Centaur also beat the solo computer.

"This is because, contrary to unscientific internet IQ tests on clickbait websites, intelligence is not a single dimension," wrote Nicky Case for the MIT Media Lab. "The 'g factor', also known as 'general intelligence', only accounts for 30–50% of an individual's performance on different cognitive tasks. So while it is an important dimension, it's not the only dimension. For example, human grandmasters are good at long-term chess strategy, but poor at seeing ahead for millions of possible moves, while the reverse is true for chess-playing AIs. And because humans and AIs are strong on different dimensions, together, as a centaur, they can beat out solo humans and computers alike."[187]

The increasing pace of change makes the future that much more challenging to predict. There are exponentially more data points to track and intertwined butterfly effect inducing factors to consider. Rapidly emerging and evolving technologies such as AI, VR/AR, quantum computing, blockchain, and the internet of things will continue to significantly disrupt and transform the way we live, the way we work, and how organisations do business. Furthermore, the unpredictable combinations of these new technologies in conjunction with new materials and manufacturing processes will allow for new inventions. These will subsequently affect customer expectations and organisational capability while rapidly shifting the Window for our clients and organisations.

Consultants, therefore, may need to become like the centaurs in Garry Kasparov's chess tournament. Armed with proprietary, modular technologies to facilitate faster, more agile analysis, design, test, build, and deployment of incremental organisational improvements in perpetually transforming organisations.

Meanwhile, consulting organisations will need to change from within, becoming more adaptable to new ways of working while embedding themselves within the fabric of their client organisations to deliver consistent, tangible, incremental value. They will need to identify new ways to differentiate, acquire, or develop modular elements that will exploit the potential of emerging technologies as they themselves continue to evolve.

Maria added, "We in business tend to think linearly. We study dynamics, but it is usually static and linear. You have, on the one hand, businesses that are set up to function linearly. Meanwhile, AI functions continuously and dynamically, meaning that there is a gap whereby organisations are not set up to truly embrace AI. That is where I believe consultants are best placed because we can help organisations make sense of this dynamic environment in the short, medium and long term."

As with any new, disruptive, and rapidly evolving technology, there will be many missteps along the way. For example, in 2016, Microsoft released a chatbot called Tay on the social platform Twitter. Tay was an experiment at the intersection of machine learning, natural language processing, and social networks. Tay was designed to learn language over time, enabling her to have conversations about any topic. However, only a few hours after Tay was exposed to the people of Twitter, she began tweeting out racist, misogynistic and anti-semitic statements. As it later turned out, it wasn't really Tay's fault. In a coordinated effort by online trolls, Tay was inundated with truly vile language, effectively proving that a learning computer is only as good as the data it absorbs. Microsoft had little choice but to shut down the account.[188]

The Peter Parker principle states that "with great power comes great responsibility". In a world where AI will play an increasingly vital role within our organisations and those of our clients, we must be mindful that AI does not propagate societal inequalities or prejudices. After all, if we were only to train AI with data from a flawed system, we could not blame the AI for the equally flawed outcomes.

Maria noted, "We need to raise awareness with our clients that it is disruptive, that it's new, but that we need to be aware of the risks and the necessary governance. Responsible AI is all about balancing the risk and the benefits."

The symbiosis of technology and people will continue to evolve in the years to come. Similarly, consultants will increasingly be supported by a sophisticated toolbox of modular technologies that will enable them to make better decisions faster. Yet, the core premise of consulting will not change. It will continue to be people coming together to solve challenges, debate, argue, and find new improvement opportunities. Everything else, however, including how consulting is done, the technologies employed, and how we embed within client organisations, will continue to dramatically evolve and change over the years to come. Our opportunity resides in understanding the trend lines and emerging technologies, acknowledging how the Window is shifting for our organisations and our clients, and then being bold and strategic enough to embrace the opportunities that ever-accelerating perpetual transformation will present.

"You miss 100% of the shots you don't take."

Wayne Gretzky

# Conclusion

When I first had the idea for this book, the concept itself was initially quite vague. Yet, I knew that it had to be a contemporary, practical guide to the world of consulting as told by people who have experienced it and have the battle scars to prove it. The insights provided by those who have kindly shared their experiences, wisdom, and time helped the themes in this book to coalesce. Interestingly, the advice and stories they shared were not of the latest technologies or methodologies. Instead, they discussed themes such as effective communication, personal growth, and building trust, through to networking, leadership, and overcoming adversity.

These are all very human considerations for what is, ultimately, a very human business. Consulting has always been about people working together to solve challenges or identifying new opportunities for improvement. It is a deceivingly simple concept, as it is one that takes no time to understand. Yet, these human considerations and all of their nuanced complexity make effective consulting something that takes a lifetime to master.

The most successful consultants I've encountered have a deep understanding and appreciation of that premise. They are humble in acknowledging that, no matter how successful they become or how many accolades they achieve, there is always room to be better. They always aspire to improve themselves, be more authentic, support those around them, represent their organisations, service their communities, and identify opportunities to benefit their clients. For them, it's as much about the journey, the relationships, and the things they learn along the way, as it is about the destination.

Even the most successful consultants have, at one time or another, failed. While it is never easy when things don't go to plan, thanks to the relationships they built along the way, the things they had learned, their perseverance and their strategic approach, they were able to come out better for the experience. We will all fail at one point or another. It is how we overcome that adversity, what we learn from it, how we work together with others, and how we move forward that will define us.

Therefore, *How (Not) to Fail at Consulting* was a fitting title to this book, with the 'Not' in parentheses, as sometimes it is just as important to know how not to fail in consulting as it is to know how to fail in consulting. Granted, that bombshell is not on par with the final scene of *The Usual Suspects*, or when we found out the origins of Hodor's name in *Game of Thrones*, or the ending of Christopher Nolan's movie *The Prestige*, but it's as good as it gets for a book about consulting.

When faced with competing priorities, external pressures, and internal struggles, there may be times when we are feeling overwhelmed. In those moments, it's essential to take a step back, take a deep breath, and put things in perspective. Our family, friends, colleagues, and support networks are there when we need them, and we should never hesitate to reach out when necessary. No matter the adversity, we will overcome any challenge through their support, combined with introspection, planning and perseverance.

We must also be mindful of those around us, as they may be facing their own challenges. We need to strive to be cheerleaders, allies, and advocates for those that need it. Empathy is a powerful instrument, not only in understanding our clients or their customers but also in understanding our teams, colleagues, family, and friends. By putting ourselves in other people's shoes, we gain perspectives different from our own, effectively expanding our worldview and allowing us to be more considerate. By genuinely listening to others, we will better appreciate their point of view, allowing us to form closer bonds and more trusted relationships.

In a world of perpetual transformation, the ever-increasing pace of change will spawn new technologies and evolve others, leading to a myriad of butterfly-effect inducing catalysts. As these innovations will profoundly disrupt the world many times over, consulting has never been a more exciting place to be. Not only are we finding new ways of working with our clients and continuously innovating, but we are also fundamentally transforming how our organisations operate and adapt to the rapidly changing world around us. In these tumultuous times, we need to be bold and strategic, taking a holistic, human-centric approach to identifying new opportunities while possessing the necessary grit and cunning to pursue them.

I sincerely hope that, in whichever small way they can, the subjects and stories we examined in this book will help you along your journey. As you go on to a successful career in consulting or elsewhere, I will leave you with three humble requests based on what we discussed in the book, as they bear repeating. First, be kind. Be kind to yourself and others, as you never know what battles they are fighting. Second, pay it forward. Support others, be an ally, and fight to create a more inclusive, diverse, and just society. Third, remember to take joy in the little things. Life comes at you fast and is gone in a blink. Take a moment every day to find something to make you smile. It could be the majesty of a sunset, the crisp, invigorating morning air, or something as simple as the digital clock that just turned to a very symmetrical 11:11.

"I've missed more than 9,000 shots in my career.
I've lost almost 300 games. 26 times, I've been trusted to take
the game winning shot and missed. I've failed over and over
and over again in my life. And that is why I succeed."

Michael Jordan

# Further reading

Personal growth is an ongoing, never-ending journey. As a means to help further expand our world view, some of this book's contributors have kindly recommended other books they have found interesting or inspirational, which will undoubtedly make for good reading. Hopefully, they will serve you well in the adventures to come.

# Andrew Finlayson

### Circle of the 9 Muses
David Hutchins
"Storytelling guide that has practical help with
structure for presentations, pitches and talks."

### Antifragile: Things that Gain from Disorder
Nassim Nicholas Taleb
"If you seek control, read this and realise you aren't in control –
but you have influence."

### Blueprint: How DNA Makes Us Who We Are
Robert Plomin
"Who are we? Do we really know? Are we part destined to be
who we are? Be prepared for DNA ethics discussions."

# Andrew Hogan

*Thinking, Fast and Slow*
Daniel Kahneman
"Fascinating insights on how we make decisions, for better and for worse."

*The Art of Travel*
Alain de Botton
"Brings a different perspective to travel and how best to appreciate the experience."

*Unbroken*
Laura Hillenbrand
"Shows the power of the human spirit under incredibly difficult circumstances."

# Andy Woodfield

**Dare to Lead**
Brene Brown
"Anything and everything from Brene is valuable, especially for leaders at all levels seeking to embrace their vulnerability as a strength."

**This is Your Moment**
Andy Woodfield
"It's a super practical and easy to read guide to help you in getting back to your unique strengths and achieving your dreams."

**Tao Te Ching**
Lao Tzu
"I love this book of extreme wisdom, some days you just need ancient wisdom like this to set you free, it works every time."

# Antoinette Kyuchukova

**_The Little Prince_**
Antoine de Saint-Exupéry
"This adventurous, magical and poetic tale runs through my veins from
early teenage years. I played the Little Prince on a school tour of northern
France and feel like the story has shaped my own outlook on life."

**_The Design of Everyday Things_**
Don Norman
"The book offers a rich, insightful and provocative perspective on design,
the human mind and engineering. It's fantastic!"

**_Quiet: The Power Of Introverts In a World That Can't Stop Talking_**
Susan Cain
"Thoughtful and powerful reminder of the value and importance of
diversity and the need to nurture authenticity at work and in life more
broadly."

# David Fowler

### *How to Avoid a Climate Disaster*
Bill Gates
"I have so much admiration for Bill Gates, for what he has achieved, and his recent philanthropy. His desire to learn and to solve problems is outstanding."

### *An Independent Man*
Eddie Jordan
"Eddie Jordan is a huge entrepreneur, and his stories of wheeling and dealing to build Jordan F1 are both interesting and hilarious."

### *The Office: The Scripts*
Ricky Gervais and Stephen Merchant
"A lesson in how not to be a boss! But I love the humour of this book, and often play to this stereotype to inject a bit of humour at work (note – it only works if the team has seen the show!)"

# Dola Fashola

***The First 90 Days***
Michael D. Watkins
"Real great gems and activities to think through as you navigate your first 90 days in a new role or new organisation. There are a few areas that will set you up for success beyond the 90 days too."

***One Minute Salesperson***
Spencer Johnson
"We are all salespeople at the heart of what we do whether we realise it or not. This book is great as it gets you to realise it's not about you or what you're selling - but about the person you're selling to."

***Customer Centricity***
Peter Fader
"A controversial look at why the customer is not always right and how to drive the strategic outcomes your business will need if it is to thrive."

# James Easterbrook

**All Marketers Are Liars**
Seth Godin
"About as neat and clear a description of what customer-centricity really means as you will find."

**Think Inside The Box**
Drew Boyd
"A helpful reminder that innovation is within everyone and a really practical guide to unlocking it."

**Where The Crawdads Sing**
Delia Owens
"Because too many business books make Jack (or James) a dull boy and this is a wonderful novel to disappear into."

# Jer Lau

### *The 7 Habits Of Highly Effective People*
Stephen R. Covey
"An oldie, but a goodie. I found this book to be a helpful and simple way of reminding ourselves of the basics to be more effective in both your personal and professional life. Building good habits is key!"

### *How to Win Friends & Influence People*
Dale Carnegie
"Another book that summarises the basic principles of how to engage with people that will be helpful in all aspects of your life."

### *Outliers*
Malcolm Gladwell
"This book helps you think about success in a different way. Sometimes there are things beyond your control that make you successful so don't feel bad if you don't achieve the same success as Bill Gates."

# Jeremy Dalton

***The Drunkard's Walk: How Randomness Rules Our Lives***
Leonard Mlodinow
"Once you read this, the curtain hiding the magic of coincidences will be raised and you'll start to see how statistics can make sense of many things in our lives that may, at first, seem unbelievable."

***Reality Check: How Immersive Technologies Can Transform Your Business***
Jeremy Dalton
"A guide to the power of virtual reality and augmented reality in business, written in simple language, backed by corporate and academic case studies."

***Humankind: A Hopeful History***
Rutger Bregman
"Humans tend to dwell on disasters and dystopia but this book sheds light on the incredible strides we've made by working together, giving some much-needed airtime to humanity's positive side."

# Jon Hughes

### *Minto for Presentations*
Barbara Minto
"The gold standard for defining and developing persuasive presentations to executives."

### *Project Management Demystified*
Geoff Reiss
"Geoff provide the foundations for both experienced practitioners and new entrants to Programme Management in an easy-to-use format with excellent tips and tricks."

### *The New Strategic Selling*
Robert B. Miller, Stephen E. Heiman, Tad Tuleja
"The bible for selling complex consulting and IT projects to senior clients."

# Maria Axente

*Atlas of AI: Power, Politics, and the Planetary Costs of Artificial Intelligence*
Kate Crawford
"Kate's book demonstrates how artificial intelligence is neither
artificial nor intelligent. Phenomenal book."

*Privacy is Power: Why and How You Should Take Back*
Carissa Véliz
"This is the best book you will read on why you are important in the digital
age, and why your privacy is the secret power you need to be flourishing as
an individual and all of us as societies."

*Weapons of Math Destruction*
Cathy O'Neil
"Explores with a high dose of critique and realism several examples of
when algorithms have harmed people and how pushing back was such
a hard job."

# Melissa Max-Macarthy

*Lean In: Women, Work, and the Will to Lead*
Sheryl Sandberg
"This literally changed my life in 2014 when I read, it gave me the
confidence to branch out and go after what I wanted.
It also helped me to understand."

*Radical Candor: How to Get What You Want by Saying What You Mean*
Kim Scott
"How to communicate with impact and inspire action."

*Making Ideas Happen*
Scott Belsky
"How to execute on my ideas /creativity with structure and certainty."

# Melville Carrie

### Blink
Malcolm Gladwell
"Confirms what you thought your brain was doing, and that you are indeed a superhuman without knowing it. It's a superb insight of realisation that your instinct can indeed, and should be trusted, once you have honed it."

### Steve Jobs
Walter Isaacson
"By far the compelling listen (audiobook) of a recent genius in their own time, revealing the insight into the man and myth that shaped our current Digital world for the better."

### F**k It
John Parkin
"An unambiguous and unashamed declaration of independent thinking and action towards things you simply cannot control."

# Richard Hepworth

*Time to Think*
Nancy Kline
"Really highlights the importance of listening to unlock the talents of those around you."

*The Silk Roads*
Peter Frankopan
"Orientates our understanding of history away from our Western bias and really shows how commerce is always evolving."

*Fermat's Last Theorem*
Simon Singh
"A brilliant book, combining my passion for maths and history, and really highlighting the shoulders of the people we stand on!"

# Richard Murton

**Brave New World**
Aldous Huxley
"I remember reading it as a young adult and thinking how ludicrously unrealistic. As the years have passed and society metamorphoses at such a pace, it now feels eerily plausible."

**The Secret History**
Donna Tartt
"It was a cult book when I was at University. Within a matter of weeks everyone had read it. It captured that moment in time; the way it was written; the setting, the characters all seemed so relatable to us as students. It was all we could talk about for a few months. Studies put on hold!"

**Long Walk to Freedom**
Nelson Mandela
"No words..."

# Stephen Knight

***Common Sense Direct Marketing***
Drayton Bird
"Taught me to always keep things simple and trust in data to
drive your decisions."

***The Trusted Advisor***
David H Maister, Robert Galford, Charles Green
"Highlighted the value of building relationships and the fragility of them,
essential reading for any consultant."

***Information is Beautiful***
David McCandless
"At a time when data was presented in a boring way everywhere,
this showed me how to present data with impact and creativity."

# Tor Gisvold

### *Snow Crash*
Neal Stephenson
"Everyone with interest in virtual worlds need to read this book,
that started a lot of the descriptors we use today."

### *Dune*
Frank Herbert
"One of the best Sci-fi/environment books ever written,
and never made into a decent film (but I live and hope)."

### *Trader's Tales from the Golden Age of the Solar Clipper*
Nathan Lowell
"A fantastic saga that describes people's everyday life on star clippers and
stations in a way that encompasses details no-one else manages to describe
as well."

# End notes

Probably as exhilarating to peruse as they were to compile and format. Yet, as all knowledge is only an iteration building on the work of others, I am thankful to those responsible for the insights and resources listed herein.

1  *Overton window — Quartz Weekly Obsession.* (2020, April 30). Quartz. https://qz.com/emails/quartz-obsession/1848715/

2  McCarthy, B. J. (2021, May 28). *U.S. Support for Same-Sex Marriage Matches Record High.* Gallup.Com. https://news.gallup.com/poll/311672/support-sex-marriage-matches-record-high.aspx

3  *The Overton Window.* (2021). The Mackinac Center. https://www.mackinac.org/OvertonWindow https://www.mackinac.org/OvertonWindow

4  *Uber Revenue and Usage Statistics* (2021). (2021, May 16). Business of Apps. https://www.businessofapps.com/data/uber-statistics/

5  A., Schmitt, A., & Greenfield, J. (2019, February 8). *All the Bad Things About Uber and Lyft In One Simple List.* Streetsblog USA. https://usa.streetsblog.org/2019/02/04/all-the-bad-things-about-uber-and-lyft-in-one-simple-list/

6  CampaignUK. (2020, September 3). *Anatoly Roytman, a key brain behind Accenture Interactive, departs.* Campaign Live. https://www.campaignlive.co.uk/article/anatoly-roytman-key-brain-behind-accenture-interactive-departs/

7  *Accenture Interactive Ranked World's Largest Digital Agency Network by Advertising Age in Annual Agency Report for Fourth Year in a Row.* (2021, April 29). Accenture. https://newsroom.accenture.com/news/accenture-interactive-ranked-worlds-largest-digital-agency-network-by-advertising-age-in-annual-agency-report-for-fourth-year-in-a-row.htm

8  Bilow, R. (2013, November 18). *Want Your Marriage To Last?* YourTango. https://www.yourtango.com/experts/rochelle-bilow/want-your-marriage-last

9  Project Management Institute. (2013). *The essential role of communications.* https://www.pmi.org/-/media/pmi/documents/public/pdf/learning/thought-leadership/pulse/the-essential-role-of-communications.pdf

10  Moore, K. (2017, July 12). *How To Better Engage Your Introverts.* Forbes. https://www.forbes.com/sites/karlmoore/2017/07/06/how-to-better-engage-your-introverts/?sh=52a07a2e3224

11  Morris, C. (2015, April 3). *12 corporate blunders that could have been avoided.* CNBC. https://www.cnbc.com/2015/04/03/12-corporate-blunders-that-could-have-been-avoided.html

12  Stampler, L. (2014, June 19). *T-Mobile's CEO: AT&T and Verizon Are "Raping You."* Time. https://time.com/2899990/t-mobile-john-legere-raping/

13  BBC News. (2021, February 12). *KPMG boss Bill Michael quits after "stop moaning" row.* https://www.bbc.co.uk/news/business-56038215

14  BBC News. (2021b, February 12). *KPMG boss Bill Michael quits after "stop moaning" row.* https://www.bbc.co.uk/news/business-56038215

15  Berman, J. (2014, April 21). *The Three Essential Warren Buffett Quotes To Live By.* Forbes. https://www.forbes.com/sites/jamesberman/2014/04/20/the-three-essential-warren-buffett-quotes-to-live-by/?sh=199a13c76543

16  FutureLearn. (2021, February 4). *Use STAR.* https://www.futurelearn.com/info/courses/writing-applications/0/steps/5405#:%7E

17  L. (2019, September 4). *4 Ways Structure Can Improve Your Communication.* Userlike Live Chat. https://www.userlike.com/en/blog/talk-with-structure

18  *MECE principle.* (2021, May 22). In Wikipedia. https://en.wikipedia.org/wiki/MECE_principle

19  Cartwright, B. (2020, January 15). *How to Calculate the Cost of Your Meetings.* Owl Labs. https://resources.owllabs.com/blog/cost-of-meetings

20  *About DDX3X, the mutation, the effects, and how the DDX3X Foundation supports research and families.* (2019, December 3). DDX3X. https://ddx3x.org/about-ddx3x/

21  Santi Cazorla. (2021, June 11). In Wikipedia. https://en.wikipedia.org/wiki/Santi_Cazorla

22  *11 operations & 668 days out: Villarreal's Cazorla on Arsenal, gangrene & magic tricks.* (2018, September 20). BBC Sport. https://www.bbc.co.uk/sport/football/45575463

23  Jones, A. (2019, September 29). *Santi Cazorla's unbelievable form is the story of the season so far...* Dream Team FC. https://www.dreamteamfc.com/c/news-gossip/454840/santi-cazorla-form-villarreal/

24  *A quote from Valley of the Dolls.* (n.d.). Good Reads. Retrieved June 14, 2021, from https://www.goodreads.com/quotes/135855-when-you-re-climbing-mount-everest-nothing-is-easy-you-just

25  Wiese, J., Buehler, R., & Griffin, D. (2016). *Backward planning: Effects of planning direction on predictions of task completion time.* Society for Judgment and Decision Making, 11(2). http://journal.sjdm.org/16/16101/jdm16101.html

26  Cobert, A. (2020, June 19). *The "Just Right" Reaction When You Mess Up at Work.* The Muse. https://www.themuse.com/advice/the-just-right-reaction-when-you-mess-up-at-work

27  Roepe, L. R. (2020, March 4). *When Leaders Make Mistakes.* SHRM. https://www.shrm.org/hr-today/news/hr-magazine/spring2020/pages/when-leaders-make-mistakes.aspx

28  Council, F. C. (2019, March 28). *How To Manage Anxiety When Owning A Mistake At Work.* Forbes. https://www.forbes.com/sites/forbescoachescouncil/2019/03/28/how-to-manage-anxiety-when-owning-a-mistake-at-work/?sh=34fd80782284

29  Morgan, N. (2011, August 11). *Why We Fear Public Speaking And How To Overcome It.* Forbes. https://www.forbes.com/sites/nickmorgan/2011/03/30/why-we-fear-public-speaking-and-how-to-overcome-it/?sh=3a9a175460b2

30  Miraldi, S. (n.d.). *The best advice for presenting is actually 2,400 years old.* LinkedIn. Retrieved June 14, 2021, from https://www.linkedin.com/pulse/best-advice-presenting-actually-2400-years-old-scott-miraldi/

31  Baldoni, J. (2020, February 6). *Give a Great Speech: 3 Tips from Aristotle.* Inc.Com. https://www.inc.com/john-baldoni/deliver-a-great-speech-aristotle-three-tips.html

32  M. (2021, April 30). *10 Tips for Improving Your Public Speaking Skills.* Professional Development | Harvard DCE. https://professional.dce.harvard.edu/blog/10-tips-for-improving-your-public-speaking-skills/

33  *It's not what you say, but how you say it.* (n.d.). Marketing Donut. Retrieved June 14, 2021, from https://www.marketingdonut.co.uk/pr/building-relationships-with-the-media/it-s-not-what-you-say-but-how-you-say-it

34  Smedley, T. (n.d.). *Is public speaking fear limiting your career?* BBC Worklife. Retrieved June 14, 2021, from https://www.bbc.com/worklife/article/20170321-is-public-speaking-fear-limiting-your-career

35  *Blind men and an elephant.* (2021, May 30). In Wikipedia. https://en.wikipedia.org/wiki/Blind_men_and_an_elephant

36  *Socialist realism in Poland.* (2021, February 9). Wikipedia. https://en.wikipedia.org/wiki/Socialist_realism_in_Poland

37  Budds, D. (2019, June 8). *Brasilia: Brazil's 'cautionary tale' for utopian urbanists.* Curbed. https://archive.curbed.com/2019/6/7/18657121/brasilia-brazil-urban-planning-architecture-design

38  Duhigg, C. (2012, February 22). *How Companies Learn Your Secrets.* The New York Times. https://www.nytimes.com/2012/02/19/magazine/shopping-habits.html

39  Dixon, M. (2021, April 13). *How Netflix used big data and analytics to generate billions.* Selerity. https://seleritysas.com/blog/2019/04/05/how-netflix-used-big-data-and-analytics-to-generate-billions/

40  *7 real-world examples of how brands are using Big Data.* (2020, April 27). Bornfight. https://www.bornfight.com/blog/7-real-world-examples-of-how-brands-are-using-big-data-analytics/

41  *Big Data and Business Analytics Market Size, Share | 2027.* (n.d.). Allied Market Research. Retrieved June 14, 2021, from https://www.alliedmarketresearch.com/big-data-and-business-analytics-market

42  Dave Thomsen, Wanderful Media. (2015, August 7). *Why Human-Centered Design Matters.* WIRED. https://www.wired.com/insights/2013/12/human-centered-design-matters/

43  Daugherty, G. (2021, April 22). *Dr. John Kellogg Invented Cereal. Some of His Other Wellness Ideas Were Much Weirder.* HISTORY. https://www.history.com/news/dr-john-kellogg-cereal-wellness-wacky-sanitarium-treatments

44  Van der Bijl-Brouwer, M., & Dorst, K. (2017). *Advancing the strategic impact of human-centred design.* Design Studies, 53, 1–23. https://doi.org/10.1016/j.destud.2017.06.003

45  *What are Personas?* (n.d.). The Interaction Design Foundation. Retrieved June 14, 2021, from https://www.interaction-design.org/literature/topics/personas

46  *What are Personas?* (n.d.). The Interaction Design Foundation. Retrieved June 14, 2021, from https://www.interaction-design.org/literature/topics/personas

47  *Journey Mapping 101.* (n.d.). Nielsen Norman Group. Retrieved June 14, 2021, from https://www.nngroup.com/articles/journey-mapping-101/

48  *Journey Mapping 101.* (n.d.). Nielsen Norman Group. Retrieved June 14, 2021, from https://www.nngroup.com/articles/journey-mapping-101/

49  Baylé, M. (2018, September 18). *Experience Design: a new discipline?* - UX Collective. Medium. https://uxdesign.cc/experience-design-a-new-discipline-e62db76d5ed1

50  Townson, B. D. (2017, November 3). *The seven tenets of human-centred design.* Design Council. https://www.designcouncil.org.uk/news-opinion/seven-tenets-human-centred-design

51  Today, J. (2014, May 3). *The business of "omotenashi."* Japan Today. https://japantoday.com/category/features/opinions/the-business-of-omotenashi

52  B2B International. (2021, May 24). *What is a customer journey map?* https://www.b2binternational.com/research/methods/faq/customer-journey-map/

53  Murray, S. (2019, February 7). *Are Management Consulting Firms Reducing their Dependence on MBAs?* FIND MBA. https://find-mba.com/articles/are-management-consulting-firms-reducing-their-dependence-on-mbas

54  Harcourt, K. (2021, January 8). *Survey Reveals the Traits of an Effective Leader.* Talent Management Talk. https://blog.mcquaig.com/survey-reveals-the-traits-of-an-effective-leader/

55  *When Empowering Employees Works, and When It Doesn't.* (2020, August 31). Harvard Business Review. https://hbr.org/2018/03/when-empowering-employees-works-and-when-it-doesnt

56  *The 3 Elements of Trust.* (2019, June 23). Harvard Business Review. https://hbr.org/2019/02/the-3-elements-of-trust

57 *The Trust Quotient and the Science Behind It - Trusted Advisor.* (2018, June 21). Trusted Advisor Associates - Training, Workshops, Trust Education. https://trustedadvisor. com/why-trust-matters/understanding-trust/the-trust-quotient-and-the-science-behind-it

58 Gourguechon, P. (2017, December 27). *Empathy Is An Essential Leadership Skill -- And There's Nothing Soft About It.* Forbes. https://www.forbes.com/sites/ prudygourguechon/2017/12/26/empathy-is-an-essential-leadership-skill-and-theres-nothing-soft-about-it/

59 *2021 Empathy Study Executive Summary.* (n.d.). Businessolver. Retrieved June 24, 2021, from https://resources.businessolver.com/c/2021-empathy-exec-summ?x=OE03jO

60 McNabb, S. (2020, May 6). *Why Having Client Empathy is Essential to Your Business.* Financial Marketing and Technology Services. https://www.gate39media.com/why-having-client-empathy-is-essential-to-your-business/

61 Henry, A., & Fishbein, R. (2019, September 26). *The Science of Breaking Out of Your Comfort Zone (and Why You Should).* Lifehacker. https://lifehacker.com/the-science-of-breaking-out-of-your-comfort-zone-and-w-656426705

62 *Mentoring Statistics: The Research You Need To Know.* (n.d.). Guider AI. Retrieved June 14, 2021, from https://www.guider-ai.com/blog/mentoring-statistics-the-research-you-need-to-know

63 *8 Employee Engagement Statistics You Need to Know in 2021* [INFOGRAPHIC]. (n.d.). Smarp. Retrieved June 14, 2021, from https://blog.smarp.com/employee-engagement-8-statistics-you-need-to-know

64 Deloitte Development LLC. (2012). *Core beliefs and culture: Chairman's survey findings.* https://www2.deloitte.com/content/dam/Deloitte/global/Documents/About-Deloitte/gx-core-beliefs-and-culture.pdf

65 Kohll, A. (2018, August 14). *How To Build A Positive Company Culture.* Forbes. https:// www.forbes.com/sites/alankohll/2018/08/14/how-to-build-a-positive-company-culture/

66 *Need theory.* (2021, May 23). In Wikipedia. https://en.wikipedia.org/wiki/Need_theory

67 Sorenson, B. S. (2021, June 11). *How Employee Engagement Drives Growth.* Gallup. Com. https://www.gallup.com/workplace/236927/employee-engagement-drives-growth.aspx

68 Henley, D. (2018, July 13). *Seven Secrets To Inspiring Your Team.* Forbes. https://www. forbes.com/sites/dedehenley/2018/07/13/seven-secrets-to-inspiring-your-team/

69 Sexton, P. (2020, November 10). *Project Delivery Performance: AIPM and KPMG Project Management Survey 2020.* KPMG. https://home.kpmg/au/en/home/insights/2020/08/ australian-project-delivery-performance-survey-2020.html

70 Project Management Institute. (2013, May). *The high cost of low performance: The essential role of communications.* https://www.pmi.org/-/media/pmi/documents/public/ pdf/learning/thought-leadership/pulse/the-essential-role-of-communications.pdf

71 Consulting.us. (2021, February 23). *Study of 900 digital transformations: Only 30% are successful.* https://www.consulting.us/news/5575/study-of-900-digital-transformations-only-30-are-successful

72 Discenza, R., & Forman, J. B. (2007). *Seven causes of project failure: How to recognize them and how to initiate project recovery.* Project Management Institute. https://www. pmi.org/learning/library/seven-causes-project-failure-initiate-recovery-7195

73 *Performing a Project Premortem.* (2014, August 1). Harvard Business Review. https:// hbr.org/2007/09/performing-a-project-premortem

74   Discenza, R., & Forman, J. B. (2007). *Seven causes of project failure: How to recognize them and how to initiate project recovery.* Project Management Institute. https://www. pmi.org/learning/library/seven-causes-project-failure-initiate-recovery-7195

75   Officevibe. (2021, March 31). *Employee feedback demystified: a guide for managers.* https:// officevibe.com/guides/employee-feedback

76   *Tips To Create A Culture Of Frequent Employee Check-ins.* (2020, November 15). Engagedly. https://engagedly.com/tips-to-create-a-culture-of-frequent-employee-check-ins

77   Wikipedia contributors. (2021, June 7). *The Boat Race.* Wikipedia. https://en.wikipedia. org/wiki/The_Boat_Race

78   Wikipedia contributors. (2021a, April 16). *Coxswain (rowing).* Wikipedia. https:// en.wikipedia.org/wiki/Coxswain_(rowing)

79   *Working or wasting time?* (2019, November 12). Korn Ferry. https://www.kornferry. com/about-us/press/working-or-wasting-time

80   *Working or wasting time?* (2019, November 12). Korn Ferry. https://www.kornferry. com/about-us/press/working-or-wasting-time

81   Leo, S. (2020, August 25). *6 benefits of one-on-one meetings (1-on-1s).* Adobe Workfront. https://www.workfront.com/blog/the-benefits-of-one-on-one-meetings

82   Wingard, J. (2018, August 14). *Reverse Mentoring: 3 Proven Outcomes Driving Change.* Forbes. https://www.forbes.com/sites/jasonwingard/2018/08/08/reverse-mentoring-3-proven-outcomes-driving-change/

83   *Why Junior Employees Should Mentor Senior Employees.* (2020, June 3). Harvard Business Review. https://hbr.org/2019/10/why-reverse-mentoring-works-and-how-to-do-it-right

84   Wong, K., Chan, A. H. S., & Ngan, S. C. (2019). *The Effect of Long Working Hours and Overtime on Occupational Health: A Meta-Analysis of Evidence from 1998 to 2018.* International Journal of Environmental Research and Public Health, 16(12), 2102. https://doi.org/10.3390/ijerph16122102

85   *Tackling mental health in the consulting industry.* (2019, January 15). MCA. https:// www.mca.org.uk/updates/tackling-mental-health-in-the-consulting-industry

86   Getting to Yes. (2021, April 8). Wikipedia. https://en.wikipedia.org/wiki/Getting_to_Yes

87   Galloway, S. (2018, April 20). *Happiness & the Gorilla.* No Mercy / No Malice. https:// www.profgalloway.com/happiness-the-gorilla/

88   *Just How Bad Is Business Travel for Your Health? Here's the Data.* (2018, August 21). Harvard Business Review. https://hbr.org/2018/05/just-how-bad-is-business-travel-for-your-health-heres-the-data

89   Deloitte LLP. (2020, January). *Mental health and employers: Refreshing the case for investment.* Deloitte. https://www2.deloitte.com/content/dam/Deloitte/uk/Documents/consultancy/deloitte-uk-mental-health-and-employers.pdf

90   The Royal College of Psychiatrists. (2008, March). *Mental Health and Work.* https:// assets.publishing.service.gov.uk/government/uploads/system/uploads/attachment_data/file/212266/hwwb-mental-health-and-work.pdf

91   Deloitte LLP. (2020, January). *Mental health and employers: Refreshing the case for investment.* Deloitte. https://www2.deloitte.com/content/dam/Deloitte/uk/Documents/consultancy/deloitte-uk-mental-health-and-employers.pdf

92   Fenton, K. (2017, February 2). *Take time to talk about mental health.* Public Health Matters. https://publichealthmatters.blog.gov.uk/2017/02/02/take-time-to-talk-about-mental-health/

93   Grant, A. (2013, December 11). *Why acquaintances, not friends, will help you find a job.* Quartz. https://qz.com/94984/why-acquaintances-not-friends-will-help-you-find-a-job/

94   Jones, S. (2021, June 9). 13 *Business Networking Statistics Everyone Should Know.* Fit Small Business. https://fitsmallbusiness.com/business-networking-statistics/

95   Granovetter, M. S. (1973). *The Strength of Weak Ties.* American Journal of Sociology, 78(6). http://snap.stanford.edu/class/cs224w-readings/granovetter73weakties.pdf

96   Ramakrishnan, V. (2020, January 8). 35 *Amazing Social Media Statistics to Start 2020 With.* Falcon.Io. https://www.falcon.io/insights-hub/topics/social-media-strategy/35-amazing-social-media-statistics-for-2020/

97   Roser, M. (2015, July 14). *Internet.* Our World in Data. https://ourworldindata.org/internet

98   Statista. (2021b, January 28). *Number of 1st level connections of LinkedIn users 2016.* https://www.statista.com/statistics/264097/number-of-1st-level-connections-of-linkedin-users/

99   *Eight Tips for Building, Maintaining, and Leveraging Your Professional Relationships.* (2021, June 10). Stanford Graduate School of Business. https://www.gsb.stanford.edu/insights/eight-tips-building-maintaining-leveraging-your-professional-relationships

100  Saxena, S. (2021a, March 30). *The Importance of Showing Appreciation.* Eva Blog. https://blog.evabot.ai/the-importance-of-showing-appreciation/

101  Spencer, J. (2019, March 21). *How to Use "the Law of Reciprocity" to Build Better Business Relationships.* Entrepreneur. https://www.entrepreneur.com/article/330557

102  Sakulku, J., & Alexander, J. (2011). *The Impostor Phenomenon.* International Journal of Behavioral Science, 6(1), 75–97. https://so06.tci-thaijo.org/index.php/IJBS/article/view/521/pdf

103  Abrams, A. (2018, June 20). *Yes, Impostor Syndrome Is Real. Here's How to Deal With It.* Time. https://time.com/5312483/how-to-deal-with-impostor-syndrome/

104  *How to Build a Personal Brand at Work.* (2019, December 10). Korn Ferry Advance. https://www.kfadvance.com/articles/building-personal-brand

105  *How to Build a Personal Brand at Work.* (2019, December 10). Korn Ferry Advance. https://www.kfadvance.com/articles/building-personal-brand

106  Baer, D. (2014, November 4). *This Cognitive Bias Explains Why Pretty People Make 12% More Money Than Everybody Else.* Business Insider. https://www.businessinsider.com/halo-effect-money-beauty-bias-2014-11?IR=T

107  Adam, H., & Galinsky, A. D. (2012). *Enclothed cognition.* Journal of Experimental Social Psychology, 48(4), 918–925. https://doi.org/10.1016/j.jesp.2012.02.008

108  Piff, P. (2013, December 20). *Does money make you mean?* TED Talks. https://www.ted.com/talks/paul_piff_does_money_make_you_mean

109  Cotterill, J. (2020, December 9). *McKinsey to repay more than $40m over South African scandal.* Financial Times. https://www.ft.com/content/c2db2a6d-693a-49e4-87e2-194183e6445b

110  Bianco-Splann, M. (2021, June 2). 5 *Reasons to Be Real: Authenticity is the New Competitive Edge.* Real Leaders. http://real-leaders.com/5-reasons-to-be-real-authenticity-is-the-new-competitive-edge/

111  Topping, A., & Barr, C. (2021, February 10). *UK ministers face pressure over gender pay gap reporting delay.* The Guardian. https://www.theguardian.com/world/2021/feb/09/uk-ministers-face-pressure-over-gender-pay-gap-reporting-delay

112  *Gender pay gap.* (2021, June 13). Wikipedia. https://en.wikipedia.org/wiki/Gender_pay_gap

113 Toossi, M., & Morisi, T. L. (2017, July). *Women In The Workforce Before, During, And After The Great Recession*. U.S. Bureau of Labor Statistics. https://www.bls. gov/spotlight/2017/women-in-the-workforce-before-during-and-after-the-great-recession/pdf/women-in-the-workforce-before-during-and-after-the-great-recession. pdf

114 History.com Editors. (2021, January 19). *Brown v. Board of Education*. HISTORY. https://www.history.com/topics/black-history/brown-v-board-of-education-of-topeka

115 Fuller, H. (2021, January 12). *The Struggle Continues*. Education Next. https://www. educationnext.org/the-struggle-continues/

116 *Racism in the United Kingdom*. (2021, June 10). Wikipedia. https://en.wikipedia.org/ wiki/Racism_in_the_United_Kingdom

117 *Timeline of LGBT history in the United Kingdom*. (2021, June 14). Wikipedia. https:// en.wikipedia.org/wiki/Timeline_of_LGBT_history_in_the_United_Kingdom

118 PriceWaterhouseCoopers. (n.d.). *We've come a long way, but we still have a long way to go*. *PwC*. Retrieved June 16, 2021, from https://www.pwc.co.uk/who-we-are/regional-sites/london/insights/we-ve-come-a-long-way--but-we-still-have-a-long-way-to-go. html

119 McElhaney, A. (2020, December 10). *Consulting Firms Are Overwhelmingly White, Data Show*. Institutional Investor. https://www.institutionalinvestor.com/article/ b1plyvx3pjzw6d/Consulting-Firms-Are-Overwhelmingly-White-Data-Show

120 Brooks, K. J. (2019, December 10). *Black professionals hold only 3.2 percent of executive jobs, 0.8 percent of CEO jobs at Fortune 500 firms, new report says*. CBS News. https:// www.cbsnews.com/news/black-professionals-hold-only-3-percent-of-executive-jobs-1-percent-of-ceo-jobs-at-fortune-500-firms-new-report-says/

121 Lloyd, B. C. (2021, May 25). *One in Four Black Workers Report Discrimination at Work*. Gallup.Com. https://news.gallup.com/poll/328394/one-four-black-workers-report-discrimination-work.aspx

122 *What is it like for Women in Consulting?* (2020, May 8). Consultiful. https://www. consultiful.com/women-in-consulting/

123 Yoshino, K. (2006, December 7). *Covering: The Hidden Assault on Our Civil Rights*. NYU Langone Medical Center. https://medhum.med.nyu.edu/view/12615

124 *2021 DEI Transparency Report*. (n.d.). Deloitte United States. Retrieved June 16, 2021, from https://www2.deloitte.com/us/en/pages/about-deloitte/articles/diversity-equity-inclusion-transparency-report.html

125 Deloitte. (2019). *Uncovering talent: A new model of inclusion*. https://www2.deloitte.com/ content/dam/Deloitte/us/Documents/about-deloitte/us-about-deloitte-uncovering-talent-a-new-model-of-inclusion.pdf

126 Clark, D., & Smith, C. (2017, December 6). *Help Your Employees Be Themselves at Work*. *Harvard Business Review*. https://hbr.org/2014/11/help-your-employees-be-themselves-at-work

127 *Seven charts that show COVID-19's impact on women's employment*. (2021, April 20). McKinsey & Company. https://www.mckinsey.com/Featured-Insights/Diversity-and-Inclusion/Seven-charts-that-show-COVID-19s-impact-on-womens-employment

128 Consultancy.uk. (2019, February 7). *Half of UK workers say employers have not progressed on D&I goals*. https://www.consultancy.uk/news/20211/half-of-uk-workers-say-employers-have-not-progressed-on-di-goals

129 Woodfield, A. (2021, January 23). *Getting real with Inclusion - Andy Woodfield*. Medium. https://medium.com/@andy_woodfield/getting-real-with-inclusion-5101d8222a39

130 Rock, D., & Grant, H. (2019, March 19). *Why Diverse Teams Are Smarter.* Harvard Business Review. https://hbr.org/2016/11/why-diverse-teams-are-smarter

131 Smith, J. (2019, October 22). *Women less likely to progress at work than male colleagues after childbirth.* Workplace Insight. https://workplaceinsight.net/women-less-likely-to-progress-at-work-than-their-male-counterparts-following-childbirth/

132 BBC News. (2021c, March 26). *Coronavirus: What is the R number and how is it calculated?* https://www.bbc.co.uk/news/health-52473523

133 *50 million users: How long does it take tech to reach this milestone?* (2018, February 21). Interactive Schools. https://blog.interactiveschools.com/blog/50-million-users-how-long-does-it-take-tech-to-reach-this-milestone

134 Berman, A. E. (2019, July 11). *Technology Feels Like It's Accelerating — Because It Actually Is.* Singularity Hub. https://singularityhub.com/2016/03/22/technology-feels-like-its-accelerating-because-it-actually-is/

135 Metz, C. (2017, June 3). *Google's AI Wins Fifth And Final Game Against Go Genius Lee Sedol.* Wired. https://www.wired.com/2016/03/googles-ai-wins-fifth-final-game-go-genius-lee-sedol/

136 Turner, A. (2021, June 1). *How Many People Have Smartphones Worldwide* (Jun 2021). BankMyCell. https://www.bankmycell.com/blog/how-many-phones-are-in-the-world

137 Nature Editorial. (n.d.). *Rise of Robot Radiologists.* Nature. Retrieved June 16, 2021, from https://www.nature.com/articles/d41586-019-03847-z

138 Nature Editorial. (n.d.-a). *How AI is improving cancer diagnostics.* Nature. Retrieved June 16, 2021, from https://www.nature.com/articles/d41586-020-00847-2

139 Prof, H., Pottebaum, T., & Wolf, P. (2019). *Autonomous Driving: Moonshot Project with Quantum Leap from Hardware to Software & AI Focus.* Deloitte. https://www2.deloitte.com/content/dam/Deloitte/be/Documents/Deloitte_Autonomous-Driving.pdf

140 Statista. (2021a, January 22). *Internet of Things - number of connected devices worldwide 2015–2025.* https://www.statista.com/statistics/471264/iot-number-of-connected-devices-worldwide/

141 Editorial Team. (2020, December 18). *Blockchain trends in 2021: Expect the unexpected.* Finextra Research. https://www.finextra.com/blogposting/19679/blockchain-trends-in-2021-expect-the-unexpected

142 Conway, L. (2021). *Blockchain Explained.* Investopedia. https://www.investopedia.com/terms/b/blockchain.asp

143 Wu, K., Liu, M., & Jie Xu, J. (2019, August 29). *How Will Blockchain Technology Impact Auditing and Accounting: Permissionless Vs. Permissioned Blockchain.* ResearchGate. https://www.researchgate.net/publication/335472340_How_Will_Blockchain_Technology_Impact_Auditing_and_Accounting_Permissionless_Vs_Permissioned_Blockchain

144 Ash, A. (2021, March 2). *The rise and fall of Blockbuster and how it's surviving with just one store left.* Business Insider. https://www.businessinsider.com/the-rise-and-fall-of-blockbuster-video-streaming-2020-1?r=US&IR=T

145 Ash, A. (2021b, March 2). *The rise and fall of Blockbuster and how it's surviving with just one store left.* Business Insider. https://www.businessinsider.com/the-rise-and-fall-of-blockbuster-video-streaming-2020-1?r=US&IR=T

146 Statista. (2021d, March 18). *Netflix: net income 2000–2020.* https://www.statista.com/statistics/272561/netflix-net-income/

147 Day, N. (2021, January 6). *Netflix earns 28.1M subscribes in 2020 so far, more than in all of 2019.* Fox Business. https://www.foxbusiness.com/markets/netflix-earns-28-1m-subscribes-in-2020-so-far-more-than-in-all-of-2019-expects-influx-of-original-content

148 Aaslaid, K. (n.d.). *50 Examples of Corporations That Failed to Innovate.* Valuer. Retrieved June 16, 2021, from https://www.valuer.ai/blog/50-examples-of-corporations-that-failed-to-innovate-and-missed-their-chance

149 Savov, V. (2016, September 30). *BlackBerry's success led to its failure.* The Verge. https://www.theverge.com/2016/9/30/13119924/blackberry-failure-success

150 Hicks, J. (2012, February 21). *Research, no motion: How the BlackBerry CEOs lost an empire.* The Verge. https://www.theverge.com/2012/2/21/2789676/rim-blackberry-mike-lazaridis-jim-balsillie-lost-empire

151 Minato, C. (2012, July 31). *THE RIM DISASTER TIMELINE: BlackBerry's Collapse, As Told By Its Ads.* Business Insider. https://www.businessinsider.com/the-rim-disaster-timeline-blackberrys-collapse-as-told-by-its-ads-2012-7?r=US&IR=T

152 Aaslaid, K. (n.d.-b). *50 Examples of Corporations That Failed to Innovate.* Valuer. Retrieved June 16, 2021, from https://www.valuer.ai/blog/50-examples-of-corporations-that-failed-to-innovate-and-missed-their-chance

153 Su, S. (2021, June 29). *Facebook Now Valued at $1 Trillion USD.* HYPEBEAST. https://hypebeast.com/2021/6/facebook-1-trillion-usd-company-valuation-info

154 Denning, S. (2019, August 26). *Why Agile's Future Is Bright.* Forbes. https://www.forbes.com/sites/stevedenning/2019/08/25/why-the-future-of-agile-is-bright/?sh=11565a9f2968

155 CA Technologies. (2017). *Discover the Benefits of Agile: The Business Case for a New Way to Work.* https://docs.broadcom.com/doc/discover-the-benefits-of-agile

156 Mark, J. J. (2021, June 14). *Heraclitus of Ephesus.* World History Encyclopedia. https://www.worldhistory.org/Heraclitus_of_Ephesos/

157 *Future Shock.* (2021, February 5). Wikipedia. https://en.wikipedia.org/wiki/Future_Shock

158 Chen, J. (2020). *Commoditization Definition.* Investopedia. https://www.investopedia.com/terms/c/commoditization.asp

159 *Wipro to acquire Capco.* (n.d.). Capco. Retrieved June 16, 2021, from https://www.capco.com/About-Us/Newsroom-and-media/wipro-to-acquire-capco-press-release

160 Mulcahy, E. (2019, October 31). *Accenture Interactive acquisitions: all its agency deals so far.* The Drum. https://www.thedrum.com/news/2019/08/12/accenture-interactive-acquisitions-all-its-agency-deals-so-far

161 Team, T. (2019, October 2). *Why Accenture's Sub-Par Consulting Performance In Q4 Wasn't A Surprise.* Forbes. https://www.forbes.com/sites/greatspeculations/2019/10/03/why-accentures-sub-par-consulting-performance-in-q4-wasnt-a-surprise/

162 Statista. (2021e, April 21). *Netflix subscribers count worldwide 2013–2021.* https://www.statista.com/statistics/250934/quarterly-number-of-netflix-streaming-subscribers-worldwide/

163 Whitten, S. (2021, January 27). *HBO Max activations double to 17.2 million in fourth quarter.* CNBC. https://www.cnbc.com/2021/01/27/hbo-max-activations-double-to-17point2-million-in-fourth-quarter.html

164 Nail, J. (2019, January 19). *Netflix Has Become HBO.* Forrester. https://go.forrester.com/blogs/netflix-has-become-hbo/

165  Katz, B. (2021, April 15). *Amazon Prime Surpasses 200M Subscribers, But It's Not Exactly on Netflix's Tail.* Observer. https://observer.com/2021/04/amazon-prime-subscribers-netflix-disneyplus/

166  Byers, D. (2021, May 27). *Amazon buys MGM for $8.5 billion.* NBC News. https://www.nbcnews.com/media/amazon-buys-mgm-85-billion-rcna1023

167  Katz, B. (2019, October 23). *How Much Does It Cost to Fight in the Streaming Wars?* Observer. https://observer.com/2019/10/netflix-disney-apple-amazon-hbo-max-peacock-content-budgets/

168  Fischer, S. (2021, February 16). *Yahoo is now a part of Verizon Media.* Yahoo! Money. https://money.yahoo.com/disney-races-catch-netflix-subscriber-152243780.html

169  Davis, D. (2020, May 21). *Amazon triples its private label product offerings in 2 years.* Digital Commerce 360. https://www.digitalcommerce360.com/2020/05/20/amazon-triples-its-private%E2%80%91label-product-offerings-in-2-years/

170  *Business and Marketing "SparkNotes": Purple Cow.* (2020, December 16). Iconic Digital Marketing Agency. https://iconicdigitalagency.com/blog/entrepreneurship/business-and-marketing-sparknotes-purple-cow/

171  Rey, J. (2019, May 3). *How Amazon created the Prime membership program.* Vox. https://www.vox.com/recode/2019/5/3/18511544/amazon-prime-oral-history-jeff-bezos-one-day-shipping

172  Galloway, S. (2021, March 19). *Let's Get Ready to Rundle.* No Mercy / No Malice. https://www.profgalloway.com/lets-get-ready-to-rundle/

173  Coppola, D. (2021, May 7). *Amazon Prime - Statistics & Facts.* Statista. https://www.statista.com/topics/4076/amazon-prime/

174  Rey, J. (2020, August 4). *Walmart+, an Amazon Prime competitor, launch delayed.* Vox. https://www.vox.com/recode/2020/7/7/21314767/walmart-plus-grocery-delivery-amazon-prime-membership-loyalty-program-walmart

175  *Amazon vs Walmart - Revenues and Profits Comparison 1999–2018.* (2020, June 19). MGM Research. https://mgmresearch.com/amazon-vs-walmart-revenues-and-profits-comparison-1999-2018/

176  Gherini, A. (2021, January 5). *The Rise Of The Rundle: A New Trend For Subscription-Based Services.* Inc.Com. https://www.inc.com/anne-gherini/the-rise-of-rundle-a-new-trend-for-subscription-based-services.html

177  *Carsharing Industry: Carsharing Market & Growth 2019.* (2019, July 11). Movmi. https://movmi.net/carsharing-market-growth-2019/

178  Key, D. (2018, August 8). *3 Reasons Why Wall Street Loves Subscription Models.* Zuora. https://www.zuora.com/guides/three-reasons-wall-street-loves-recurring-revenue-models/

179  Galloway, S. (2021, March 19). *Let's Get Ready to Rundle.* No Mercy / No Malice. https://www.profgalloway.com/lets-get-ready-to-rundle/

180  *How To Make Money From Membership Economics.* (n.d.). Global Banking and Finance. Retrieved June 16, 2021, from https://www.globalbankingandfinance.com/how-to-make-money-from-membership-economics/

181  Whitler, K. A. (2016, January 20). *How The Subscription Economy Is Disrupting The Traditional Business Model.* Forbes. https://www.forbes.com/sites/kimberlywhitler/2016/01/17/a-new-business-trend-shifting-from-a-service-model-to-a-subscription-based-model/?sh=63b37aa24a5f

182  Saran, C. (2019, December 12). *Stanford University finds that AI is outpacing Moore's Law.* ComputerWeekly.Com. https://www.computerweekly.com/news/252475371/Stanford-University-finds-that-AI-is-outpacing-Moores-Law

183 Breckenfelder, J. (2020, December 17). *Competition among high-frequency traders and market liquidity*. VOX, CEPR Policy Portal. https://voxeu.org/article/competition-among-high-frequency-traders-and-market-liquidity

184 Pappalardo, J. (2011, October 27). *New Transatlantic Cable Built to Shave 5 Milliseconds off Stock Trades*. Popular Mechanics. https://www.popularmechanics.com/technology/infrastructure/a7274/a-transatlantic-cable-to-shave-5-milliseconds-off-stock-trades/

185 PricewaterhouseCoopers. (2017). *Sizing the prize: What's the real value of AI for your business and how can you capitalise?* https://www.pwc.com/gx/en/issues/analytics/assets/pwc-ai-analysis-sizing-the-prize-report.pdf

186 Quach, K. (2018, May 11). *Don't try and beat AI, merge with it says chess champ Garry Kasparov*. The Register. https://www.theregister.com/2018/05/10/heres_what_garry_kasparov_an_old_world_chess_champion_thinks_of_ai/

187 Case, N. (2018, January 8). *How To Become A Centaur*. Journal of Design and Science. https://jods.mitpress.mit.edu/pub/issue3-case/release/4

188 Schwartz, O. (2021, September 30). *In 2016, Microsoft's Racist Chatbot Revealed the Dangers of Online Conversation*. IEEE Spectrum. https://spectrum.ieee.org/in-2016-microsofts-racist-chatbot-revealed-the-dangers-of-online-conversation

# www.hownottofailatconsulting.com

If you have any questions about the topics discussed in this book or have the know-how to help those who do, join the discussion on Facebook, Twitter, LinkedIn, or YouTube.

Your support, in the form of likes, follows, or exceedingly kind reviews, is always very much appreciated, as it may help others discover this book.

# Jack Przemieniecki

An experienced consultant, entrepreneur, and advocate for human-centred design, Jack has spent over twenty years working with innovative start-ups, entrepreneurial agencies, and industry-leading consultancies. Having worked across four continents with some of the world's most recognisable brands, he has seen the good, the bad and the ugly sides of the consulting world. He continues to help organisations and start-ups identify innovative opportunities, mentors and supports others within numerous communities, and advocates for a more inclusive, diverse, and just society. When not writing or working, he can be found staying active, discovering new restaurants, enjoying a good movie, or continuing to explore the world.

Printed in Great Britain
by Amazon

14349637R00234